WebSphere Application Server 7.0 Administration Guide

Manage and administer your WebSphere Application Server to create a reliable, secure, and scalable environment for running your applications

Steve Robinson

BIRMINGHAM - MUMBAI

WebSphere Application Server 7.0 Administration Guide

First published: August 2009

Production Reference: 1070809

Published by Packt Publishing Ltd.
32 Lincoln Road
Olton
Birmingham, B27 6PA, UK.

ISBN 978-1-847197-20-7

www.packtpub.com

Cover Image by Vinayak Chittar (vinayak.chittar@gmail.com)

Credits

Author
Steve Robinson

Reviewers
Meenakshi Verma

Owen Chung

Prabu Swamidurai

Acquisition Editor
Sarah Cullington

Development Editor
Ved Prakash Jha

Technical Editor
Dhiraj Bellani

Aditi Srivastava

Editorial Team Leader
Abhijeet Deobhakta

Project Team Leader
Priya Mukherji

Project Coordinator
Leena Purkait

Proofreader
Laura Booth

Indexer
Hemangini Bari

Production Coordinator
Dolly Dasilva

Cover Work
Dolly Dasilva

About the Author

Steven Charles Robinson is a young entrepreneur and leading UK WebSphere consultant. He has been consulting in IT since 1997 and has been involved in projects throughout the globe. He has worked for fortune 500 companies around the world and is currently working for SCRev.com, a specialist consultancy dedicated to helping service companies achieve capability maturity in software configuration and release management, specifically focusing on J2EE (Enterprise Edition) best practice and deployment readiness.

Steve started out originally as a consultant in the IBM Lotus Notes/Domino product suite, where he excelled in middleware integration technologies to ensure homogenous environments could exist in the new heterogeneous world. Having worked for many different industries, Steve has had a plethora of experience in the integration of most technologies across many different systems and cultures. He is also an accomplished programmer in including C, Java, and the Microsoft .NET development tools.

Steve has gleaned many insights due to the amount of large enterprise projects he has been involved with and his passion for documentation and process improvement is recognized by all those he works with.

Steve is married and lives with his family in England. He spends his time either writing, or researching new products and technologies for client projects along with investigating new ways to automate technologies where possible. Steve is also known for his contribution to the WebSphere Internet community through one of his many top-ranking WebSphere knowledge portals www.webspheretools.com.

Acknowledgement

To my loving wife and "bestest buddy" Jacqui; without you I would not be the person I am today. You keep me grounded, while I dream my biggest dreams. I would also like to thank my mother Carillon Faery who is a gift to the planet for her constant love and energy. Mum, you give me inspiration. I also dedicate this book to my children, Brooke, Jodie, Carly and Mike who in their own unique ways give me encouragement, enjoyment and individual insights. I would also like to thank my brother Jaime, who believes in me so much and encourages me to write more often.

I thank the colleagues who reviewed my book, Owen Chung, Prabu Swamidurai, and James Thomas. Thanks guys, you helped me ensure that the content was accurate.

I would also like to thank the following Packt Publishing staff: Sarah Cullington, who helped me find my writing style; Leena Purkait—Project Coordinator, who kept me on the ball with timings; and Ved Prakash Jha—Development Editor, who helped me keep my writing in form and to the point.

About the Reviewers

Meenakshi Verma has been part of the IT industry since 1998. She is experienced in putting up solutions across multiple industry segments using SAP Business Intelligence (BI), SAP Business Objects, and Java/J2EE technologies. She is currently based in Toronto, Canada and is working with Enbridge Gas Distribution.

Meenakshi has been helping with technical reviews for books published by Packt publishing across varied enterprise solutions. Her earlier work includes JasperReports for Java Developers, Java EE 5 Development using GlassFish Application Server, Practical Data Analysis and Reporting with Business Intelligence Reporting Tools (BIRT), Enterprise JavaBeans (EJB) 3 Developer's Guide, and Learning DOJO.

I'd like to thank my Father (Mr. Bhopal Singh) and Mother (Mrs. Raj Bala) for laying a strong foundation in me and giving me their unconditional love and support. I also owe thanks and gratitude to my husband (Atul Verma) for his encouragement and support throughout the review of this book and many others; my four-year-old son (Prieyaansh Verma) for giving me the warmth of his love despite my hectic schedules; and my brother (Sachin Singh) for always being there for me.

Owen Chung is a software configuration manager who has worked in the telecommunications and banking industries in the United Kingdom and Australia. He has worked with WebSphere solutions for the past four years. He is self-employed in his company Red Cliff Management Limited.

I would like to thank my dearest other half Vislinda Alba Bacanto for her love and endless support. My parents Winston and Sarah Chung for providing all they could so I could have a better life in a new country and my brother Adrian for his tireless sense of mirth and amusement.

Prabu Swamidurai is a WebSphere consultant specializing in large scale WebSphere implementations in financial and retail industries in the UK. He is certified in several IBM products and has worked with the WebSphere products over 11 years. He has a master's degree in Physics and Computer Science.

He can be contacted via his web site www.webspherespecialist.com.

Thanks to Latha for her love and encouragement.

Table of Contents

Preface   **1**

Chapter 1: Installing WebSphere Application Server   **7**

Installation planning   **8**

Installation scenarios   9

    Profile types   10

Preparation and prerequisites   **10**

Graphical installation   **10**

Installing the base binaries   11

    Downloading the WAS for Linux trial   11

    Uploading the trial install to your Linux server   13

    Installing as root   16

    Running the launchpad   17

    Installation wizard welcome screen   18

    Software license agreement   18

    System prerequisites check   19

    Optional features   20

    Installation directory   21

    WebSphere Application Server environments   21

Profile creation   25

Installation registry files   38

Installation logs   39

Profile manager logs and files   40

    Logs   40

    Files   40

Admin console   **40**

Silent installation   **43**

Creating a response file   44

Editing a response file   45

Running the installer silently   45

Examining installation logs   45

Summary   **45**

Chapter 2: Deploying your Applications — 47

Inside the Application Server — 48
JVM — 49
Web container — 49
Virtual hosts — 49
Environment settings — 49
Resources — 50
JNDI — 50
Application file types — 50
Deploying an application — 52
Starting and stopping your applications — 58
Data access applications — 61
Data sources — 61
Preparing our sample database — 62
JDBC providers — 66
Creating a JDBC provider — 66
Creating a J2C alias — 70
Creating a data source — 72
Deploying a data access application — 75
Selecting installation options — 76
Mapping modules to servers — 77
Providing JSP reloading options for web modules — 77
Mapping shared libraries — 77
Mapping resource references to resources — 78
Mapping virtual hosts for web modules — 78
Mapping context roots for web modules — 79
Reviewing the deployment steps — 79
Using the application — 80
Summary — 81

Chapter 3: Security — 83

J2EE security — 83
Global security — 84
Global security registry types — 84
Turning on global security — 85
Standalone custom registry — 87
Local operating system — 92
Creating a Linux user — 92
Standalone LDAP — 94
Download OpenLDAP — 94
Installing OpenLDAP — 95
Configuring OpenLDAP — 95

Adding a user to LDAP	99
Configuring an LDAP registry in WebSphere	104
Administrative roles	108
Mapping users and groups to administrative roles	110
Summary	**113**
Chapter 4: Administrative Scripting	**115**
Automation	**116**
The ws_ant tool	**116**
Deploying an application using ws_ant	118
The wsadmin tool	**123**
Interactive commands	124
Individual commands	126
Profile scripts	128
Command script files	128
Listing installed applications with Jython	129
Installing an application using Jython	129
Querying application status	132
Summary	**139**
Chapter 5: WebSphere Configuration	**141**
File structure	**141**
The WebSphere file system	142
The product binaries file structure	142
The profile file structure	143
XML configuration files	**144**
Cell level XML files	145
Node level XML files	146
Server level XML files	146
Important properties files	**147**
The soap.client.props file	147
The sas.client.props file	147
Logs	**148**
JVM logs	148
Configuring logs	150
Changing log file locations	151
Changing log styles	153
FFDC logs	153
Viewing JVM logs	154
Viewing logs in the admin console	154
Viewing logs on the file system	154
Linux tail command	154
Linux grep command	156

JVM settings	**157**
Changing JVM settings using the admin console	158
Class loaders	**159**
Class loading basics	160
WebSphere class loaders	161
Application server class loader	161
Configuring server class loaders	162
Application class loader	163
Configuring application class loaders	163
Web module class loader	164
Configuring module class loading	165
Class loading isolation	165
Summary	**166**
Chapter 6: WebSphere Messaging	**167**
Java messaging	**168**
Java Message Service	168
JMS features	170
JMS concepts	170
JMS API	**172**
WebSphere messaging	**173**
Default JMS provider	173
WebSphere SIB	174
Creating a SIB	175
Configuring JMS	177
Creating queue connection factories	177
Creating queue destinations	179
Installing the JMS demo application	180
JMS Test Tool application	183
WebSphere MQ overview	**185**
Overview of WebSphere MQ example	185
Installing WebSphere MQ	185
Running the WMQ installer	187
Creating a queue manager	188
Creating a WMQ connection factory	192
Creating a WMQ queue destination	195
Reconfiguring the JMS demo application	196
Summary	**198**
Chapter 7: Monitoring and Tuning	**199**
Tivoli Performance Viewer	**200**
Enabling Tivoli Performance Viewer	201
Key TPV categories	205
Summary Reports	206
Key performance modules	206

Starting Tivoli Performance Viewer	208
PMI for external monitoring	**215**
Request metrics	**216**
Enabling request metrics	217
Components to be instrumented	218
Trace level	218
Request metrics destination	218
Request metrics in SystemOut.log	219
Retrieving performance data with PerfServlet	220
Dynamic caching	**222**
JVM tuning	**223**
JVM core and heap dumps	224
Requesting a Java core dump using Jython	224
Requesting a heap dump using Jython	225
Requesting a Java core dump using the kill command	225
JVM-triggered heap dump	226
Analysing a Java core (thread) dump	229
IBM Thread and Monitor Dump Analyzer for Java	230
Installing the JCA tool	230
Generate a Java core dump to view the thread lock	231
Other analysis tools	235
Setting the initial and maximum heap sizes	236
Tuning your heap size	236
Summary	**237**
Chapter 8: Administrative Features	**239**
The administrative agent	**240**
Creating an administration profile	241
Profile Management Tool	241
Starting the administrative agent	245
Administrative agent console	246
Registering an application server node	247
Creating a second application server node	250
Removing the administrative agent	**255**
IBM HTTP Server	**257**
Starting IBM HTTP Server	261
The WebSphere plugin	**262**
Installing the WebSphere plugin	263
Manual configuration of the plugin	265
Generate plugin	269
Summary	**270**
Chapter 9: Administration Tools	**271**
Dumping namespaces	**272**
Example name space dump	274

EAR expander   **275**

Oveview of the WebSphere Application Server toolkit   **277**

Installing the WebSphere Application Server toolkit   278

Running the Application Server toolkit   278

Log analysis using the ASTK   279

Creating a new project   280

Importing log files   281

Applying filters   284

Selecting columns   285

Loading symptom databases   286

Inspecting J2EE applications   289

Summary   **293**

Chapter 10: Product Maintenance   **295**

Understanding updates   **296**

Update process overview   **296**

Product update types   **297**

Preparing for updates   **299**

Locating updates   **300**

Fix Central   300

Update installers   **303**

Creating a backup   **303**

Installing a new Update Installer   **304**

Downloading the Update Installer   304

Installing the graphical Update Installer   305

Applying an update using the Update Installer   307

Silent updates   **311**

Logs   **312**

Troubleshooting tips   **313**

Summary   **315**

Index   **317**

Preface

As a J2EE (Enterprise Edition) administrator, you require a secure, scalable, and resilient infrastructure to support and manage your J2EE applications and service-oriented architecture services.

The WebSphere suite of products from IBM provides many different industry solutions and WebSphere Application Server is the core of the WebSphere product range from IBM.

WebSphere is optimized to ease administration and improve runtime performance. It runs your applications and services in a reliable, secure, and high-performance environment to ensure that your core business opportunities are not lost due to application or infrastructure downtime.

Whether you are experienced or new to WebSphere, this book will provide you with a cross-section of WebSphere Application Server features and how to configure these features for optimal use. This book will provide you with the knowledge to build and manage performance-based J2EE applications and service-oriented architecture (SOA) services, offering the highest level of reliability, security, and scalability.

Taking you through by examples, you will be shown the different methods for installing WebSphere Application Server and will be shown how to configure and prepare WebSphere resources for your application deployments. The facets of data-aware and message-aware applications are explained and demonstrated, giving the reader real-world examples of manual and automated deployments.

WebSphere security is covered in detail showing the various methods of implementing federated user and group repositories. Key administration features and tools are introduced, which will help WebSphere administrators manage and tune their WebSphere implementation and applications. You will also be shown how to administer your WebSphere server standalone or use the new administrative agent, which provides the ability to administer multiple installations of WebSphere Application Server using one single administration console.

What this book covers

Chapter 1, Installing WebSphere Application Server covers how to plan and prepare your WebSphere installation and shows how to manually install WebSphere using the graphical installer and how to use a response file for automated silent installation. The fundamentals of application server profiles are described and the administrative console is introduced.

Chapter 2, Deploying your Applications explains the make-up of Enterprise Archive (EAR) files, how to manually deploy applications, and how Java Naming and Directory Interface (JNDI) is used in the configuration of resources. Connecting to databases is explained via the configuration of Java database connectivity (JDBC) drivers and data sources used in the deployment of a data-aware application.

Chapter 3, Security demonstrates the implementation of global security and how to federate lightweight directory access protocol (LDAP) and file-based registries for managing WebSphere security. Roles are explained where users and groups can be assigned different administrative capabilities.

Chapter 4, Administrative Scripting introduces ws_ant, a utility for using apache Ant build scripts to deploy and configure applications. Advanced administrative scripting is demonstrated by using the wsadmin tool with Jython scripts, covering how WebSphere deployment and configuration can be automated using the extensive WebSphere Jython scripting objects.

Chapter 5, WebSphere Configuration explains the WebSphere installation structure and key XML files, which make up the underlying WebSphere configuration repository. WebSphere logging is covered showing the types of log and log settings that are vital for administration. Application Server JVM settings and class loading are explained.

Chapter 6, WebSphere Messaging explains basic Java message service (JMS) messaging concepts and demonstrates both JMS messaging using the default messaging provider and WebSphere Message Queuing (MQ) along with explanations of message types. Use of Queue Connection Factories, Queues, and Queue Destinations are demonstrated via a sample application.

Chapter 7, Monitoring and Tuning shows how to use Tivoli Performance Monitor, request metrics, and JVM tuning settings to help you improve WebSphere performance and monitor the running state of your deployed applications.

Chapter 8, Administrative Features covers how to enable the administrative agent for administering multiple application servers with a central administrative console. IBM HTTP Server and the WebSphere plug-in are explained.

Chapter 9, Administration Tools demonstrates some of the shell-script-based utilities vital to the WebSphere administrator for debugging and problem resolution.

Chapter 10, Product Maintenance shows how to maintain your WebSphere Application Server by keeping it up-to-date with the latest fix packs and feature packs.

What you need for this book

You can now download the latest version, RHEL 5.3, known as Tikanga, as a trial from www.redhat.com. If you cannot obtain Red Hat, you can also use CentOS 5.3 which is a community-supported, freely-available operating system based on Red Hat Enterprise Linux and is freely available for download from http://www.centos.org. If you find any variances from the exercises in this book, you can search http://www.webspheretools.com for tips on how to install and configure Red Hat or Centos. All of the software applications required are either trial or open source software applications, which are freely available on the Internet, and the download URLs are provided along with instructions of how to install and configure the software required for each exercise.

Below is a list of the software applications used in this book:

- WebSphere Application Server 7 Trial
- WebSphere MQ 7 Trial
- Open LDAP
- Oracle XE (Oracle Database 10g Express Edition)
- Xming
- PuTTY

Conventions

In this book, you will find a number of styles of text that distinguish between different kinds of information. Here are some examples of these styles, and an explanation of their meaning.

Code words in text are shown as follows: "Since the manageHR.xml file has a project declaration which specifies the default target being build-all, as shown below, the build-all target will be called if no target name is specified on the command line."

A block of code is set as follows:

```
[<project name="Manage HR Lister Application Deployment"
default="build-all" basedir=".">]
```

Any command-line input or output is written as follows:

```
print "Hello World"
```

New terms and **important words** are shown in bold. Words that you see on the screen, in menus or dialog boxes for example, appear in the text like this: "clicking the **Next** button moves you to the next screen".

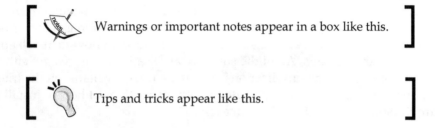

Warnings or important notes appear in a box like this.

Tips and tricks appear like this.

Reader feedback

Feedback from our readers is always welcome. Let us know what you think about this book—what you liked or may have disliked. Reader feedback is important for us to develop titles that you really get the most out of.

To send us general feedback, simply send an email to feedback@packtpub.com, and mention the book title via the subject of your message.

If there is a book that you need and would like to see us publish, please send us a note in the **SUGGEST A TITLE** form on www.packtpub.com or email suggest@packtpub.com.

If there is a topic that you have expertise in and you are interested in either writing or contributing to a book on, see our author guide on www.packtpub.com/authors.

Customer support

Now that you are the proud owner of a Packt book, we have a number of things to help you to get the most from your purchase.

Downloading the example code for the book

Visit http://www.packtpub.com/files/code/7207_Code.zip to directly download the example code.

The downloadable files contain instructions on how to use them.

Errata

Although we have taken every care to ensure the accuracy of our content, mistakes do happen. If you find a mistake in one of our books—maybe a mistake in the text or the code—we would be grateful if you would report this to us. By doing so, you can save other readers from frustration, and help us to improve subsequent versions of this book. If you find any errata, please report them by visiting http://www.packtpub.com/support, selecting your book, clicking on the **let us know** link, and entering the details of your errata. Once your errata are verified, your submission will be accepted and the errata added to any list of existing errata. Any existing errata can be viewed by selecting your title from http://www.packtpub.com/support.

Piracy

Piracy of copyright material on the Internet is an ongoing problem across all media. At Packt, we take the protection of our copyright and licenses very seriously. If you come across any illegal copies of our works, in any form, on the Internet, please provide us with the location address or website name immediately so that we can pursue a remedy.

Please contact us at copyright@packtpub.com with a link to the suspected pirated material.

We appreciate your help in protecting our authors, and our ability to bring you valuable content.

Questions

You can contact us at questions@packtpub.com if you are having a problem with any aspect of the book, and we will do our best to address it.

1
Installing WebSphere Application Server

To begin our journey, we will need to install IBM **WebSphere Application Server (WAS)**. WebSphere is based on Java and can run on many platforms from Windows through to Unix and even Mainframes. We have chosen Linux Red Hat as our IBM certified **Operating System (OS)**. For the remainder of this book, we will discuss WebSphere Administration from a Linux/Unix standpoint using Red Hat (RHEL) version 4 update 6 as our Linux distribution. It is easy to acquire Linux Red Hat trial ISO images which can be downloaded from the Internet; it is also readily available on CD from your local PC store. We use Linux as opposed to Windows as using WebSphere on Linux lends to being Unix-ready. What we mean is that by learning to install and administer Websphere using Linux, you will be well-prepared and equipped to work with WebSphere for Linux or WebSphere for Unix versions. The skills learned in this book are transferable to WebSphere installations and configurations on all the supported versions of Unix; for example, Solaris, AIX and HP-UX, and other versions of Linux like SUSE. It must also be mentioned that Websphere for Linux can also be installed on CentOS and Fedora and also Ubuntu, which are all open source versions of Linux; however, they are not supported by IBM.

In this chapter, we will cover the following topics:

- Planning an application server install
- Installation scenarios
- Preparation and prerequisites
- Graphical installation
- Installing base binaries
- Understanding profile types
- Installing profiles

- Verifying and installation
- Administration console
- Silent installs

Installation planning

Before we begin any WebSphere installation, we would ask the three questions below to help prepare and plan for an installation.

- What version of Websphere is required to support your applications?
    - ° Investigations are made to ensure that your application will run in the version of Websphere you intend to install. A key point is to understand what version of the Java WebSphere version support. You can go to the following URL to view a WebSphere version compatibility matrix: http://en.wikipedia.org/wiki/Websphere. You may have to speak to your application developers or application vendors to accurately asses JVM requirements.

- Are there any OS tweaks for the platform required for the chosen version of Websphere?
    - ° It is important to understand what version of OS you are going to use. First decide which platform you are going to install on and then research what the prerequisites are for that platform. Each platform may have certain Operating System (OS) changes or optimizations which are stipulated for correct installation of WAS.

- What version of OS and fix packs are required to support the chosen version of WebSphere?
    - ° Not only do you need to understand the base installation version, you may also want to understand what the latest fix packs are to ensure that your version of Websphere is fully up-to-date. You can go to the following URL to find the latest WebSphere fix pack version: http://www-01.ibm.com/support/docview.wss?rs=180&uid=swg27004980#ver70. We will cover more about maintenance and fix packs in Chapter 10.

As mentioned above, we have chosen to use Red Hat Enterprise Linux in this book, as it is the most commonly used IBM certified Linux distribution used for Websphere; however, it is recommended that you visit the following IBM URL and read up on the prerequisites for installing Websphere Application Server 7.0 on Linux platforms `http://www-01.ibm.com/support/docview.wss?rs=180&uid=swg27012369`.

Installation scenarios

Before beginning an installation, it is advised that you think about the type of WAS install you wish to perform. There are several installation scenarios and knowing which components are available might influence your chosen installation path. You may also wish to think about coexistence or interoperability with other WAS implementations or helper services. Helper services are other applications and/or technologies that may be required for your applications to run correctly on WebSphere and function as per their design. This means you may have to consider installation requirements in addition to those of WAS.

The WAS installation process allows for two main actions. The first being the base binaries which are the core executables and the second being a profile. The base binaries are the product mechanics made up of executables and shells scripts, and can be shared by one or many profiles. Profiles exist so data can be partitioned away from the underlying core. Simply put, a profile contains an Application Server. When an Application Server is running, the server process may read and write data to underlying configuration files and logs. So, by using profiles, transient data is kept away from the base product. This allows us to have more than one profile using the same base binaries and also allows us to remove profiles without affecting other profiles. Another reason for separating the base binaries is so that we can upgrade the product with maintenance and fix packs without having to reconfigure our Application Server profiles. A conceptual diagram is shown below.

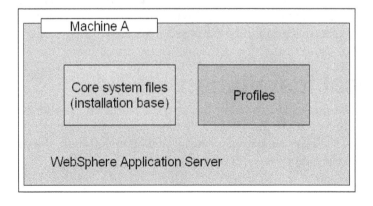

Profile types

During the installation process, you can decide to install different profile types.
There are two main profile types: application server profile or a management profile.
Your installation scenarios will determine which combination of profile types you
will be selecting during the installation wizard. Below is a table explaining the
different profile types:

Profile Type	Description
Application server	WebSphere has the ability to have multiple application server definitions using the same underlying base binaries. Each profile defines the attributes and configurations for a given application server.
	Each standalone application server can optionally have its own administrative console application, which you use to manage the application server.
	We will cover how to install a profile later in the chapter.
Management profile	A Management profile defines an administrative agent which provides a single interface (administrative console) to administer multiple application servers.
	We will cover the administrative agent in Chapter 8.

Preparation and prerequisites

Before we start with the WebSphere Application Server installation, we need to
ensure the correct installation media is available and that the operating system
prerequisites have been met. It is also important to ensure that there is enough free
disk space on your Linux file system and that you have a large enough /tmp folder.
A recommended size for the /tmp folder is 1 Gigabyte; this will also later cater to
deployment of large applications. The installer program checks for required space
before calling the installation wizard and will inform you that there is not enough
disk space; however, it is good to be prepared upfront.

Graphical installation

For our first installation, we are going to use the Installer in graphical mode to install
and configure our WAS. We are going to install our WAS in two parts. Part 1 will
be installation of the base binaries and part 2 will be installation of a profile. In each
part, we will list the actions as a set of steps.

Installing the base binaries

The WebSphere 7 trial installation process is almost identical to the official product release, the major difference being that you will get more supporting information with the official product media and that a few extras show up in the installation wizards.

Downloading the WAS for Linux trial

Normally, the installation media for WebSphere can be obtained on CD or downloaded from IBM using an online passport advantage account. If your organization has a passport advantage account, then media CDs can also be requested to be delivered as part of your license agreement. Nowadays, it is more common that software is delivered by wire (via the Internet). For our installation media, we are going to use the demo trial, which can be downloaded from the IBM developer works site at the following location: `http://www.ibm.com/developerworks/downloads/ws/was/`. Below is a screenshot of what the IBM download site looks like:

 Helpful hint: If you do not already have an IBM login, then you will need to register and complete a small questionnaire. Once completed, you will be directed to the trials download page.

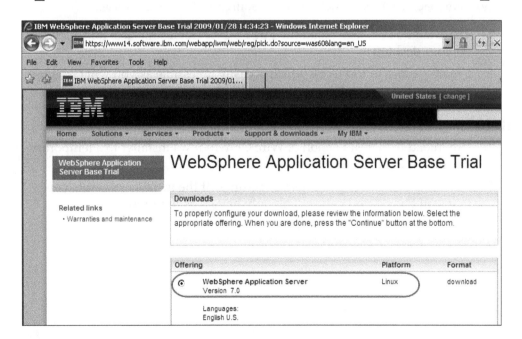

Download the trial for Linux from the site mentioned above. The file you are looking to download is called `was.cd.7000.trial.base.linux.ia32.tar.gz`. You may need to locate the download by name, that is, WebSphere Application Server for the Linux platform.

Select and download the file to a temporary location, for example, `c:\temp`, on your desktop and transfer the installation binary to your Linux machine via secure **File Transfer Protocol (FTP)**.

It is recommended that you copy the files onto your Linux box into a folder where you can keep the install binaries for later reference, for re-install, or for adding new features post-installation. You can use a secure FTP client or secure copy client, depending on your preference of file transfer tools. It is best to use a secure shell (SSH) for all conversation with your Linux server and so we will be using the open tools WinSCP (Secure Copy) and PuTTY. WinSCP is an open source SFTP and FTP client for Microsoft Windows which we will use for file transfers to and from our Linux server. PuTTY is a terminal emulator application which is often used as a client for the SSH and Telnet protocols and we will use it for shell access.

Installing PuTTY

PuTTy can be downloaded from `http://www.chiark.greenend.org.uk/~sgtatham/putty/download.html`. Both tools are open source and are free for use.

1. To install PuTTY, download the PuTTY executable and save it in a location on your desktop.
2. Create a shortcut to PuTTy which is easily accessible as you will be using PuTTY to connect to Linux.

Installing WinSCP

1. Download the latest version of WinSCP windows installer to a temporary location, that is, `c:/temp/`.
2. Run the installer using the default settings. If the installer prompts you to install PuTTY, indicate you already have it as required.

Uploading the trial install to your Linux server

The step-by-step procedure to install the trial version to your LINUX server is as follows:

1. After the trial has been downloaded, upload the file to your Linux server using WinSCP.

 Check disk space to ensure you can complete the installation. You can use the Linux command df -k to see how much file system space you have.

2. Once you have uploaded the trial, log in with a secure shell (for example, PuTTY) as root, navigate to the `tar.gz` file location, and decompress the file by using the Linux unzip tool called gunzip as shown by the command below. gunzip expands files that have been reduced by gzip, which shrinks files using compression algorithms.

    ```
    gunzip ./was.cd.7000.trial.base.linux.ia32.tar.gz
    ```

3. The `tar.gz` file will now become a tar file and we can decompress the tar file by using the Linux command `tar` as follows.

    ```
    tar -xvf ./was.cd.7000.trial.base.linux.ia32.tar
    ```

Explanation of options used in the tar command:

* `options -xv`: decompress with verbose screen logging
* `option f`: the filename we wish to decompress.

After extracting the installation files, navigate to the folder where you decompressed the tar file to. If you do a listing of the directory, you will see a shell script named `launchpad.sh`, as seen in the screenshot below:

```
-rwxr-xr-x    1 root root      5440 Sep  1 05:24 launchpad.sh
-rw-r--r--    1 root root      1113 Sep  1 05:24 launchpad.ini
-rw-r--r--    1 root root       225 Sep  2 23:50 Version.txt
-rw-r--r--    1 root root     68230 Sep  2 23:50 notices.txt
-rw-r--r--    1 root root      4610 Sep  2 23:50 non_IBM_license.txt
-rw-r--r--    1 root root       336 Sep  2 23:50 Copyright.txt
drwxr-xr-x    3 root root      4096 Sep  3 03:28 JDK
drwxr-xr-x   11 root root      4096 Sep  3 03:29 WAS
drwxr-xr-x   35 root root      4096 Sep  3 03:29 launchpad
```

Since our installation requires the use of a graphical user interface (GUI), before we start the installation we need to ensure that we set up PuTTY correctly for use with X Windows. The X Windows system (commonly X or X11) is a protocol that provides a GUI for Unix-based systems.

To set up PuTTY for use with X Windows, we need to enable X11 forwarding. We do this by changing the X11 option in the properties of PuTTY as found in the **Connection | SSH | X11** option in the **Category** panel tree, as seen in the screenshot below:

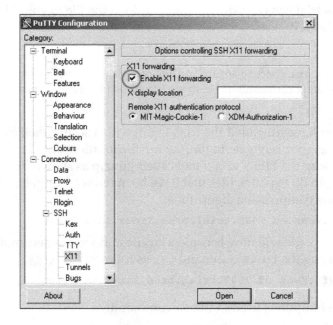

To test X Windows, we will also need a Windows X server. Xming is an open X Windows server which we will use. Xming can be downloaded from the following URL:

`http://www.straightrunning.com/XmingNotes/`

Once installed, we can run Xming and do a quick test with our SSH session to ensure that X Windows is working. When Xming is running, you will see an **X** icon in the Windows system tray on your desktop, similar to the one shown in the following screenshot:

It is recommended that you also install **Xming-fonts** to ensure that all WebSphere-related installation products run error-free. Without the correct X-fonts installed, certain installation products can fail. Installing Xming-fonts ensures that there are appropriate fonts available which are used by installers. You can download Xming-fonts from the same Xming web site and install over the top of the base Xming installation.

Once you have set X11 forwarding in PuTTY, you can run the `xclock` command to test if X Windows is running. If it is, you will see a clock popup if Xming and PuTTY are working correctly.

Note: To connect from our PC desktop machine to an X Windows session, we will need to export the display. To export our display, we will need to get the IP address of our PC. We can do this by using a command prompt and typing the Windows command `ipconfig`, as shown in the following figure:

```
C:\WINDOWS\system32\cmd.exe

Microsoft Windows XP [Version 5.1.2600]
(C) Copyright 1985-2001 Microsoft Corp.

C:\Documents and Settings\SteveR>ipconfig

Windows IP Configuration

Ethernet adapter Wireless Network Connection:

        Connection-specific DNS Suffix  . :
        IP Address. . . . . . . . . . . . : 192.168.0.3
        Subnet Mask . . . . . . . . . . . : 255.255.255.0
        Default Gateway . . . . . . . . . : 192.168.0.1

Ethernet adapter Local Area Connection:

        Media State . . . . . . . . . . . : Media disconnected

C:\Documents and Settings\SteveR>
```

Once we know our local PC's IP address, we can then type the following command:

export DISPLAY=<localhost>:0.0

(The last set of digits here are your IP address.)

We can now type xclock and we will see a clock popup as an independent X Window.

Before running the WebSphere trial installation script, we need to check the umask. The umask setting controls which permissions will be masked (not set) for any newly created files, for example, 022. By using the Linux command umask, we can check the current umask. It needs to be set to 022. We can set this by typing the command umask 022 in a secure shell. Using the umask command ensures that all new files will be set with the 8-bit inverse permission of 755. This translates as follows: the owner of the file gets rwx (Read, Write, Execute) permissions and groups and others will have rx (Read, Execute) permissions. In simple terms, the root user will be able to view and navigate files as well as edit and run scripts. All users in the group root will have only read and execute permissions, the same as any other user, which means they can only view and navigate files in the WebSphere installation tree of files. Discussing the details of Unix file permissions is beyond the scope of this book. There are many online tutorials that can give you a quick overview of Unix file permissions.

Installing as root

WebSphere should be installed as root and after the installation is complete the ownership of the installation binaries should be changed to an appropriate non-root user. How this is done is not covered in this book. It is recommended that a non-root user and appropriate associated group be created. Once WAS has been installed using root, the ownership is changed to the new user and this user is then used to administer WAS at the Linux shell level. To keep things simple in all our exercise, we will be installing and running WebSphere instances as the root user so that our WebSphere installation will work with all the third-party products we will install throughout this book, without having to get sidetracked by security and folder permission errors.

Running the launchpad

Once you have X Windows working, launch the installation wizard by running the installation wizard launchpad using the following command:

```
./launchpad.sh
```

The following figure shows the installation launchpad:

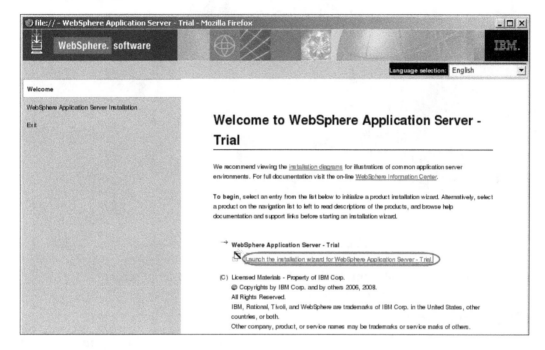

You will be presented with the IBM Launchpad. As you can see, there is a link to **installation diagrams**. It is recommended that you familiarize yourself with these diagrams as they explain visually the possible installation scenarios very well.

To continue with the actual install, click **Launch the installation wizard for WebSphere Application Server –Trial** as shown in the preceding screenshot.

Installation wizard welcome screen

You will be presented with the installation wizard welcome screen as seen below:

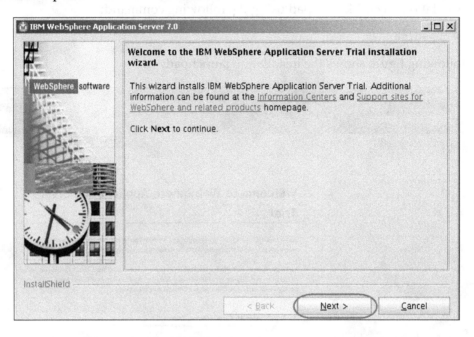

Clicking on **Next** will take you to the software license agreement screen.

Software license agreement

It is a requirement that you accept the license agreement; this is also a requirement which we will see later in the *Silent installation* section.

Click **Next** to move on to the prerequisites check.

System prerequisites check

The installer will check to ensure that your Linux OS meets the required prerequisites. If your OS is not patched to the correct level, you may see a screen similar to the one below:

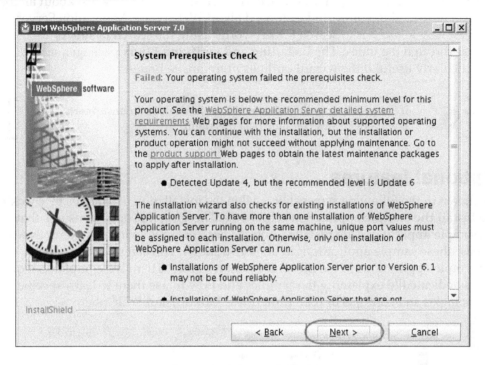

You can fix the operating system by applying appropriate patches/updates which is a Linux administration activity. If the wizard prompts you with an error, you may have to consult your Linux distribution's web site for more information. The installation wizard will prompt you for certain Linux dependencies required for the installation to progress.

Linux OS patches are often downloaded from sites on the Internet which offer RPMs. If there are no Linux patches required, simply ignore and continue. If you are prompted for patches to be made, it is recommended that you quit the installation at this point and ensure the prerequisites are completed as the installation is restarted. If you don't care, you can move on.

This is one of the reasons why we chose Red Hat Linux as it is a certified platform for IBM WebSphere. If you are unsure about platform prerequisites, it is recommended that you consult the online IBM Information Center Portal for IBM WebSphere which is located at this address: `http://publib.boulder.ibm.com/infocenter/wasinfo/v7r0/index.jsp`. This Info Centre web site will provide just about all the detailed information you would ever need about WebSphere Application Server. The best way to use it is to search for keywords using the search facility or to browse through the index. The **Installing and verifying Linux packages** section is particularly useful if the wizard outlines prerequisite issues.

> If the installation wizard detects a major fault or an unsupported OS, it will not let you continue past this point.

Optional features

As shown in the following screenshot, enable the installation of samples by checking the **Install the Sample applications** checkbox. Checking this option ensures that the sample applications are installed into the base binaries so in later exercises we can use these sample applications in demonstrations. You can read more about the sample applications in the IBM Information Centre. There is a complete set of pages dedicated to explaining the samples and how to use them to learn specific technologies and concepts of J2EE (Enterprise Edition) and WebSphere.

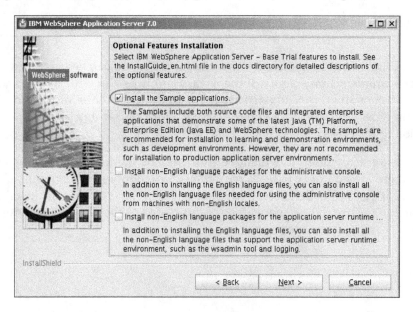

Click **Next** to continue to move on and set the installation folder locations.

Installation directory

You can change the installation directory. Often in production environments the default option is not used. It may be useful to shorten the folder names, which will make it easier for administration later when we need to navigate through the WebSphere file systems. For our purposes, we are going to change the default folder from /opt/IBM/WebSphere/AppServer to /apps/was7. Take note of this path as we will now refer to this path as the <was_root> path.

WebSphere Application Server environments

Depending on which installation scenario you chose, you will now have to select a type of installation. The type of installation chosen will determine whether a profile is created or not.

There are three types of installation options listed by the wizard as shown in the following table:

Installation Option	Description
Management profile	A management profile includes an administrative agent server and services for managing multiple application server environments. An administrative agent manages application servers that are on the same machine.
Standalone application server	A standalone application server environment runs your enterprise applications. The application server is managed from its own administrative console and functions independently of all other application servers.
Base binaries	WebSphere Application Server version 7.0 requires at least one profile to be functional. Select this option only if one or more profiles will be created after installation completes successfully.

Since it is good practice to understand the possibilities in which WebSphere can be installed, we are not going to use the wizard default of standalone application server. We are going to choose **None** which will install the base binaries only. The binaries in their own right are not useful unless at least one application server profile is created. After the base binaries are installed, we will use another tool called the Profile Management Tool to demonstrate how to independently create an application server profile.

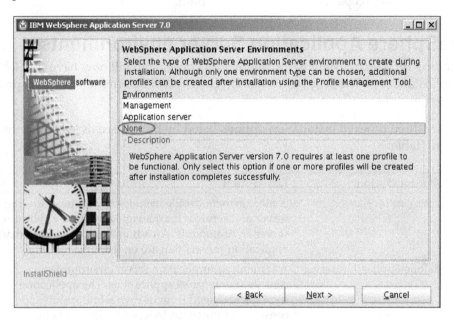

When asked if you want to proceed without creating a profile, click **Yes**.

The installation wizard will now search for installable fixes; however, since we have not prepared any, the installer will continue. We will cover maintenance and fix packs later on in Chapter 10, however, in reality, you would want to now update WebSphere with the latest fix pack to ensure that the base binaries are fully up-to-date. This will ensure that any subsequent profiles will also contain the latest fixes. Click **Next** to move on to the installation summary screen.

Before the next screen loads, the installation wizard will double-check that the current user has permissions to install to the folder specified in locations. Since we are installing as **root** in our example, it really doesn't matter as we have full system privileges. For production environments, it may not be possible to install as root due to company policy. Some companies may allow **sudo** access. Sudo to root access is an administrative feature that allows users to do root work as another user and an audit log captures all the commands that are issued. As discussed previously, we can install as non-root user; however, for demonstration we have elected to use root access to minimize issues in our learning because root access is granted full system privileges.

When you click **Next**, the installation process will now run and install the base binaries. Once completed, we will be presented with an installation report, as seen in the following screenshot.

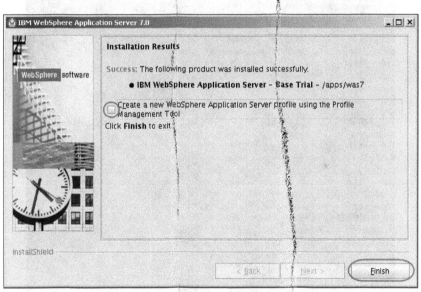

You can click **Finish** to complete the installation.

Earlier in the installation wizard we chose to defer the running of the Profile Management Tool so we could later demonstrate the manual creation of a profile. This means that all we have installed at this point is the base binaries.

By looking at the files installed by the installer, we will see what makes up the base binaries. You will also notice that the folder permissions are rwxr-xr-x (755), which is a result of the 022 umask we set before we ran the installation wizard. The screenshot below shows a typical list of the <was_root> directory.

 The presence of the **uninstall** folder contains an uninstaller which we can use to uninstall WAS.

We will now do a quick check to see if the base binaries have installed correctly by running the WebSphere command script installver.sh (which is found in the bin folder). We can generate a report which will identify the state of the installation.

From now on, we will refer to folders relative to the base install folder; for example, using the syntax `<was_root>/<folder_path>` will mean the WebSphere base installation folder plus the path we are working with. In our examples, we have a `<was_root>` of `/apps/was7` because we set the installation path as such in the installation wizard. Since you may not follow this convention, to make it simpler we will make all paths relative to `<was_root>` which you can substitute with the base folder naming convention you have chosen.

Run the following command:

```
<was_root>/bin/installver.sh
```

The result of running the command above will be a report similar to the following:

```
I CWNVU0470I: [ivu] Starting to analyze: workspace
I CWNVU0480I: [ivu] Done analyzing: workspace

I CWNVU0470I: [ivu] Starting to analyze: workspace.query
I CWNVU0480I: [ivu] Done analyzing: workspace.query

I CWNVU0470I: [ivu] Starting to analyze: wsadie.bundle
I CWNVU0480I: [ivu] Done analyzing: wsadie.bundle

I CWNVU0470I: [ivu] Starting to analyze: wsba.impl
I CWNVU0480I: [ivu] Done analyzing: wsba.impl

I CWNVU0470I: [ivu] Starting to analyze: wsfp.wsaddressing.impl
I CWNVU0480I: [ivu] Done analyzing: wsfp.wsaddressing.impl

I CWNVU0470I: [ivu] Starting to analyze: wsnotification
I CWNVU0480I: [ivu] Done analyzing: wsnotification

I CWNVU0470I: [ivu] Starting to analyze: wssecurity.impl
I CWNVU0480I: [ivu] Done analyzing: wssecurity.impl

I CWNVU0400I: [ivu] Total issues found : 0
I CWNVU0340I: [ivu] Done.
```

Profile creation

By themselves, the base binaries serve no purpose. We must create a profile which is essentially an application server definition. We use the **Profile Management Tool (PMT)**. The tool is an X Windows tool. To run it, type

```
<was_root>/bin/ProfileManagement/pmt.sh
```

As shown in the next screenshot, when the PMT has loaded, the option to create a profile will be available.

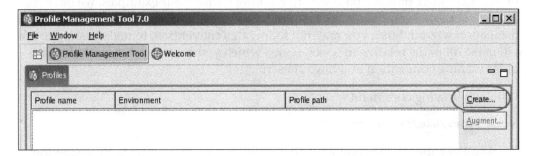

Click **Create** to start the profile creation wizard. You will then be presented with the **Environment Selection** screen. In the **Environment Selection** screen, we are now going to create a profile which will define our application server.

Select **Application server** from the list of options, as shown in the screenshot below:

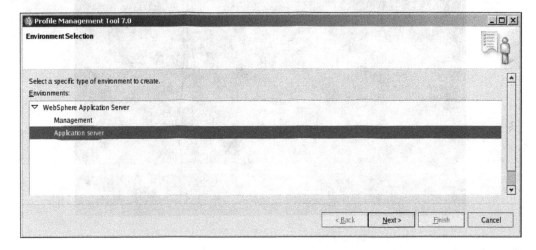

At this time, we are only interested in a standalone application server. If we wanted to administer multiple application servers with a single administration console, then we can create a management profile to have a single administration interface which can manage multiple application server nodes. We will cover more about the administrative agent in Chapter 8.

Click **Next** to move on to the **Profile Creation options** screen shown in the following screenshot:

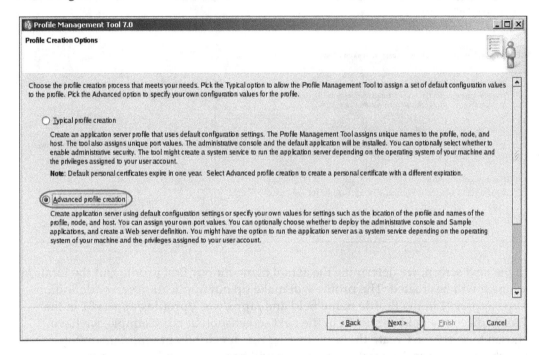

In the **Profile Creation options** screen as shown above, select **Advanced profile creation** as shown in the above screenshot. Choosing this option allows for greater choice and flexibility and control of our profile creation as opposed to using a default configuration.

Click on **Next**.

Since we opted for the sample applications to be made available during our base install, we now have the option to now install sample applications as part of our new profile. We do not wish the sample applications to be installed in our new application server profile. The sample applications will still exist in the base installation, but we are not using them in this profile. Uncheck the **Deploy the Sample applications** checkbox as shown below, then click **Next** to continue.

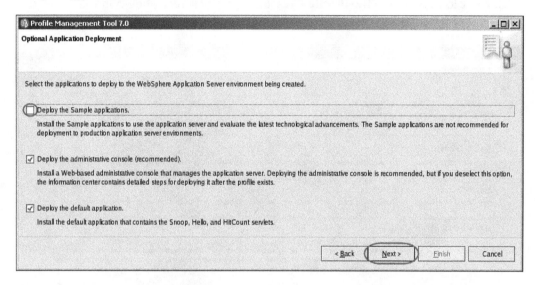

In the next screen, we determine the actual name for our first profile and the location where it will be created. The profile will make up our application server definition. Type **appsrv01** in the **Profile name** field and **/apps/was7/profiles/appsrv01** in the **Profile directory** field as shown in the next screenshot. In our example, we have chosen to select the **Create the server using the development template** option, which speeds up server start-up. Since we will be starting and stopping the server many times during our learning, it is recommended we turn this option on to save time when waiting for server restarts. For production, we would turn this option off. Click **Next** to move on to the next screen.

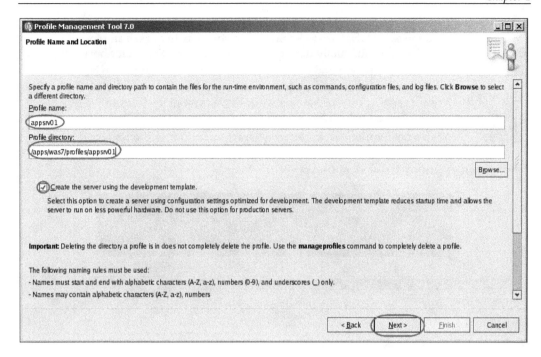

 Using lowercase for all folder names makes it easier to remember the case when typing folder paths in Linux, as Linux is case-sensitive.

The next screen is the **Node and Host Names** screen. The **Node name** is an important part of the installation process. It is recommended to keep this name as short as possible. We will cover the concept of nodes in later chapters.

The **Server name** is the actual name of the application server's JVM. This name will be referred to in logging and configuration, which we will address in later chapters.

The **Host name** will automatically be taken from the OS hosts file and can be changed in the wizard at this point to suit your requirements. You can use a hostname, IP address, or **Fully Qualified Domain Name (FQDN)**. If you decide to change the hostname in the wizard, ensure that the change is reflected in your host file or DNS as required.

If you use an FQDN, first test that it is resolvable. In our eexamples, we will be using a manually derived hostname for simplicity. Our hostname will be **WebSphere** and our domain name is **redhat.com**. The FQDN will be **websphere.redhat.com**. This is not a real Internet domain. We are running on a private network so we can call it whatever we like, as long as our OS host file is configured correctly.

We do not require a DNS server to be set up for our examples.

Below is an example of our host file:

```
[root@localhost bin]# cat /etc/hosts
# Do not remove the following line, or various programs
# that require network functionality will fail.
127.0.0.1          localhost.localdomain    localhost
192.168.0.94       websphere.redhat.com     websphere
```

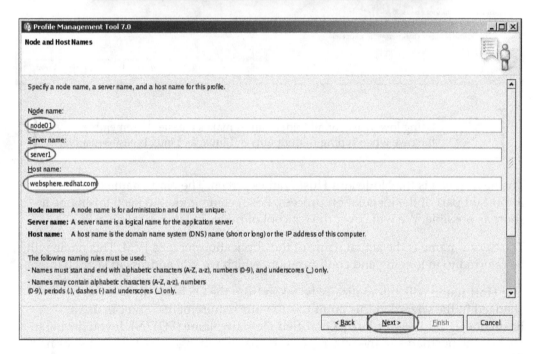

As shown in the preceding screenshot, we want to enter the following values, as listed in the table below into the fields on the **Nodes and Host Names** screen.

Field Name	Field Value
Node name	node01
Server name	server1
Host name	Use localhost or whatever FQDN you wish to use.
	We have used **websphere.redhat.com**

To move on to the **Administrative Security** screen, click **Next**.

In the **Administrative Security** screen, we will disable administrative security for now and re-enable it in Chapter 3. It is recommended for production environments that you enable administrative security right from the start to secure against unwanted changes being made to your server configuration by non-administrators. Leave the option **Enable administrative security** unchecked and click **Next** to move on to the security certificate screens.

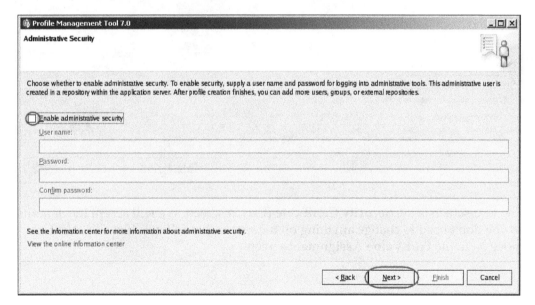

As shown below, the next screen is the **Security Certificate (Part 1)** screen. This is a new feature of the WebSphere 7 installation wizard. In previous versions of WebSphere, the security certificate screens were not available. The options available are to either use default certificates, use an existing keystore, or create one from another **Certificate Authority** (**CA**). For now, we will use the default keystore as generated by the installer. Certificates which are used for SSL are beyond the scope of this book. We will accept the default settings for this screen as shown below. Click **Next** to go to the **Security Certificate (Part 2)** screen.

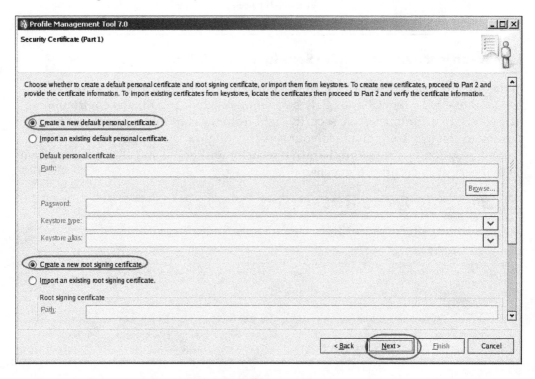

The next screen is the **Security Certificate (Part 2)** screen. We will accept the defaults, so you don't need to change anything on the screen that follows. Just click **Next** to move on to the **Port Value Assignment** screen.

WAS requires several ports during runtime. It is wise to ensure that no other application is already using the ports that you wish to use. The wizard is quite clever and will detect port usage and recommend free ports; however, it is recommended that you use the Linux command `netstat -an` to ensure that no other applications are using these ports. Use the following steps to check for used ports:

1. Open a secure shell to your Linux server using PuTTY.

2. Type the following command:

   `Netstat -an`

3. In the report that is generated, you are looking to see if ports have already been used, as shown below:

```
unix   2        [ ]            DGRAM                          6552
unix   2        [ ]            DGRAM                          6536
unix   2        [ ]            DGRAM                          6517
unix   2        [ ]            DGRAM                          5980
unix   2        [ ]            DGRAM                          5922
unix   3        [ ]            STREAM         CONNECTED       5593
unix   3        [ ]            STREAM         CONNECTED       5592
unix   2        [ ]            DGRAM                          5481
unix   2        [ ]            DGRAM                          5417
```

In the table below, you will be able to see what ports WebSphere uses.

Port Name	Default Port Value
Administrative console port	9060
Administrative console secure port	9043
HTTP transport port	9080
HTTPS transport port	9443
Boostrap port	2809
SIP port	5060
SIP secure port	5061
SOAP connector port	8880
Administrative interprocess communication port	9633
SAS SSL ServerAuth port	9401
CSIV2 ServerAuth listener port	9403
CSIV2 MultiAuth listener port	9402
ORB listener port	9100

Since this is our first WAS profile on the Linux machine, we will use the defaults recommended by the wizard, as shown in the screenshot below:

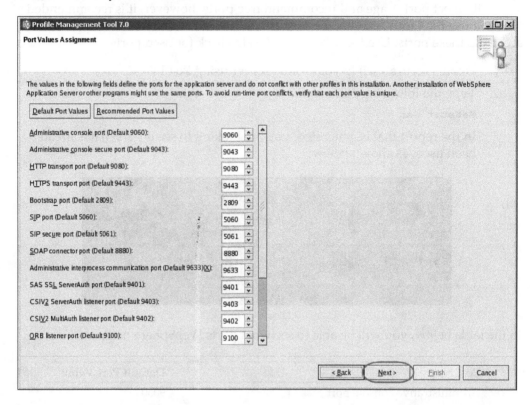

The administrative console port is very important. We will use this port to gain access to the administration console. Please take note of this port detailed as the **Administrative console port (Default 9060)** field as seen in the screenshot above.

Click **Next** to go to the next step of the installation, where we choose whether we want WebSphere to automatically restart on reboot.

If you wish to have WebSphere automatically start up again when Linux is rebooted, then you can enable this option. If enabled, the wizard will generate an automatic start and stop script in the init.d directories as required by the Linux runlevels. We will not be discussing Linux runlevels in this book; please consult your Linux documentation or search the Internet.

We don't require WebSphere to start on reboot, so we will leave the **Run the application server process as a Linux service** checkbox unchecked.

Helpful hint: Automatic start and stop scripts are recommended for production environments. However, Linux administrators may wish to craft their own start-up scripts. If you wish to learn how these start-up scripts work, then enable the creation of the Linux Service Definition to view the resulting script and it is also recommended that you consult how Linux runlevels work.

 If you wish to add a service definition post-install and have appropriate access, you can run the WebSphere `<was_root>/bin/wasservice.sh` command script, which will create the appropriate start and stop scripts.

The next screen that is displayed is about Web Server definitions. We will be covering Web Server definitions in Chapter 8. For now, we will skip this screen, leaving the **Create a Web server definition** checkbox unchecked. Click **Next** to move on to the **Profile Creation Summary** screen.

The final step of the wizard is **Profile Creation Summary**. The wizard presents a summary of your configuration options. If you are not happy with your configuration, you can go back and change your settings. If your settings are correct, then you can click **Create**, which will start the profile creation, as seen in the screenshot below:

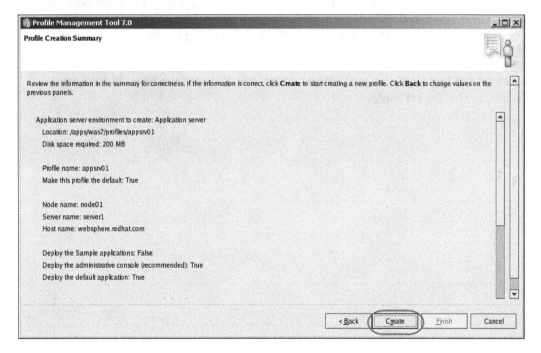

Once the profile creation is complete, you can choose to run the **First steps** console which provides a few checks which you can run to verify that the installation and profile creation was successful.

To verify your installation, it is best to ensure that you run the **First steps** console. Launch the console by selecting the on-screen option and clicking **Finish**, as seen in the following screenshot:

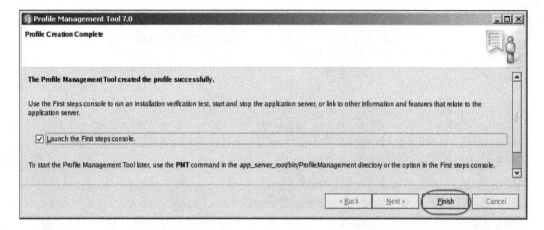

After the wizard has completed the install and profile creation, there are several checks that you can do to ensure that your installation and profile creation was successful. By running the **First steps** console, we can get quick proof that the WAS is functional.

Click on the **Installation verification** option in the **First steps** console as shown below, to run the **ivf** tool.

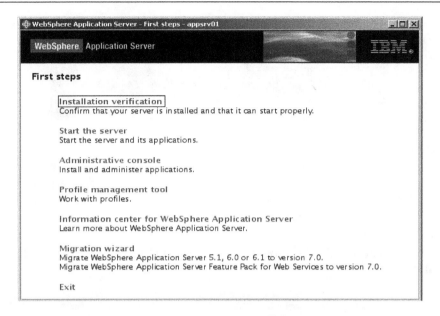

A report similar to the one below will be generated:

The tool will report the line **The installation verification is complete** (highlighted in the screenshot) if there were no problems with the installation.

Now that we have proven the application server was able to start, we can now stop the server by clicking on **Stop the server**, as seen in the following screenshot:

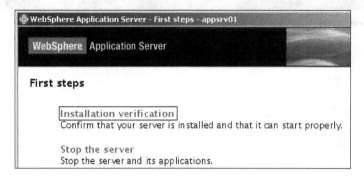

The **First steps** console should now report that **server1** has stopped. The following screen shows this:

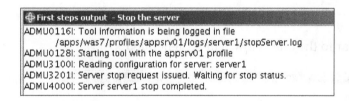

We have now successfully installed the WebSphere Application Server.

Installation registry files

During the installation process, the installer will create a `vdp.properties` file. This file is located in the current user's home directory. Since we installed using **root**, the file is located in `/root`.

Since the installer is based on the install shield product, it creates the `vdp.propeties` file, a product registry, which lists WebSphere products and features that have been installed.

The `vpd.properties` file is for informational purposes only and should not be relied on to accurately list installed applications. When the product is uninstalled using the uninstaller, the `vdp.properties` file is updated. However, there are known limitations with this registry and when product features are removed or updated the registry may not follow suit. The `installRegistryUtils` command can be used to list the installed products and can be used to help identify issues after uninstalls. It is another tool that can aid in verifying if your installation is successful and can be a source of information during troubleshooting of a malformed installation.

Another useful utility is the `./versionInfo.sh` command located in <was_root>/bin, which when run reports the current installation version and applied fix packs. This command is covered in Chapter 10.

Installation logs

The installer logs events as it is installing the WAS product. If there is a problem with your installation, you can consult the logs. The `log.txt` file is located in the

<was_root>/ logs/install/ folder.

You can use the Linux command `view` (read only version of `vi`) or your favorite Linux text editor to look at the file.

Here is an example of the last few lines of the installation log, post a successful installation.

```
(Dec 29, 2008 6:16:14 PM), Process, com.ibm.ws.install.ni.ismp.
actions.SettleNIFRegistryAction, msg1, Current install/uninstall
process is successful. Process type is: install
(Dec 29, 2008 6:16:14 PM), Process, com.ibm.ws.install.ni.ismp.
actions.SetExitCodeAction, msg1, CWUPI0000I: EXITCODE=0
(Dec 29, 2008 6:16:14 PM), Process, com.ibm.ws.install.ni.ismp.
actions.ISMPLogSuccessMessageAction, msg1, INSTCONFSUCCESS
```

Log files are the lifebloods of WAS. They are used for problem solving and runtime status. We will delve more into logging in Chapter 5.

Profile manager logs and files

Similar to the installation logs, the Profile Management Tool (PMT) also leaves a small foot print of logs detailing the profile creations.

Logs

During the creation of a profile, the PMT logs to a file called `pmt.log` in the `<was_root>/logs/manageprofiles` folder. This log file can be used to help diagnose causes of issues when a profile creation fails. This file most probably will not need to be consulted very often.

Files

After a profile is created, a useful file called `AboutThisProfile.txt` is created in the profile's logs folder; for example, `<was_root>/profiles/appsrv01/logs`.

This file can be useful to determine basic information about the profile like ports and general settings.

> Also located in the logs folder is a file called `ivtClient.log`, which contains the logging information as seen in the first step verification steps.

Admin console

To test our application server is functioning correctly, we will log in to the administration console. The administration console is a web application which is used to configure the WebSphere Application Server. You can use it to perform tasks such as:

- Add, delete, start, and stop application servers
- Deploy new applications to a server
- Start and stop existing applications, and modify certain configurations
- Add, delete, and edit resource providers
- Configure security, including access to the administrative console
  - Details are covered in Chapter 3
- Collect data for performance and troubleshooting purposes
  - Details are covered in Chapter 7

Currently, the application server is in a stopped state. Before we can log in to the admin console, we must start the newly created application server. To start the application server, we can use a special command script. Command scripts are found in the `<was_root>/bin` directory.

There are two scripts that we will use often throughout the book to start and stop WAS.

Script Name	Description
`startServer.sh`	Used to start a given application server. Usage: `startServer.sh <servername>`
`stopServer.sh`	Used to start a given application server. Usage: `startServer.sh <servername>`

To start our application server, we will use the `startServer.sh` command as follows:

`<was_root>/bin/startServer.sh server1`

Once you run the script, you will see the following output in your SSH session:

```
ADMU0116I: Tool information is being logged in file
           /apps/was7/profiles/appsrv01/logs/server1/startServer.log
ADMU0128I: Starting tool with the appsrv01 profile
ADMU3100I: Reading configuration for server: server1
ADMU3200I: Server launched. Waiting for initialization status.
```

When the server has actually started, you will see an extra line mentioning that the server has started and its associated Unix **Process ID (PID)**.

```
ADMU3000I: Server server1 open for e-business; process id is 3813
```

Now that the application server has started, we can navigate to the admin console URL. We can craft the URL as follows.

`http://<hostname>:<port>/ibm/console`

We have noted earlier that an important port to note was the admin_default port, which in our case is 9060. By using this port and the IP address of our server, we can access the admin console using a URL similar to the URL demonstrated below:

`http://192.168.0.94:9060/ibm/console`

If we made a host-file modification on our desktop machine, we would be able to use a hostname or FQDN to access the admin console; for example,
`http://websphere.redhat.com:9060/ibm/console`

If we were able to browse from the local machine where the application server was running, we could use `http://localhost:9060/ibm/console`.

When we navigate to the admin console URL, we see the following page:

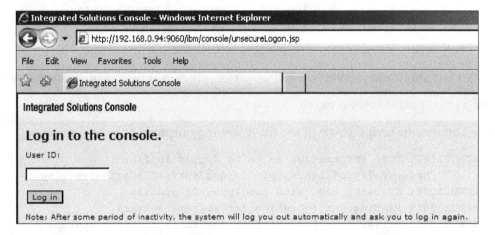

During the installation, we opted to not turn on global security, and so we can log in using any username and no password is required. For the purpose of this book, we will log in as **wasadmin** as shown below:

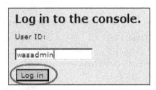

Once logged in, we can see the administration console welcome screen and the main navigation panel on the left-hand side (LHS). Looking at the LHS panel shown in the following screenshot, we can see a list of all the configuration items, that is, features and resources that are available for WAS administration.

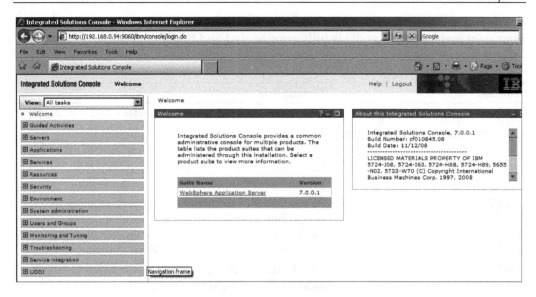

The administration panel provides a GUI that allows administrators to administer WAS. There is also an interactive command line interface called wsadmin.sh created for administering WAS without using the admin console. We will cover administrative scripting in Chapter 4.

Silent installation

So far, we have covered using the GUI approach to install WAS. The installation wizard can also be run silently. By using special response files, we can pre-set installation settings and the installation will not require any user input.

Using response files is the technique used in automatic installations where servers are built to a known standard and naming convention. This ensures that each new WAS is installed exactly the same each time. This is critical for production environments to ensure each server is configured the same way. This lends to easier support and fewer errors are introduced into environments, which is a key factor in supporting production systems. Another reason that it is vital to know how to use silent installations is that some organizations do not install X Windows on production servers for security reasons.

Below is a list of the main sections where you can change properties to customize your own installation. The file is fully commented and is self-explanatory. It only takes a short while to edit as required to craft a customized silent installation.

Section	Description
License Acceptance	This must be edited to true for a silent install to work.
Non-root Installation Limitations	This option indicates whether you accept the limitations associated with installing as a non-root user.
Prerequisite Checking	By default, the installer checks the system for prerequisites. You can change how this is done.
File Permission Checking	By default, the installer does not check whether the user account that is running the installation has sufficient permissions to perform the installation. You can change this to be more permission-aware.
Installation Type	The default installType setting is to install without the samples. You can change this option.
Administrative Security	To configure administrative security, an administrative username and password must be specified. Additionally, if the Application Server Samples are installed, a password is also required for the Samples user.
Installation Location	Specify a valid directory path into which the product can be installed.
Trace Control Output	Trace output is saved as both text and XML files by default, but it can be restricted to only one output format. Tracing can be used to help diagnose installation issues.
Profile Settings	Determine whether to create a management or standalone profile. The following sections explain the settings for management profile or standalone profile configuration options, which are located at the end of the response file.

Creating a response file

Locate the sample response file. It is located in `<was_install_root>\WAS`. The response file is named `responsefile.base.txt`. Copy and rename the file to `response.txt`. This will preserve the original file as a backup in case we need it again later.

Editing a response file

Edit the response file (`response.txt`) as required for your environment.

Running the installer silently

Run the installer in silent mode by passing the name of the response file as a command line parameter. Here is an example:

```
<was_install_root>installer -options "/<responsefile.
path>/<responsefile.txt>" -silent
```

You can tail the logs mentioned above to show progress of an install. We will look at the tail command in more detail in Chapter 5.

Examining installation logs

After the silent installation has completed, examine the logs for success. The logs are located in `<profile_root>/logs/install/log.txt`. By examining these logs, you can see if there were any errors during the installation. `<profile_root>` is the notation syntax we will use to determine the root of the application server profile.

Summary

In this chapter, we covered how to install an application server and learned that there are different optional installation scenarios. Depending on requirements, there are multiple ways to install WAS. The manual techniques shown above have given a cross-section of possible install variations and demonstrated how flexible the installation process is. We covered the ability to use a silent installation by using a customized response file and that silent installs dramatically speed up an installation. When installations are frequent, a response file approach ensures less installation errors due to the fact that it requires no human intervention and once configured and tested, it can be run again and again without introducing errors that are often introduced when information needs to be typed into fields as required by the graphical installer. We were also introduced to the start and stop command scripts and had a brief look at the administration console. A reoccurring theme in this chapter was the use of evaluating logs to ensure our installations were successful and error-free. Ensuring we have a stable base set of binaries and correct, configured profile will ensure our application server is less likely to contain errors related to the actual installation process.

2
Deploying your Applications

We have installed an application server, now we will want to deploy applications.
Applications can be installed manually or in an automated fashion using scripts. In this
chapter, we will cover how to manually deploy a J2EE (Enterprise Edition) application,
covering automated deployments in Chapter 4. As we walk through this chapter,
we will show you how to deploy two applications. One application does not require
database connectivity; the second is a database aware application which requires some
WebSphere configuration to provide database connectivity to the application.

In this chapter, we will cover the following topics:

- Application server internals
- The web container
- Virtual hosts
- WebSphere ports
- Data sources
- Java Naming and Directory Interface (JNDI)
- Application deployment
- J2EE applications
- Enterprise Archive (EAR)
- Web Archive (WAR)
- Java Archive (JAR)

Inside the Application Server

Before we look at deploying an application, we will quickly run over the internals of **WebSphere Application Server (WAS)**. The anatomy of WebSphere Application Server is quite detailed, so for now, we will briefly explain the important parts of WebSphere Application Server, discovering more about the working internals as we work through each of the remaining chapters.

The figure below shows the basic architecture model for a WebSphere Application Server JVM. There are many more components which we will cover in later chapters.

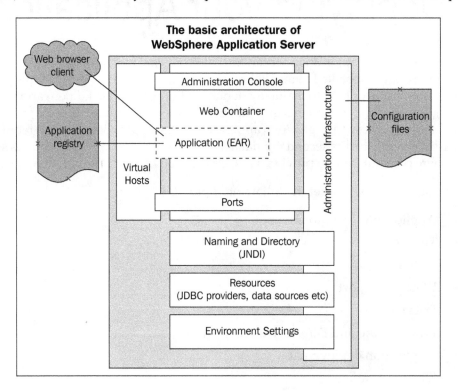

An important thing to remember is that the WebSphere product code base is the same for all operating-systems (platforms). The Java applications that are deployed are written once and can be deployed to all versions of a given WebSphere release without any code changes.

JVM

All WebSphere Application Servers are essentially Java Virtual Machines (JVMs). IBM has implemented the J2EE application server model in a way which maximises the J2EE specification and also provides many enhancements creating specific features for WAS. J2EE applications are deployed to an Application Server.

Web container

A common type of business application is a web application. The WAS web container is essentially a Java-based web server contained within an application server's JVM, which serves the web component of an application to the client browser.

Virtual hosts

A virtual host is a configuration element which is required for the web container to receive HTTP requests. As in most web server technologies, a single machine may be required to host multiple applications and appear to the outside world as multiple machines. Resources that are associated with a particular virtual host are designed to not share data with resources belonging to another virtual host, even if the virtual hosts share the same physical machine. Each virtual host is given a logical name and assigned one or more DNS aliases by which it is known. A DNS alias is the TCP/ host name and port number that are used to request a web resource, for example: `<hostname>:9080/<servlet>`.

By default, two virtual host aliases are created during installation. One for the administration console called `admin_host` and another called `default_host` which is assigned as the default virtual host alias for all application deployments unless overridden during the deployment phase. All web applications must be mapped to a virtual host, otherwise web browser clients cannot access the application that is being served by the web container.

Environment settings

WebSphere uses Java environment variables to control settings and properties relating to the server environment. WebSphere variables are used to configure product path names, such as the location of a database driver, for example, `ORACLE_JDBC_DRIVER_PATH`, and environmental values required by internal WebSphere services and/or applications.

Resources

Configuration data is stored in XML files in the underlying configuration repository of the WebSphere Application Server. Resource definitions are a fundamental part of J2EE administration. Application logic can vary depending on the business requirement and there are several types of resource types that can be used by an application. Below is a list of some of the most commonly used resource types.

Resource Types	Description
JDBC (Java database connectivity)	Used to define providers and data sources
URL providers	Used to define end-points for external services, for example, web services
JMS providers	Used to define messaging configurations for Java Message Service, **Message Queuing (MQ)** connection factories and queue destinations, and so on.
Mail providers	Enable applications to send and receive mail, typically using the SMTP protocol.

JNDI

The **Java Naming and Directory Interface (JNDI)** is employed to make applications more portable. JNDI is essentially an API for a directory service which allows Java applications to look up data and objects via a name. JNDI is a lookup service where each resource can be given a unique name. Naming operations, such as lookups and binds, are performed on contexts. All naming operations begin with obtaining an initial context. You can view the initial context as a starting point in the namespace. Applications use JNDI lookups to find a resource using a known naming convention. Administrators can override the resource the application is actually connecting to without requiring a reconfiguration or code change in the application. This level of abstraction using JNDI is fundamental and required for the proper use of WebSphere by applications.

Application file types

There are three file types we work with in Java applications. Two can be installed via the WebSphere deployment process. One is known as an EAR file, and the other is a WAR file. The third is a JAR file (often re-usable common code) which is contained in either the WAR or EAR format. The explanation of these file types is shown in the following table:

File Type	Description
JAR file	A JAR file (or Java ARchive) is used for organising many files into one. The actual internal physical layout is much like a ZIP file. A JAR is generally used to distribute Java classes and associated metadata. In J2EE applications, the JAR file often contains utility code, shared libraries, and EJBS. An EJB is a server-side model that encapsulates the business logic of an application and is one of several Java APIs in the Java Platform, Enterprise Edition with its own specification. You can visit `http://java.sun.com/products/ejb/` for information on EJBs.
EAR file	An Enterprise Archive file represents a J2EE application that can be deployed in a WebSphere Application Server. EAR files are standard Java archive files (JAR) and have the file extension `.ear`. An EAR file can consist of the following: • One or more web modules packaged in WAR files • One or more EJB modules packaged in JAR files • One or more application client modules • Additional JAR files required by the application • Any combination of the above The modules that make up the EAR file are themselves packaged in archive files specific to their types. For example, a web module contains web archive files and an EJB module contains Java archive files. EAR files also contain a deployment descriptor (an XML file called `application.xml`) that describes the contents of the application and contains instructions for the entire application, such as security settings to be used in the runtime environment.
WAR file	A WAR file (Web Application) is essentially a JAR file used to encapsulate a collection of JavaServer Pages (JSP), servlets, Java classes, HTML and other related files which may include XML and other file types depending on the web technology used. For information on JSP and servlets, you can visit `http://java.sun.com/products/jsp/`. • Servlets can support dynamic web page content; they provide dynamic server-side processing and can connect to databases. • Java ServerPages (JSP) files can be used to separate HTML code from the business logic in web pages. Essentially, they too can generate dynamic pages; however, they employ Java beans (classes) which contain specific detailed server-side logic. A WAR file also has its own deployment descriptor called `web.xml` which is used to configure the WAR file and can contain instructions for resource mapping and security.

When an EJB module or web module is installed as a standalone application, it is automatically wrapped in an Enterprise Archive (EAR) file by the WebSphere deployment process and is managed on disk by WebSphere as an EAR file structure. So, if a WAR file is deployed, WebSphere will convert it into an EAR file.

Deploying an application

As WebSphere administrators, we are asked to deploy applications. These applications may be written in-house or delivered by a third-party vendor. Either way, they will most often be provided as an EAR file for deployment into WebSphere. You may remember this from Chapter 1, where we created a profile and opted not to install an EAR file called the default application. For the purpose of understanding a manual deployment, we are now going to install the default application. The default application can be located in the `<was_root>/ installableApps` folder. The following steps will show how we deploy the EAR file.

Open the administration console and navigate to the **Applications** section and click on **New Application** as shown below

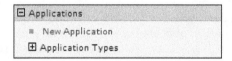

You now see the option to create one of the following three types of applications:

Application Type	Description
Enterprise Application	An EAR file on a server configured to hold installable Web Applications, WAR, Java archives, library files, and other resource files.
Business Level Application	A business-level application is an administration model similar to a server or cluster. However, it lends itself to the configuration of applications as a single grouping of modules.
Asset	An asset represents one or more application binary files that are stored in an asset repository, such as Java archives, library files, and other resource files. Assets can be shared between applications.

Click on **New Enterprise Application**.

As seen in the following screenshot, you will be presented with the option to either browse locally on your machine for the file or remotely on the Application Server's file system. Since the EAR file we wish to install is on the server, we will choose the **Remote file system** option.

 It can sometimes be quicker to deploy large applications by first using **Secure File Transfer Protocol (SFTP)** to move the file to the application server's file system and then using remote, as opposed to transferring via local browse, which will do an HTTP file transfer which takes more resources and can be slower.

The following screenshot depicts the path to the new application:

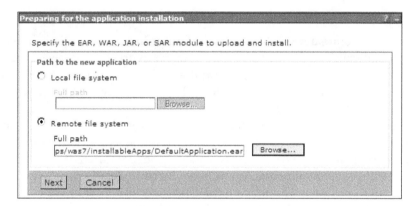

Click **Browse....** You will see the name of the application server node. If there is more than one profile, select the appropriate instance. You will then be able to navigate through a web-based version of the Linux file system as seen in the following screenshot:

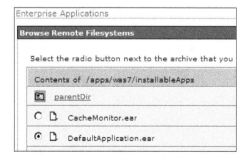

Locate the `DefaultApplication.ear` file. It will be in a folder called `installableApps` located in the root WebSphere install folder, for example, `<was_root>/installableApps` as shown in the previous screenshot.

Click **Next** to begin installing the EAR file.

On the **Preparing for the application installation** page, choose the **Fast Path** option. There are two options to choose.

Install option	Description
Fast Path	The deployment wizard will skip advanced settings and only prompt for the absolute minimum settings required for the deployment.
Detailed	The wizard will allow, at each stage of the installation, for the user to override any of the J2EE properties and configurations available to an EAR file.

The **Choose to generate default bindings and mappings** setting allows the user to accept the default settings for resource mappings or override with specific values. Resource mappings will exist depending on the complexity of the EAR. Bindings are JNDI to resource mappings. Each EAR file has pre-configured XML descriptors which specify the JNDI name that the application resource uses to map to a matching (application server) provided resource. An example would be a JDBC data source name which is referred to as `jdbc/mydatasource`, whereas the actual data source created in the application server might be called `jdbc/datasource1`. By choosing the **Detailed** option, you get prompted by the wizard to decide on how you want to map the resource bindings. By choosing the **Fast Path** option, you are allowing the application to use its pre-configured default JNDI names.

We will cover the details of resources in later chapters. For now, we will select **Fast Path** as demonstrated in the following screenshot:

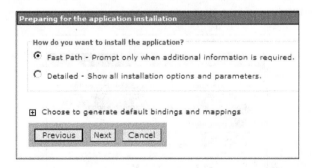

Click on **Next**.

In the next screen, we are given the ability to fill out some specific deployment options. Below is a list of the options presented in this page.

Option value	Description/Values
Precompile JavaServer Pages files	Specify whether to precompile **JavaServer Pages (JSP)** files as a part of installation. The default is not to precompile JSP files.
Directory to install application	Specifies the directory to which the **Enterprise Application Resource (EAR)** file will be installed.
	You can change this if you want the application to be physically located outside of the WebSphere file structure.
Distribute application	The default is to enable application distribution. You can override this and choose to not distribute the application across multiple nodes.
Use Binary Configuration	Specifies whether the application server uses the binding, extensions, and deployment descriptors located within the application deployment document, the deployment.xml file (default), or those located in the EAR file.
Deploy enterprise beans	The tool generates the code needed to run enterprise bean (EJB) files. You must enable this setting when the EAR file is assembled and the EJBDeploy is not run during packaging.
	Its default value is false.
Application name	A logical name for the application. The default name is the same as the EAR file. An application name must be unique within a cell.
Create MBeans for resources	Specifies whether to create MBeans for resources, such as servlets or JSP files, within an application when the application starts.
	The default is to create MBeans.
Override class reloading settings for Web and EJB modules	Specifies whether the WebSphere Application Server runtime detects changes to application classes when the application is running.
	If this setting is enabled and if application classes are changed, then the application is stopped and restarted to reload updated classes.
	The default is not to enable class reloading.

Option value	Description/Values
Reload interval in seconds	Specifies the number of seconds to scan the application's file system for updated files.
Process embedded configuration	Specifies whether the embedded configuration should be processed. An embedded configuration consists of files such as `resource.xml` and `variables.xml`. When selected or true, the embedded configuration is loaded to the application scope from the `.ear` file.
File Permission	• Allows all files to be read but not written to • Allows executables to execute • Allows HTML and image files to be read by everyone
Application Build ID	A string that identifies the build version of the application. Once set, it cannot be edited.
Allow dispatching includes to remote resources	Web modules included in this application are enabled as remote request dispatcher clients that can dispatch remote includes. Default = true.
Allow servicing includes from remote resources	Web modules included in this application are enabled as remote request dispatcher servers that are resolved to service remote includes from another application. Default = true.
Business level application name	Specifies whether the product creates a new business-level application with the enterprise application that you are installing or makes the enterprise application a composition unit of an existing business-level application.
Asynchronous Request Dispatch Type	Specifies whether web modules can dispatch requests concurrently on separate threads.
Allow EJB reference targets to resolve automatically	Specifies whether the product assigns default JNDI values for or automatically resolves incomplete EJB reference targets.

For this deployment, we will leave the majority of these values as default. Except we will override the EAR application name to be:

```
DefaultApplication
```

as opposed to

```
DefaultApplication.ear
```

Click on **Next** to move on to the **Map modules to server** page.

Map the application to the appropriate server. At this stage, we only have one application server profile; however, we discussed in Chapter 1 that we can administer several application servers and we are going to look at managing multiple server nodes in Chapter 8. For this application, we will see two resources contained in the application. An EJB and a WAR file. We want to ensure that both of these are mapped to the same server **server1** which we created in Chapter 1. Select both checkboxes and click **Apply** to ensure the application modules are bound to server1, as shown in the following screenshot:

Clusters and servers:

WebSphere:cell=websphereNode01Cell,node=node01,server=server1   [Apply]

Select	Module	URI	Server
☐	Increment EJB module	Increment.jar,META-INF/ejb-jar.xml	WebSphere:cell=websphereNode01Cell,node=node01,server=server1
☐	Default Web Application	DefaultWebApplication.war,WEB-INF/web.xml	WebSphere:cell=websphereNode01Cell,node=node01,server=server1

Accept defaults and click **Next**.

You will now be presented with a summary of the options chosen during the configuration of the deployment. Click **Finish** and the wizard will expand the uploaded EAR file into a temporary folder and override any files as required.

Up until now, all the work that has been done by the wizard has been in a temporary folder called wstemp, found at the root of the application server's profile. Here is an example of what that might look like:

```
<profile_root>wstemp/anonymous1231468782776/workspace/cells/
websphereNode01Cell/applications/DefaultApplication.ear
```

Once the EAR file has been deployed, a report will be given where you will be asked to save. This will store the EAR file to the installedApps folder, which is in the following location:

```
/<profile_root>/appsrv01/installedApps/websphereNode01Cell.
```

The EAR file in the installedApps folder is expanded and is the runtime version of the application, meaning this is what WebSphere considers to be the actual application.

There is another important area known as the application registry and an EAR file will also exist there too, containing the actual EAR file which was uploaded. The applications registry is located at:

```
<profile_root>/config/cells/websphereNode01Cell/applications
```

Click **Save** to continue. The application has now been deployed.

Navigate to the **Applications** section of the administration console and click **WebSphere enterprise applications** and you will get a list of installed applications.

Starting and stopping your applications

In the **WebSphere enterprise applications** screen, we will see a list of applications which have been installed and their current state. Below is a table explaining the actions which can be performed against one or more selected applications.

Option	Description
Start	When an application is stopped, you will see a ✖ icon.
	To start, select one or more applications and click on the **Start** button.
Stop	When an application is started, you will see a ⇨ icon.
	To stop, select one or more applications and click the **Stop** button.
Install	As a part of deploying an application, you install application files on a server. Depending on EAR/WAR complexity, the deployment wizard will dynamically produce a guide of steps which requires user input.
Uninstall	Select applications you wish to uninstall. It is recommended you stop applications first.
Update	Used to apply delta updates. Only the application code elements that have been changed in the application since last deployment are updated while the application remains running.
Rollout Update	If an application is deployed across multiple nodes, you can use the Rollout Update option which replaces the application one node at a time. Using this method reduces the amount of time that any single node member is unavailable for service during application deployment.
Remove File	Deletes a file of the deployed application or module. Remove File deletes a file from the configuration repository and from the file system of all the nodes where the file is installed.

Option	Description
Export	Allows the application to be exported as an EAR file. Can be used to back up an application version.
Export DDL	By using the Export DDL option, you can export DDL (Data Definition) files located within database-aware EJB modules.
Export File	Allows the exporting of a specific file from an enterprise application or module.

We are going to start the default application. Select **DefaultApplication** and click on the **Start** action, as shown in the following screenshot:

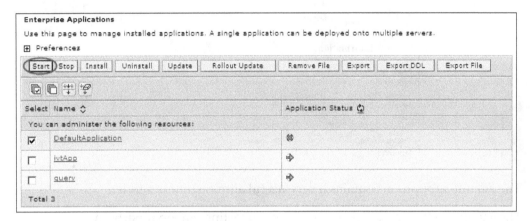

When an application has successfully started, you will a message similar to the one shown below:

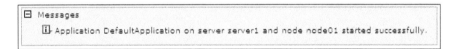

Now, **DefaultApplication** is started, we can use a web browser to navigate to the URL http://<host_name>:9080/snoop.

The following screen will load.

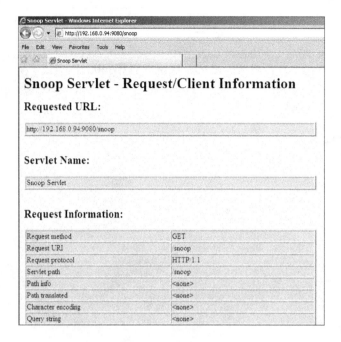

The default application contains a very useful administration servlet.

The snoop servlet is an excellent tool to use in testing. Snoop reports on the following attributes:

- Servlet context initialization parameters
- URL invocation request parameters
- Preferred client locale
- Context path
- User principal
- Request headers and their values
- Request parameter names and their values
- HTTPS protocol information
- Servlet request attributes and their values
- HTTP session information
- Session attributes and their values

Data access applications

We have just deployed an application that did not require database connectivity. Often, applications in the business world require access to a RDBMS to fulfill their business objective. If an application requires the ability to retrieve from, or store information in, a database, then you will need to create a data source which will allow the application to connect and use the database (DB).

Looking at the figure below, we can see the logical flow of the sample data access application that we are going to install. The basic idea of the application is to display a list of tables that exist in a database schema. Since the application requires a database connection, we need to configure WebSphere before we can deploy the application. We will now cover the preparation work before we install our application.

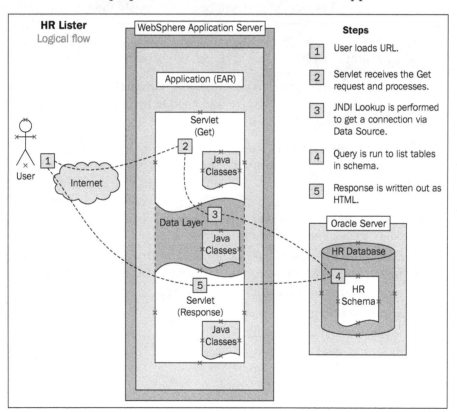

Data sources

Each data source is associated with a JDBC provider that is configured for access to a specific database type. The data source provides connectivity which allows an application to communicate with the database.

Preparing our sample database

Before you create a data source, you need to ensure that the appropriate client database driver software is installed. For our demonstration, we are going to use Oracle Express Edition (Oracle XE) for Linux which is the free version of Oracle. We are using version Oracle XE 10g for Linux and the download size is about 210MB, so it will take time to download. We installed Oracle XE using the default install option for installing an RPM. The administration process is fully documented on Oracle's web site and in the documentation which is installed with the product.

We could have chosen to use many open source/free databases, however their explanations and configurations would detract from the point. We have chosen to use Oracle's free RDBMS called Oracle XE, and JDBC with Oracle XE is quite easy to configure. By following these steps, you will be able to apply the same logic to any of the major vendors' full RDMS products, that is, DB/2, Oracle, SQL Server, and so on. Another reason why we chose Oracle XE is that it is an enterprise-ready DB and is administered by a simple web interface and comes with sample databases.

We need to test that we can connect to our database without WebSphere so that we can evaluate the DB design. To do this, we will need to install Oracle XE. We will now cover the following steps one by one.

1. Download Oracle XE from Oracle's web site using the following URL: `http://www.oracle.com/technology/products/database/xe/index.html`.

2. Transfer the `oracle-xe-10.2.0.1-1.0.i386.rpm` file to an appropriate directory on your Linux server using WinSCP (Secure Copy) or your chosen Secure FTP client.

3. Since the XE installer uses X Windows, ensure that you have Xming running. Then install Oracle XE by using the `rpm` command, as shown here:

    `rpm -ivh oracle-xe-10.2.0.1-1.0.i386.rpm`

4. Follow the installer steps as prompted:

    ◦ HTTP port = 8080

    ◦ Listener port = 1521

    ◦ SYS & SYSTEM / password = oracle

    ◦ Autostart = y

 Oracle XE requires 1024 minimum swap space and requires 1.5 GB of disk space to install.

Ensure that Oracle XE is running. You can now access the web interface via a browser from the local machine; by default, XE will only accept a connection locally. As shown in the following figure, we have a screenshot of using Firefox to connect to OracleXE using the URL `http://localhost:8080/apex`. The reason we use Firefox on Linux is that this is the most commonly installed default browser on the newer Linux distributions.

When the administration application loads, you will be presented with a login screen as seen in the following screenshot. You can log in using the username **SYSTEM** and password `oracle` as set by your installation process.

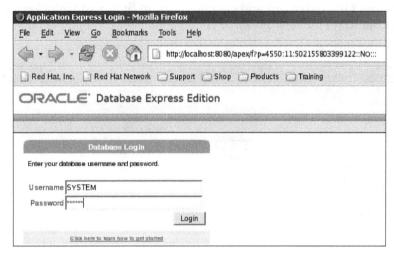

Oracle XE comes with a pre-created user called HR which is granted ownership to the HR Schema. However, the account is locked by default for security reasons and so we need to unlock the HR user account. To unlock an account, we need to navigate to the **Database Users | Manage Users** screen, as demonstrated in the following screenshot:

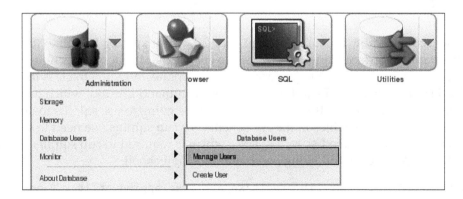

You will notice that the icon for the **HR** user is locked. You will see a small padlock on the HR icon, as seen in this figure:

Click on the **HR** user icon and unlock the account as shown in the following figure. You need to reset the password and change **Account Status** to **Unlocked**, and then click **Alter User** to set the new password.

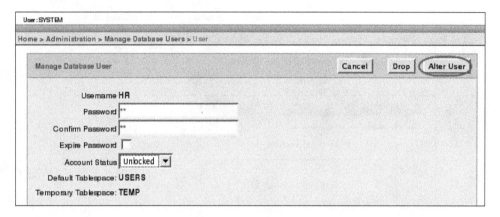

The following figure shows that the HR account is unlocked:

The HR account is now unlocked as seen above. Log out and log back into the administration interface using the HR user to ensure that the account is now unlocked. Another good test to perform to ensure connectivity to Oracle is to use an Oracle admin tool called sqlplus. Sqlplus is a command line tool which database administrators can use to administer Oracle. We are going to use sqlplus to do a simple query to list the tables in the HR schema. To run sqlplus, we need to set up an environment variable called $ORACLE_HOME which is required to run sqlplus. To set $ORACLE_HOME, type the following command in a Linux shell:

```
export ORACLE_HOME=/usr/lib/oracle/xe/app/oracle/product/10.2.0/server
```

If you have installed Oracle XE in a non-default location, then you may have to use a different path.

To run sqlplus, type the following command:

`<oracle_home>/bin/sqlplus`

The result will be a login screen as shown below:

```
SQL*Plus: Release 10.2.0.1.0 - Production on Sat Apr 25 01:24:30 2009

Copyright (c) 1982, 2005, Oracle.  All rights reserved.

Enter user-name: 
```

You will be prompted for a username. Type the following command:

`hr@xe<enter>`

For the password, type the following command:

`hr<enter>`

When you have successfully logged in, you can type the following commands in the SQL prompt:

- `SELECT TABLE_NAME FROM user_tables<enter>`
- `/<enter>`

The / command means execute the command buffer. The result will be a list of tables in the HR schema, as shown in the following screenshot:

```
SQL> SELECT TABLE_NAME FROM user_tables
  2  /

TABLE_NAME
------------------------------
REGIONS
LOCATIONS
DEPARTMENTS
JOBS
EMPLOYEES
JOB_HISTORY
COUNTRIES

7 rows selected.
```

We have now successfully verified that Oracle works from a command line, and thus it is very likely that WebSphere will also be able to communicate with Oracle. Next, we will cover how to configure WebSphere to communicate with Oracle.

JDBC providers

Deployed applications use JDBC providers to communicate with RDBMS.

- The JDBC provider object provides the actual JDBC driver implementation class for access to a specific database type, that is, Oracle, SQL Server, DB/2, and so on.

- You associate a data source with a JDBC provider. A data source provides the connection to the RDBMS.

- The JDBC provider and the data source provide connectivity to a database.

Creating a JDBC provider

Before creating a JDBC provider, you will need to understand the application's resource requirements, that is, the data sources that the application references. You should know the answer to the following questions:

- Does your application require a data source? Not all applications use a database.

- The security credentials required to connect to the database. Often databases are secured and you will need a username and password to access a secure database.

- Are there any web components (Servlets, JSP, and so on) or EJBs which need to access a database.

Answering these questions will determine the amount of configuration required for your database connectivity configurations.

To create a JDBC provider, log into the administration console and click on the **JDBC Provider** link in the **JDBC** category of the **Resources** section located in the left-hand panel of the administration console as shown below.

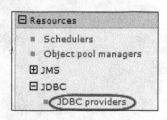

We need to choose an appropriate scope from the **Scope** drop-down pick list. Scope determines how the provider will be seen by applications. We will talk more about scope in the JNDI section. For now, please choose the **Cell** scope as seen below.

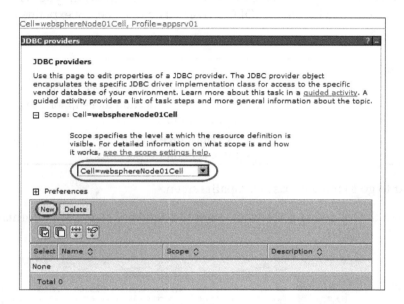

Click **New** and the new JDBC provider wizard is displayed.

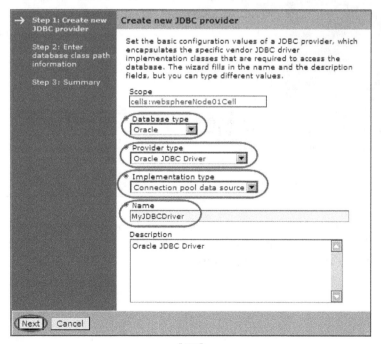

Select the **Database type** as **Oracle**, **Provider type** as **Oracle JDBC Driver**, **Implementation type** as **Connection pool data source**, and **Name** for the new JDBC provider. We are going to enter **MyJDBCDriver** as the provider name as seen in the previous screenshot. We also have to choose an **Implementation type**. There are two implementation types for Oracle JDBC Drivers. The table below explains the two different types.

Implementation Type	Description
Connection pool data source	Use **Connection pool data source** if your application does not require connection that supports two-phase commit transactions...
XA Datasource	Use **XA Datasource** if your application requires two-phase commit transactions.

Click **Next** to go to the database classpath screen.

As shown in the following screenshot, enter the database class path information for the JDBC provider.

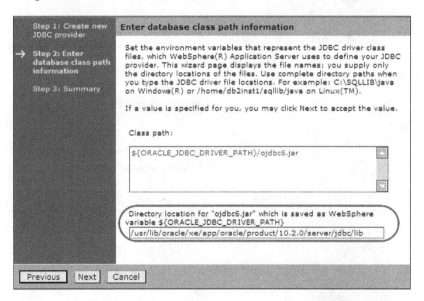

As long as you have installed Oracle XE using the default paths, you will be able to use the following path in the **Directory location** field: `/usr/lib/oracle/xe/oracle/product/10.2.0/server/jdbc/lib`.

Click **Next** to proceed to the next step, where you will be presented with a summary as shown in the following screenshot. Review the JDBC provider information that you have entered and click **Finish**.

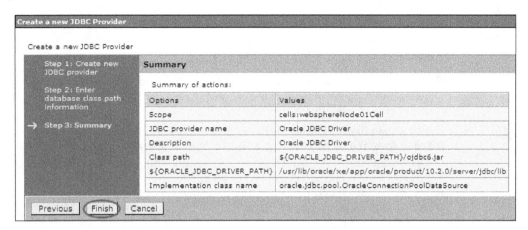

You will now be prompted to save the JDBC provider configuration. Click **Save**, as shown in the following screenshot. Saving this will persist the configuration to disk the resources to `resources.xml`.

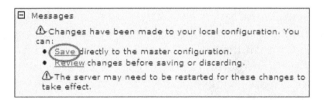

Before we finish, we need to update the JDBC Provider with the correct JAR file as the default one is not the one that we wish to use as it was assuming a later Oracle driver which we are not using. To change the driver, we must first select the driver that we created earlier called **MyJDBCDriver** as shown in the following screenshot:

In the screen presented, we are going to change the **Classpath** field from:

```
${ORACLE_JDBC_DRIVER_PATH}/ojdbc6.jar
```

to

```
${ORACLE_JDBC_DRIVER_PATH}/ojdbc14.jar
```

> Since WAS 7.0 is the latest version of WebSphere, the wizard already knows about the new version of the oracle 11g JDBC Driver. We are connecting to Oracle XE 10g and the driver for this is `ojdbc14.jar`.
>
> The classpath file can contain a list of paths or JAR file names which together form the location for the resource provider classes. Class path entries are separated by using the *ENTER* key and must not contain path separator characters (such as ; or :). Class paths can contain variable (symbolic) names that can be substituted using a variable map. Check your driver installation notes for specific JAR file names that are required.

Click **Apply** and save the configuration.

Creating a J2C alias

If a database has security enabled, which is the case for most RDBMS, we will need to somehow provide the username and password for the connection. By creating a J2C alias, we can create an authentication resource independent from the provider and data source. Using this approach, we can change the alias if the database username and password are changed without reconfiguring the provider or data source. This is a key concept and WebSphere provides levels of abstraction to allow the configuration of resources independent form each other. So, in a way, you could say that the JDBC Provider, data source, and J2C alias are loosely-coupled.

Navigate to the **Security** section in the left-hand navigation panel and click on the **Global security** link as seen in the following screenshot:

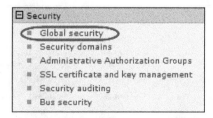

Expand the **Java Authentication and Authorization Service** category in the **Authentication** section found in the bottom right-hand side of the **Global security** screen.

Click on **J2C authentication data** as shown in the following figure:

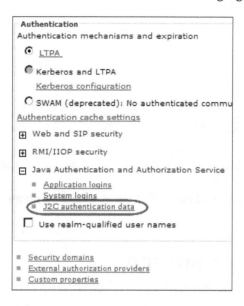

You will be presented with a screen where you can click **New** to create a new J2C authentication alias. Please enter **HR** for the **Alias** and **hr** for the **User ID** and **hr** for **Password** as shown in the following screenshot:

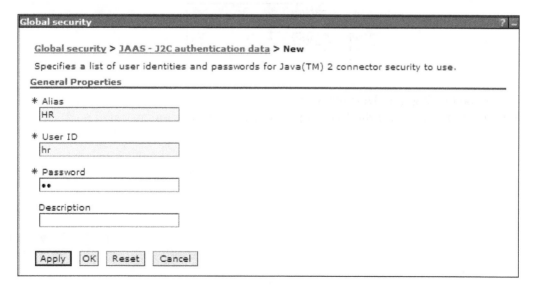

Oracle usernames and passwords are not case sensitive.

Click **Apply** and then **Save**.

A new alias will be created, as shown below.

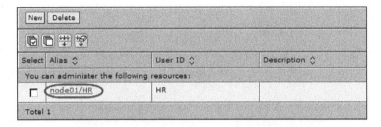

We will reference this J2C authentication alias when we create our data source in the following steps.

Creating a data source

In the next steps, we will use the administrative console to create a new data source.

Open the administrative console and navigate to the **JDBC** section in the left-hand side panel and click on **Data sources** as shown in the following screenshot:

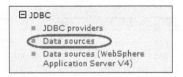

We will be looking at JNDI (Java Naming and Directory Interface) scope in later chapters. For now, select the **Cell** scope and click **New** as demonstrated next.

You will now be asked to fill out the data source information.

Enter the value **MyDataSource** in the **Data source name** field and the value **jdbc/mydatasource** in the **JNDI name** field as shown in the following image.

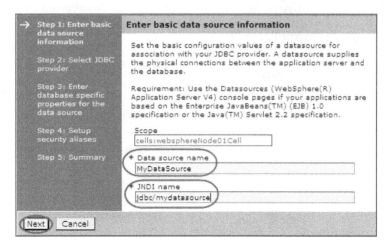

The JNDI name provides a naming context for the data source as used in resource lookups by application code. Click **Next** to move on to the next screen where you will be asked to select a JDBC provider for your data source. The following image demonstrates this.

Select the JDBC provider that we created previously.

Click **Next**, and in the next screen, enter the following value in the **URL** field: **jdbc:or acle:thin:@192.168.0.94:1521/xe**

In our example, we are using an oracle thin client URL. An Oracle thin client URL allows Websphere to connect to Oracle via a URL which is made up of the following syntax: `<driver_type>:@<host>:<port>/<service_name>`. It can be broken up as follows:

`<driver_type>` = `jdbc:oracle:thin`

`<host>` = `192.168.0.94` (the IP address of your Linux machine; it could even be localhost as Oracle is installed on the same machine as WebSphere)

`<port>`=`1521` (Default oracle listener port)

`<service_name>` = `xe` (the Oracle instance and service name)

Click **Next** to set up a security alias. In this screen, there are several fields.

There are two options to apply the J2C alias. They are listed below.

Authentication alias	Description
Component-managed	Use when the resource configured in the EJB's deployment descriptor res-auth property is set to `Application`.
Container-managed	Use when the resource configured in the EJB's deployment descriptor res-auth property is set to `Container`.

Since our application is controlling access to the database, we are going to use a component-managed alias. We will now select our J2C authentication alias mapping our user id and password to the data source as shown in the image below, so it can connect to the database.

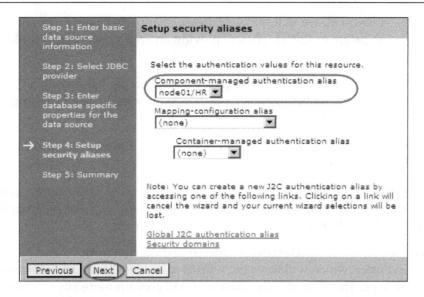

Click **Next** to view the summary screen and click **Finish** and then save. You will now see the data source listed in the data sources panel.

Test the data source by selecting the data source you wish to test and click **Test Connection**. If the data source is configured correctly, you will see a message similar to the one below.

Deploying a data access application

Now that we have created a JDBC provider and a data source which uses the provider, we are now ready to deploy a data access application. Our application comes in the form of an EAR file called HRLister.ear, which can be downloaded from the PACKT Publishing web site at the following location: www.packtpub.com.

The HRLister EAR file contains a single web application which, in turn, contains a servlet called listtable. The application is used to show how to deploy an application which uses a resource reference. The resource reference uses a JNDI lookup to find the data source and allow the application to connect to the HR database.

Our application contains several deployment descriptors; one is called application.xml and the other is called web.xml. The two descriptors detail certain configuration information which will be used by WebSphere during deployment.

During our deployment, we will select the detailed approach so we can see what kinds of steps are required when deploying an application which contains resource references.

Similarly, we will navigate to the **Applications** panel on the left-hand side navigation panel of the admin console, selecting **WebSphere enterprise applications** from the **application types** tree list.

To begin the deployment, click the **Install** button in the **Enterprise Applications** section as seen in the main panel.

If you have not already done so, download the HRLister.ear file into c:/temp on your desktop, click on the **Browse** button to browse for the EAR file in c:/temp, and click **Next** to continue.

On the next page, select the **Detailed-Show all installation options and parameters** radio option button which will force the wizard to ask for information during the deployment steps. The wizard is dynamic and will contain more steps depending on the contents of the EAR file. The workings of the sample HRListerEAR EAR file are quite simple; however some EAR files can contain many J2EE artefacts which result in a greater number of steps to complete the deployment process.

Below is a list of the steps we will be presented with by the installation wizard during the installation process.

Selecting installation options

Click **Next** to enter the **Select installation options** screen, and change the **Application name** from **HRListerEAR** to **HRLister**. This is a logical name and does not affect the running of the application.

In environments that contain multiple streams of development, it may be prudent to name each application with a standard naming scheme to determine which version of the application is at what stage of the development process.

Mapping modules to servers

Leave all other options as default and click **Next** to enter the **Map modules to servers** screen.

Because we have a web application, we need to ensure that the application can map to the appropriate virtual host. A virtual host already exists by default as explained earlier and is allowing HTTP connections to port 9080, the default HTTP port as set by WebSphere.

If we have more than one virtual host, we can choose at this stage to map the web application(s) contained in the EAR file to separate ports. Since our application only contains one web application, we do not wish to change it and will use the default host. If we did wish to change it, we would select the web module and map it to an available virtual host and click **Apply** which would store the mapping.

Leave the screen set as it is and click **Next** to move on to the next screen where we will set some loading options.

Providing JSP reloading options for web modules

In the **Provide JSP reloading options for Web modules** screen, we can once again leave the defaults. The **JSP reloading** option allows the web server to reload JSPs, which allow for hot deployment of artefacts. This means that we can replace JSPs on the file system and WebSphere will automatically pick up those changed. JSPs are compiled into servlets to work inside the web container and these options decide whether they are cached after the first compile or not.

Click **Next**.

Mapping shared libraries

The **Map Share Libraries** section allows the configuration of shared libraries. A shared library is a JAR file that is used by more than one module in an EAR file. An EARfile can contain many web modules and EJB modules and they can be designed to share common code routines. We do not have any other modules in the applications and no shared JARS, so we do not need to worry about shared libraries in this deployment.

We can click **Next**.

Once again, we have no shared libraries so we need not worry about this page. Click **Next** to go to the **Map resource references to resources** page.

Mapping resource references to resources

On the **Map resource references to resources** page we can see that there is a field called **Target Resource JNDI Name** as shown in the figure below, and it already has the JNDI name **jdbc/mydatasource**. If you recall from our datasource creation, this was the JNDI name that we gave to our data source which we want to use to connect to the Oracle database. The reason that this wizard page is presented is to give us an option to override the JNDI name of the data source that we wish to use. The idea here is about decoupling the application from the data source. This level of abstraction means that an administrator can choose which data source is to be used as opposed to the application. There might be a requirement to change the database and move the data to a different data source. This can be done via the wizard at deployment time and also post-deployment by changing the application settings in the administrative console.

The web.xml file contained in the web module defines an internal name that the application uses for the data source. In this application example, it uses the name jdbc/hrdatasource, however, we configured our WebSphere data source to be jdbc/mydatasource. This screen is used to map the two together. This is a very powerful concept of J2EE application design and allows for deployment time changes based on administration decisions which do not affect the application code, providing flexibility of deployment.

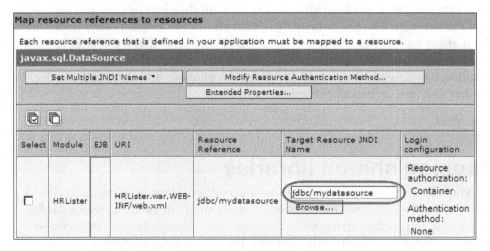

Click **Next** to open the **Map virtual hosts for Web modules** page.

Mapping virtual hosts for web modules

Here, we leave the default settings and use the default_host which will assign the web module to port 9080. Click **Next**.

Mapping context roots for web modules

The next page of the wizard is where we set the application **Context Root**. The context root is used to calculate the base path of the application. All URIs should be relative to the context root; this allows for the application's runtime URL to be changed as required. Each application URI must be unique. If multiple web applications exist in an EAR, or multiple web applications across multiple EAR are installed on the server, then the context root can be overridden by the administrator. The `application.xml` file contains the default context root and we can override it here if we wish. At this time, we will leave it set to `hrlister`.

Reviewing the deployment steps

Click **Next** to review the summary of the wizard's deployment steps and click **Finish** when you are happy. A report similar to the following will be presented detailing the installation process.

```
Installing...

If there are enterprise beans in the application, the EJB deployment process can take several minutes. Do not save the configuration until the process completes.

Check the SystemOut.log on the deployment manager or server where the application is deployed for specific information about the EJB deployment process as it occurs.

ADMA5016I: Installation of HRLister started.

ADMA0115W: Resource assignment of name jdbc/mydatasource and type javax.sql.DataSource, with JNDI name jdbc/mydatasource is not found within scope of module HRLister with URI HRLister.war,WEB-INF/web.xml deployed to target WebSphere:cell=websphereNode01Cell,node=websphereNode01,server=server1.

ADMA5068I: The resource validation for application HRLister completed successfully, but warnings occurred during validation.

ADMA5058I: Application and module versions are validated with versions of deployment targets.

ADMA5005I: The application HRLister is configured in the WebSphere Application Server repository.

ADMA5053I: The library references for the installed optional package are created.

ADMA5005I: The application HRLister is configured in the WebSphere Application Server repository.

ADMA5001I: The application binaries are saved in /apps/was7/profiles/appsrv01/wstemp/514564814/workspace/cells/websphereNode01Cell/applications/HRLister.ear/HRLister.ear

ADMA5005I: The application HRLister is configured in the WebSphere Application Server repository.

SECJ0400I: Successfully updated the application HRLister with the appContextIDForSecurity information.

CWSAD0040I: The application HRLister is configured in the Application Server repository.

ADMA5005I: The application HRLister is configured in the WebSphere Application Server repository.

ADMA5113I: Activation plan created successfully.

ADMA5011I: The cleanup of the temp directory for application HRLister is complete.

ADMA5013I: Application HRLister installed successfully.

Application HRLister installed successfully.

To start the application, first save changes to the master configuration.

Changes have been made to your local configuration. You can:
• Save directly to the master configuration.
• Review changes before saving or discarding.
```

If there are no errors shown in the summary, you can click **Save** to persist the applications deployment. If there are errors found at this point, you will need to review the logs to see what the problem could be. If you were to find a problem, you can choose not to save the configuration.

After saving to the master configuration, you will be redirected back to the main **Enterprise Applications** screen, where you will see the HR Lister application currently in the stopped state.

Using the application

Select the **HRLister** application, as shown in the following screenshot, and click **Start** to start the application.

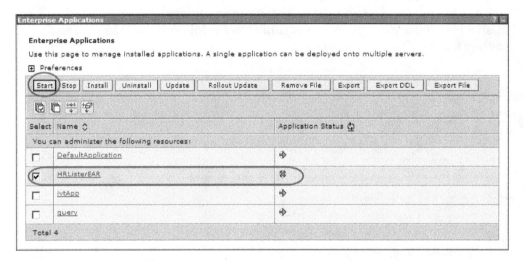

Once the HR Lister application has started, open a browser and navigate to the following URL:

`http://<host_name>:9080/hrlister/listtable`

The URL can be broken up as follows:

`<host_name>:<port>/<context_root>/<URL>`

`<host_name>` = iaddress or hostname

`<port>` = 9080, the default host port for WebSphere

`<URI>` = the resource name, that is, the ListTable servlet

As it loads, the ListTable servlet will connect to the HR database and list the tables in the HR schema, as shown in the following screenshot:

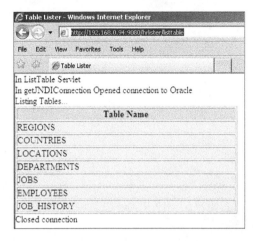

Congratulations! You have now successfully installed and configured a data access application.

Summary

In this chapter, we learned about Java Virtual Machines (JVMs), the web container, virtual hosts,and about deploying applications. We have covered the three different file types used in J2EE applications. A JAR file contains Java utility classes, EJBs, and sometimes shared libraries alongside other manifest information. WAR files are the containers for web application artefacts and EAR files can contain a mixture of WARs and JARs. We deployed two types of applications, one being a simple web application and the other being a data access application which was connected to a database. In this chapter, we focused on Oracle, however, we know that we could use any other database vendor and WebSphere can be easily configured to talk to other RDBMS types. We focused on manual deployments in the installation of applications and later, in Chapter 4, we will cover how to automate deployments using administrative scripting.

3
Security

Security is an important part of any application server configuration. In this chapter, we will cover securing the WebSphere Application Server's administrative console and how to configure different types of repositories containing the users and groups of authorized users who are given different levels of access to administer a WebSphere server.

In this chapter, we will cover the following topics:

- J2EE (Enterprise Edition) security
- Global security
- File-based repositories
- Local **Open Source (OS)** repository
- Standalone **Lightweight Directory Access Protocol (LDAP)** repository
- Open LDAP
- Administrative roles

J2EE security

WebSphere security is based on the J2EE application programming model. The J2EE security model is designed to separate the application's need for security and administration of security, allowing applications to be portable between vendors who have a slightly different implementation of the J2EE security model. There are two aspects of security which need to be explained, which are authentication and authorisation. Authentication is essentially asking, "Are you who you say you are?" Authorization is simply a case of, once we know who you are, "What are you allowed to do?". WebSphere employs repositories to register and store users and groups. Groups organize users together for a common action and users are assigned as members of groups. Knowing this, we will now move on to learn how to secure our WebSphere server.

Global security

In Chapter 1, during the installation process of WebSphere Application Server, we opted not to turn on global security and thus we did not have to supply a password to log in to the Administrative console. We logged in using the username **wasadmin** and we were not prompted for a password. The truth of the matter is that we could have actually used any name as the console was not authenticating us at all. To protect our WAS from unauthorized access, we need to turn on global security.

It is important to secure the administration of WebSphere even if the applications being installed are not using security. It is paramount to ensure we have control of our WebSphere environments. The larger your team is the more important this becomes. In time, other people in your organization will get to know the URLs of your WebSphere servers and if they are not secured you do not really know who is making changes without your approval. Securing the console stops inadvertent access and can ensure that only trained administrators are sanctioned to access and make configurations to environments. This is integral to keeping your WebSphere environment stable.

Here is a brief list of the steps required to implement global security.

- Verify which supported registries are available for your operating system
- Acquire the information required to connect to the user registry
- Define the users and groups which will be given administrative access in the selected registry
- Define which users you wish to assign administrative access to

Global security registry types

Global security is enabled to secure your WAS server, however, to do so requires a user registry. A user registry contains the user and group names for authentication and authorization purposes. Once configured, an application server will connect to the registry and perform lookups to acquire user credentials used in areas where authorization is required.

There are four types of registry—Standalone custom registry, local operating system, standalone LDAP registry, and federated repositories-as explained in the table below.

Registry Type	Description
Standalone LDAP registry	Only used LDAP defined users and groups and required LDAP configuration.
Local operating system	Specified the registry for the local OS.
Standalone custom registry	Allows a custom registry that is essentially based on Java code implementation.
Federated repositories	Manages users and groups across multiple repositories using a virtual realm. The registries can also be made up of the combinations of the other registry types.

First, we are going to demonstrate the creation and configuration of a file-based repository, then cover use of the local operating system as a repository, followed by our preferred method of using an LDAP repository.

Turning on global security

To turn on global security, log in to the Admin console and navigate to the **Security** section of the left-hand side navigation panel and click **Global security**, as shown in the following screenshot:

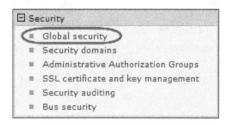

You will now be taken to the main **Global security** configuration page as shown in the following screenshot:

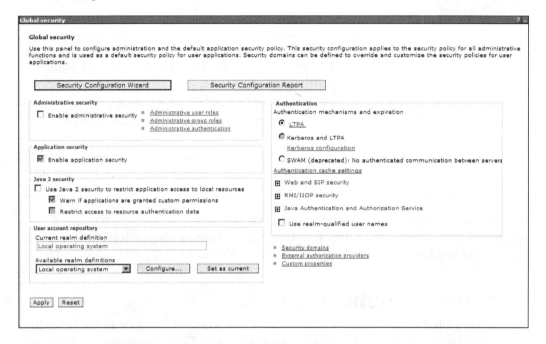

WebSphere provides a wizard to set up basic security using an internal repository. What we are going to do is run the wizard to secure our admin console.

Click the **Security Configuration Wizard** button as shown in the previous screenshot. You will be presented with an option to decide on the extent of your security protection. Leave the screen defaults and click **Next** to move on to the next page, where you will select which type of repository you wish to use.

> **Use Java 2 security to restrict application access to local resources,** as seen in the **Security Configuration Wizard**, is used when you do not trust the application's code. Since in most cases you trust the code you are installing in your EAR/WAR files, you do not need to turn this option on.

On the **Select user repository** page, you have four options to choose from as previously.

> The default repository is built into WebSphere and is based on the platform you are running on.

Standalone custom registry

The simplest way to provide administrative security is to use a file-based standalone custom registry. In our first example, we are going to start by selecting **Standalone custom registry** during our use of the Global security wizard, as shown in the following screenshot:

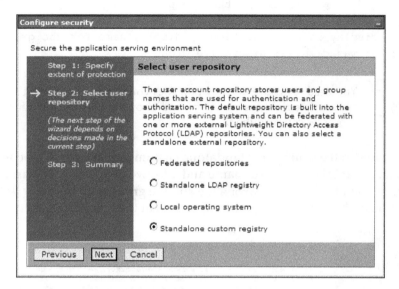

Select **Standalone custom registry** in the **Select user repository** screen and click **Next**.

Before we can continue, we need to set up two properties files—one for users and one for groups. These properties files will contain authorized users and groups. Our custom registry will use these two files.

We need to create a folder called `<was_root>/fileRegistry` on our Linux box. In this folder, we will create a file called `user.props` with the following contents:

```
# Format:
# name:passwd:uid:gids:display name
# where name     = userId/userName of the user
#       passwd = password of the user
#       uid     = uniqueId of the user
#       gid     = groupIds of the groups that the user belongs to
#       display name = a (optional) display name for the user.
wasadmin:wasadmin:101:101:WebSphere Administrator
```

We will then create a second file named `groups.props` and the contents of the file will be as follows:

```
# Format:
# name:gid:users:display name
# where name    = groupId of the group
#        gid    = uniqueId of the group
#        users  = list of all the userIds that the group contains
#        display name = a (optional) display name for the group.
admins:101:wasadmin:Administrative group
```

 You need to ensure that any new files you create are assigned appropriate rights using `chmod` and `chown` to ensure WebSphere processes can read the file.

As shown below in the **Configure standalone custom registry** page, type **wasadmin** in the **Primary administrative user name** and add two properties. The **usersFile** property will point to the `users.props` file and the **groupsFile** property will point to the location of the `groups.props` file, as shown in the following screenshot:

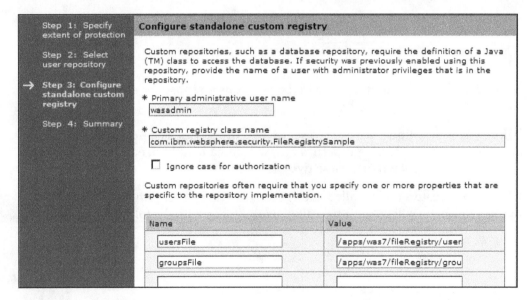

Custom registry class name is already filled in with a Java class that exists in the internals of WebSphere that contains the code for WebSphere to use the `user.props` and `groups.props` files. We will not go into detail as to how this class is coded.

Click **Next** to view the summary, and then click **Finish** to complete your file-based repository.

You will now need to bounce WAS, and then when you next try to log in to the administrative console, you will be prompted for a username and password.

Now that you have enabled global security, you will be starting to find that your application server will have issues while starting and stopping.

When Global security is enabled, a username and password is now required to start and stop the application server. Let's say you are trying to stop the application server using the stop shell script we learned in Chapter 1.

`<was_profile_root>/bin/stopServer.sh server1`

You might see the following error:

```
ADMU0116I: Tool information is being logged in file
           /apps/was7/profiles/appsrv01/logs/server1/stopServer.log
ADMU0128I: Starting tool with the appsrv01 profile
ADMU3100I: Reading configuration for server: server1
X connection to localhost:10.0 broken (explicit kill or server
shutdown).
```

If you do get an **X connection** error when trying to stop a server, it means that a login pop-up dialog cannot be displayed for the user to authenticate with as X Windows is not running. The solution could be to simply run XMing, the X Windows server we used in Chapter 1. Once X Windows is running, the next time you try to stop a server, a login pop-up dialog will allow you to type in the username and password. It can be very annoying having to continuously type in a username and password every time you bounce your server. To stop this, we can alter a file called `soap.client.props`.

The `soap.client.props` file is located in the `<was_profile_root>/propeties` folder, as shown in the following screenshot:

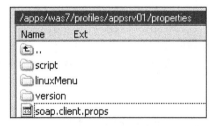

Edit the file using the vi command and change the `com.ibm.SOAP.securityEnabled` setting's value from `false` to `true`. Change the `com.ibm.SOAP.loginUserid` setting's value to `com.ibm.SOAP.loginUserid=wasadmin` and the `com.ibm.SOAP.loginPassword` setting value to `wasadmin`.

The changes just made can be seen in the following code:

```
#------------------------------------------------------------
# SOAP Client Security Enablement
# - security enabled status  ( false[default], true  )
#------------------------------------------------------------
com.ibm.SOAP.securityEnabled=true

#------------------------------------------------------------
# - authenticationTarget     ( BasicAuth[default], KRB5. These are the
only supported selection
#                               on a pure client for JMX SOAP Connector
Client. )
#------------------------------------------------------------
com.ibm.SOAP.authenticationTarget=BasicAuth

com.ibm.SOAP.loginUserid=wasadmin
com.ibm.SOAP.loginPassword=wasadmin
```

Save the `soap.client.props` file. Now when you stop and start WAS, you will no longer be prompted for a username and password. We will cover encoding the administrative password when we cover *Administrative tools* in Chapter 7.

If you have problems getting to the port 9060, then it might be because now that we have global security enabled, the console now wants to redirect to port 9043, which is the secure HTTP port for the admin console. Your Linux security might not allow this port. Log in to your Linux distribution as root and change the Linux security options to allow port 9060 and port 9043. This is done by re-configuring your Linux firewall implementation, most often achieved by editing the iptables configuration or simply turning off your firewall using the linux system-config-securitylevel utility.

Once global security is enabled, when you try to log in to the standard login URL `http://<host_name>:9060/ibm/console`, you will then be presented with a screen informing you that you are being redirected to a secure site and a warning that you have received a **Secure Sockets Layer (SSL)** certificate from an unknown **Certificate Authority (CA)** will be shown in the browser.

If you are using Internet explorer, Click **Continue to this website (not recommended)**, if you are using Firefox 3.0, click **Or you can add an exception** and follow the appropriate steps.

Browser versions change and each vendor might show different SSL certificate warnings, worded in different ways, with slightly different recommendations, to solve the problem. Be aware, all they are trying to do is alert you to the fact that the SSL certificates come from an untrusted certificate authority and you have the choice to continue or not.

After you have opted to continue, trusting the SSL certificate, you will then be redirected to the administrative login screen as shown below. However, it will now be using the following secure administrative URL:

Note the use of the HTTPS protocol and the port **9043**, as shown in the following screenshot:

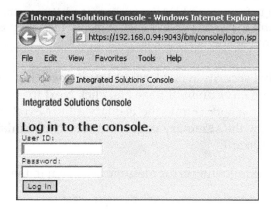

Type **wasadmin** for the username and **wasadmin** for the password and click **Log in** to gain access to the administrative console.

In our next example, we are going to discuss how to use the local operating system. Implementing a file-based repository requires the least effort and can often seem the best way to secure WebSphere. However, being a file-based repository, it means that anyone who has access to the Unix operating system can gain access to the props files containing your usernames and groups and alter the files. Using a file-based repository is not recommended for production.

Local operating system

We are now going to turn on global security with the **Local operating system** option, which is the default option for global security. We mentioned in Chapter 1 that installing WAS to run as root is not ideal and often not the most secure way to run WebSphere in Linux. However, to use the local operating system as a user registry, we need to have WebSphere running as root. Since root is required for local operating system usage it means it is not the best method for production environments because it requires a lower level of administration and is not easily managed. We will still cover it as an option as it is often a good way to secure a Windows desktop version of WebSphere when you are testing WebSphere configurations or developing locally and using a local version of WebSphere to test your J2EE applications.

 How to federate an LDAP repository is a better method and more suitable to production-like environments. LDAP repositories will be covered after this section.

This time in the **Global security** wizard, select **Local operating system** on the **Secure the application serving environment** page and click **Next** to configure the local operating system. Type wasadmin into the **Primary administrative user name** field and click **Next** to review the **summary** page. And then click **Finish** on the summary page to complete the wizard.

You should now get the following error message as shown in the following screenshot:

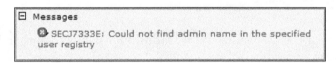

The reason that there is an error is that the wasadmin user does not exist as a user in the local operating system and so we cannot complete the wizard. We need to create a user in Linux.

Creating a Linux user

By using the addUser Linux command, we can add a new user and password. To create a new user, we must also create an associated group that the user must belong to.

The groupadd command is used to create a new group account. The new group will be entered into the system files as needed with appropriate configuration files being updated.

There are two types of groups. The first type of groups is a primary user group and the other is called a secondary group.
All user account related information is stored in /etc/passwd, /etc/shadow and /etc/group files to store user information. Consult the Linux documentation for use of groups.

All Linux OS user accounts must belong to a group, so first we are going to create a group called was by typing the following command into an SSH session to our Linux box.

/usr/sbin/groupadd was

To create a user, use the useradd command to add a new user and automatically add the user to an existing group (or create a new group and then add the user). If the group does not exist, create it. The syntax for creating a group is: **useradd -g {group-name} username**. Please note that the small -g option means adding the new user to the initial login group (primary group). The group name must exist. Type the following command to create a new user called wasadmin and add wasadmin to the was group.

/usr/sbin/useradd wasadmin -g was

We can check to see that the user is created by typing the following command:

cat /etc/passwd | cut -d":" -f1

For the WebSphere Application Server Local OS security registry to work on Linux, a shadow password file must exist. The shadow password file is named shadow and is located in the /etc directory. If the shadow password file does not exist, an error occurs while trying to complete the local OS global security option.

To create the shadow file, run the following Linux command:

pwconv

A /etc/shadow file will be created from the /etc/passwd file. After creating the shadow file, you can enable local operating system security successfully.

Now that we have created a local user and a shadow file using basic Linux administration, we can use this new user's name in the Security wizard and we will be able to complete the wizard's process. You may have to start the wizard again if you took too long and the console timed out. If so, restart the local OS global security process using the wizard and remember to save your configuration once you have completed the wizard.

Once the **Global security** wizard is complete, you need to stop and start (bounce) the application server for security to take effect. Once WAS has started back up, we will now be presented with a login screen, which will be the same as in the file-based example previously.

We have now learned how to secure our WebSphere server using the local operating system. However, this means that the user will only exist on this physical Linux machine, and in reality, this is not practical in an environment where there are many Linux/Unix machines running WebSphere. Also, we may wish to allow many different types of users to access the console with different rights and we would continually need to update our OS with users who really are never going to do any work in Linux.

What we really need is a user directory which can be shared by all WebSphere servers and this is why WebSphere should primarily be configured to use an LDAP directory, which provides the ability to have a centrally administrated user and group directory independent from WebSphere. Using a central user directory allows administration of passwords without worrying about how many Linux machines may have to be updated to allow a password to be changed, which can be tedious if you have to go around and update each server's local admin user when you want to change your WebSphere administration password. Common sense dictates that you also don't want a different password each time you log in to a different WebSphere Application Server.

Standalone LDAP

Manually configuring Lightweight Directory Access Protocol is quite a long-winded task. What we will cover in the next few pages is how to configure WebSphere to use an LDAP registry as opposed to the more easier, yet less secure file-based security option. Using LDAP requires the use of an LDAP directory. There are many products in the market place and your organization will have a solution from one of the big vendors, such as Microsoft's ADAM, which is a light-weight implementation of Active Directory or IBM's Tivoli Directory Server. These two are very common LDAP implementations. However, we are going to use Open LDAP, an open source LDAP implantation. Before we configure our WebSphere LDAP registry, we need to download, install, and configure OpenLDAP.

Download OpenLDAP

Download the latest version of OpenLDAP from the following URL:

`http://www.openldap.org/software/download/`

At the time of writing, the last stable version of OpenLDAP is version 2.4.11 and we downloaded the tar file called `openldap-stable-20080813.tgz`.

Installing OpenLDAP

Create a new folder on your Linux server, that is, /apps/openldap using the following command. If the folder path doesn't exist, it will be created.

mkdir -p /apps/openldap

Upload the tar file to your Linux box into the /apps/openldap folder.

Un-tar and de-compress the file using the following command:

tar -x -z -f ./openldap-stable-20080813.tgz

A directory called openldap-2.4.13 will be created. Change into this directory using the following command:

 cd openldap-2.4.11

Listing the contents of this directory will look something like the following screenshot:

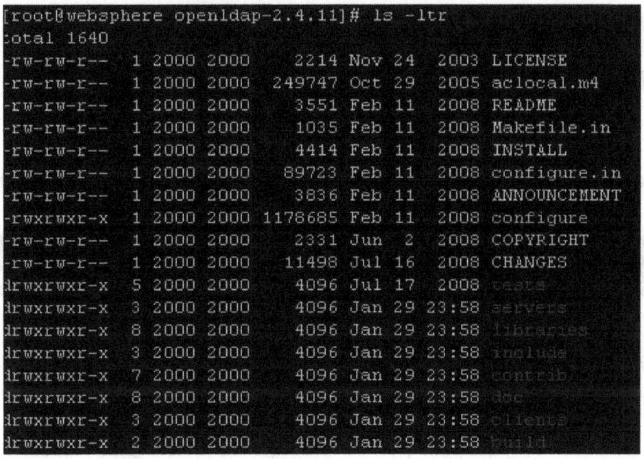

Configuring OpenLDAP

To configure OpenLDAP, type the following command:

./configure

This will run a script which will check your Linux configuration and outline any dependencies or libraries that are missing. The script should end with the following statement: **Please run "make depend" to build dependencies**.

1. Run the following command:

   make depend

2. Then run the following command:

   make

3. Then run the following command:

   Make test

4. Then run the following command:

   Make install

OpenLDAP is now installed and the configuration files can be found in `/usr/local/etc/openlda`

Once the software has been built and installed, you are ready to configure slapd(8) for use at your site. Slapd is the Standalone LDAP Daemon process which is the actual LDAP service program on Linux.

We are going to configure OpenLDAP to run in a local directory service mode — the simplest form of OpenLDAP directory usage.

1. To start slapd, type:

   /usr/local/libexec/slapd

2. Once started, you can type:

   ps -ef | grep slapd | grep -v grep

   and you will see something similar to the following screenshot:

```
[root@localhost openldap-2.4.11]# ps -ef | grep slapd | grep -v grep
root      4094      1  0 09:07 ?        00:00:00 /usr/local/libexec/slapd
```

3. To stop slapd, type:

   kill -9 `cat /usr/local/var/run/slapd.pid`

4. Edit the `ldap.conf` file located in the `/usr/local/etc/openldap` folder.

5. And add the following two lines:

   HOST   websphere.redhat.com
   BASE dc=webpshere,dc=redhat,dc=com

6. Save the `ldap.conf` file.

7. Edit the `slapd.conf` file located in the same folder as `ldap.conf` above. Navigate to the section shown below.

   ```
   ############################################################
   # BDB database definitions
   ############################################################
   ```

8. Edit the `suffix` line to be as follows:

```
Suffix    ""dc=websphere,dc=redhat,dc=com"
```

9. Edit the `rootdn` line to be:

```
rootdn           "uid=root,dc=websphere,dc=redhat,dc=com"
```

10. Ensure slapd is running and type:

    slappasswd

11. Enter `ldapadmin` as the password.

12. A key similar to {SSHA}dound2tIC9bmTCGM2gWYoyR6XXvfivn3 will be generated.

13. Edit the `slapd.conf` file, find the lines:

```
# Use of strong authentication encouraged

rootpw        secret
```

14. Comment the line out and set `rootpw` to the new key which was generated above, as shown below:

```
#rootpw            secret
rootpw             {SSHA}dound2tIC9bmTCGM2gWYoyR6XXvfivn3
```

Here is some background information about **Lightweight Directory Interchange Format (LDIF)** files. To import and export directory information between LDAP-based directory servers, or to describe a set of changes which are to be applied to a directory, the file format known as LDIF, for LDAP Data Interchange Format, is typically used. A LDIF file stores information in object-oriented hierarchies of entries.

A common LDIF file looks like this:

```
dn: o=Packt, c=UK
o: Packt
objectclass: organization
dn: cn=Bob Jackson, o=Packt, c=UK
cn: Bob Jackson
sn: Jackson
mail: bob.jackson@webpshere.redhat.com
objectclass: person
```

A description of LDIF attributes is shown below:

LDIF Attribute Name	Description
DN (distinguishedName)	This is a hierarchical name element, often used to promote uniqueness.
O	Represents the name of an organizational unit. Use this attribute to identify your organization.
objectclass	Object class refers to the type of object this LDAP represents. Often a person or organizational unit.
CN (commonName)	The name of the person or group
SN (Surname)	SN often requires an attribute representing a user's last name.

The next step is to create an LDIF file called webpshere.ldif — the root user's home directory, that is /root/webpshere.ldif containing the following attributes:

```
dn: dc=websphere,dc=redhat,dc=com
objectclass: dcobject
objectClass: organization
o: Pakt Publishing
dc: websphere
```

Finally, we just run this command to add your root account in LDAP:

/usr/local/bin/ldapadd -x -D 'uid=root,dc=websphere,dc=redhat,dc=com' -W -f /root/websphere.ldif

You will then be asked for your secret password. Type in ldapadmin.

The result will be as shown:

```
[root@localhost openldap-data]# /usr/local/bin/ldapadd -x -D 'uid=root,dc=we
bsphere,dc=redhat,dc=com' -w ldapadmin -f /root/websphere.ldif
adding new entry "dc=websphere,dc=redhat,dc=com"
```

If you list /usr/local/var/openldap-data, you will see the configuration files of the directory as shown in the following screenshot:

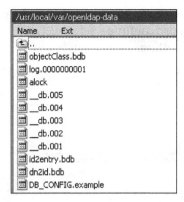

To test that ldap is working, we can type the following:

```
Ldapsearch -x
```

The result should be something similar to the following screenshot:

```
[root@localhost openldap]# ldapsearch -x
# extended LDIF
#
# LDAPv3
# base <dc=webpshere,dc=redhat,dc=com> (default) with scope subtree
# filter: (objectclass=*)
# requesting: ALL
#

# search result
search: 2
result: 32 No such object

# numResponses: 1
```

Adding a user to LDAP

We now need to use an LDAP client to administer our LDAP directory and add users. We will download open source LDAP client called **jexplorer**, which we will use as our LDAP administration client.

Go to http://www.jxplorer.org/ and download the windows installer, for example, select the **JXv3.2_install_windows** option from available installers on the site's download page. Once downloaded, run the installer and launch JXplorer. It must be noted that JXplorer is a Java application, and as such, it requires an appropriate **Java Runtime Environment** (**JRE**) to be installed before it can be used. When you install a JRE, the JRE path is automatically added in your system PATH variable which tells the Java application where to find a JRE to run the Java application. You can download the latest JRE from the following URL:

http://www.java.com/en/download/

Once JXplorer is running, click **Connect** and you will be prompted with the option to configure a connection record, defining which LDAP server you are connecting to and appropriate connection settings, as shown below.

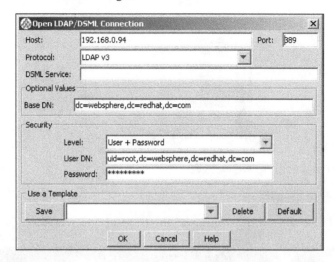

In our example, we are using the following values as shown in the preceding screenshot:

Field	Value
Host	`<machine ip address or hostname>`
Base DN	dc=websphere,dc=redhat,dc=com
Level	User + Password
User DN	uid=root,dc=websphere,dc=redhat,dc=com
Password	ldapadmin

It is wise to save your connection as a template using the **Save** button in the **Use a Template** section. Ensure that Linux machines' firewall allows 339, otherwise you might get an error like the one below.

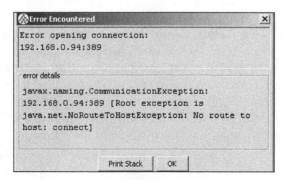

To open a Linux port, we will need to run a Linux administration command to alter your firewall settings. Run the following command to allow clients to connect to the LDAP port 339.

```
iptables -A INPUT -i eth0 -p tcp --sport 389 -m state --state ESTABLISHED
-j ACCEPT
```

An explanation of the command line is given below:

Code Element	Description
`iptables -A INPUT`	This sets the IP rule to be appended into the INPUT table.
`-i eth0`	This rule applies to the eth0 interface.
`-p tcp --sport 389`	This sets the protocol to TCP and the source port is 443.
`-m state --state ESTABLISHED -j ACCEPT`	This sets a match on the state of established. That means if the connection has been established, it will be accepted.
	However, this rule will deny any new connections as the rule needs the state of NEW.

Once you have enabled port 339 in your firewall settings, then you will be able to administer the LDAP directory using the jexplorer client. The following screenshot shows the main entry page if you have successfully logged into the LDAP directory.

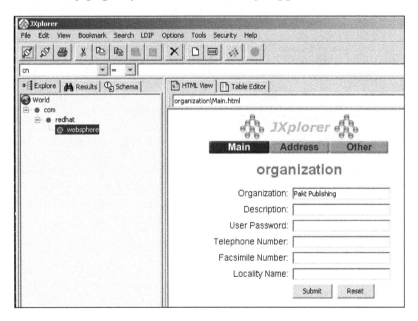

In LDAP, an object class defines the collection of attributes that can be used to define an entry. The LDAP standard provides these basic types of object classes:

- Groups in the directory, including unordered lists of individual objects or groups of objects
- Locations, such as the country name and description
- Organizations in the directory
- People in the directory

For instance, the commonName, or cn, attribute is used to store a person's name. A person named Bob Jackson can be represented in the directory as:

```
cn: Bob Jackson
```

We are going to create some users (people).

To create a new user, right-click on the **websphere** node in the directory tree in the explorer table, and then click on the **New** toolbar as shown immediately below.

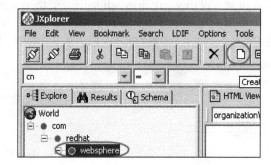

Check that the DN of the parent entry in the **Parent DN** text box is correct.

Enter the **Relative Domain Name (RDN)** of the new entry in the **Enter RDN** text box. For example, if you want to add John Smith to the Administration Department, you may enter **cn=wasadmin**. Select a class (object type) from the **Available Classes:** and then click **Add** to add the object to the list of the classes, as shown in the following screenshot:

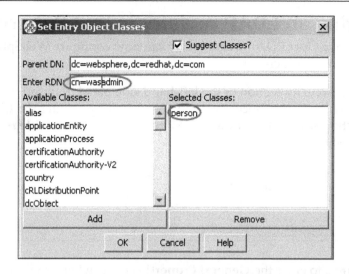

Click **OK** to create the new JDAP user. Once created, you will then be able to double-click the **userPassword** property and change the user's password.

The fields in bold within the main attribute table are mandatory. We need to edit the sn (surname) attribute. We used **wasadmin** for both cn and sn.

After you have created the **wasadmin** user, please create another user called **Bob Jackson**. We do not set the password for **Bob Jackson**.

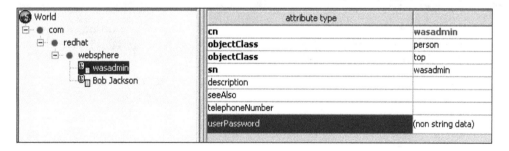

At this stage, the user has been created in the root DN. You may wish to add organizational hierarchy to administer your users. Administration of LDAP is not covered by the scope of this book. We have essentially created two new users which will be given two different roles—one being an administrator, the other being an operator user who can only do basic administration functions in the administrative console.

We now have what we need to demonstrate using LDAP-based users to administer WebSphere.

Configuring an LDAP registry in WebSphere

Now that we have OpenLDAP working, we can now configure WebSphere to use the LDAP directory we have created.

Navigate to the **Security** section of the left-hand side panel in the administrative console and click on **Global security**. In the **Security** page, under the **User account repository** section, select **Standalone LDAP registry** from **Available realm definitions**, as shown below.

Click **Configure...** to enter the **General Properties** page, where you can configure all the appropriate settings to configure WAS to use an LDAP repository. As shown below, type **wasadmin** in the **Primary administrative user name** field. This is the primary user WebSphere will use for the server identity.

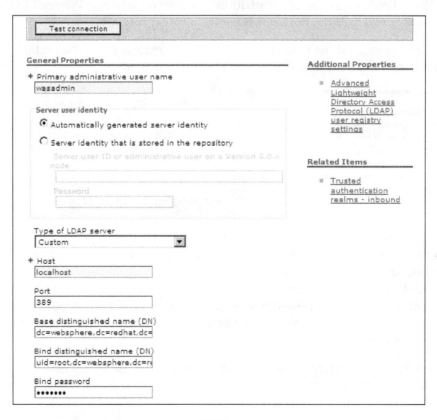

As shown in the previous screenshot, fill in the remaining fields with the values as shown in the following table:

Field Name	Value Entered
Host	**localhost**. (Using localhost allows you to not worry about what domain name system fully qualified name [DNS FQN] you have configured)
Port	**339** (Default LDAP port)
Base distinguished Name (DN)	**dc=websphere,dc=redhat,dc=com**
Bind distinguished name (DN)	**uid=root,dc=websphere,dc=redhat,dc=com**
Bind password	**ldapadmin**

Once you have completed filling in the required fields, click **Apply** and you will then be prompted with the following message:

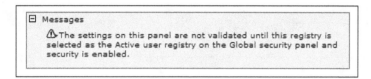

Navigate back to the previous **Global security** page and select **Standalone LDAP registry** from the **Available realm definition** pick-list and click the **Set as current** button as shown below.

Click **Apply** and you will be prompted to save the configuration. Click **Save** to persist the security changes to the master configuration. You will find that an error message will be presented with a **Primary administrative user ID does not exist in the registry** error message as shown below.

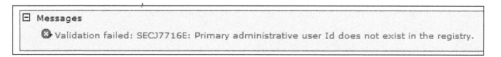

The reason for the error above is that the default LDAP configuration for **Custom** in WebSphere is set to look for the uid attribute for a common name. However, we have created a user in LDAP using the cn attribute, which is the standard used by default in OpenLDAP. We can either edit our LDAP directory and add extra LDAP attributes to our person objects, or we can customize the WebSphere LDAP configuration. We will change our LDAP registry settings using the administrative console advanced LDAP options.

To edit advanced LDAP setting, click on **Advanced Lightweight Directory Access Protocol (LDAP) user registry settings** in the configuration page for a **Standalone LDAP Registry**, as shown in the following screenshot:

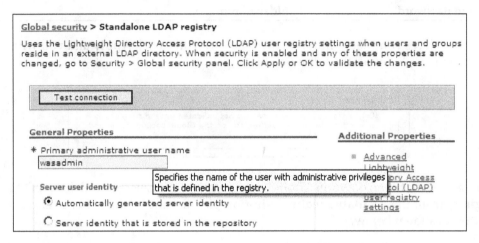

You will now be presented with the option to change LDAP attributes as shown in the following screenshot:

A default set of predefined filters exist, which are provided for each LDAP server that the WebSphere supports. You can modify these filters to fit your LDAP configuration

The **User filter** field contains a LDAP string, which provides the LDAP search filter which is used to obtain information about users and groups from an LDAP directory server.

We need to change the **User filter** field from **(&(uid=%v)(objectclass=Person))**

to **(&(cn=%v)(objectclass=Person))**.

and the **User ID map** field from ***:uid to*:cn**, as shown in the previous screenshot, to ensure that WebSphere queries the LDAP directory correctly.

Click **Apply** and **Save**.

If all the settings are correct, you will be presented with the following message:

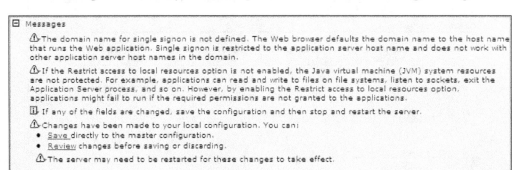

Click **Save** to save to the master configuration. Bounce WAS for the LDAP settings to take effect.

You now have configured WebSphere to use an LDAP registry. What we now need to do is ensure that each user is assigned appropriate administrative roles.

Administrative roles

We need a way to assign different levels of privileges to different users, thus controlling what groups of people can do. We may want some people to have only the ability to start and stop applications, we may wish to allow others full configuration access. WebSphere implements a way of delegating privileges through the use of administrative roles. There are ten predefined roles in WebSphere 7, as outlined in the following table, which users are mapped to.

Administrative Role	Description
Monitor	A user or group with the monitor role can do the following: • View the WebSphere Application Server configuration • View the current state of the Application Server
Configurator	Assigned monitor privilege plus the ability to configuration. For example, a configurator role can do the following: • Create a resource • Map an application server • Install and uninstall an application • Deploy an application • Assign users and groups-to-role mapping for applications • Set up Java 2 security permissions for applications
Operator	Assigned monitor privileges and can stop and start the server and monitor the server status in the administrative console.
Administrator	An individual or group which can be assigned this role will have the operator and configurator privileges, plus additional privileges that are granted for administration.
Iscadmins	Available to administrative console users. Users who are granted this role have administrator privileges for managing users and groups in the federated repositories.
Deployer	Use this role to grant users the ability to completely deploy an application and configure application runtime settings.
Admin Security Manager	By using the Admin Security Manager role, you can assign users and groups to the administrative user roles and administrative group roles.
Auditor	This role allows users to modify the configuration settings for security auditing and the role includes the monitor role. This allows the auditor to view but not change the rest of the security configuration.

 Users and groups can be added or removed from administrative roles using the WebSphere Application Server administrative console by a user given the appropriate authority and the administrator role is for this purpose.

Mapping users and groups to administrative roles

To manage administrative user roles, we will need to navigate to the **Administrative security** section of the **Global security** page where we started our global security configuration.

Clicking the **Administrative user roles** link will result in a configuration page which will allow us to assign administrative roles to our LDAP users. As seen in the following image, we already have a role assigned to wasadmin because it was set to be the primary administrative user in our global security configuration.

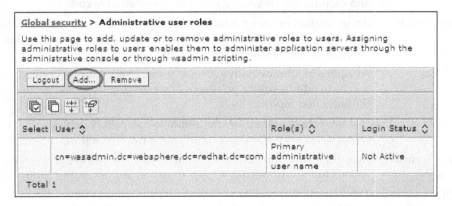

To add a new role mapping, click **Add** and you will be directed to a screen where you can assign other LDAP users to other roles. We want to assign the **Operator** role to the LDAP user we created earlier named **Bob Jackson**. Select **Operator** from the **Role(s)** pick list and type **bob*** in the **Search string** field. When you click **Search**, a query will be made to LDAP using the wildcard filter to look for any user whose **cn** starts with bob.

The result of the search will return matches. The users found in LDAP that match the find will be listed in the **Available** field. Select the user **Bob Jackson** from the **Available** field and click the arrow pointing right to assign **Bob Jackson** the **Operator** role. You will see the user move from the available list to the **Mapped role** list as shown as follows:

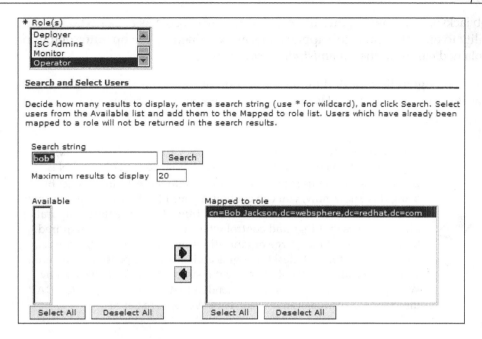

Click **OK** to return to the **Administrative user roles** screen and click **Save** to save the mapping to the master configuration as shown below.

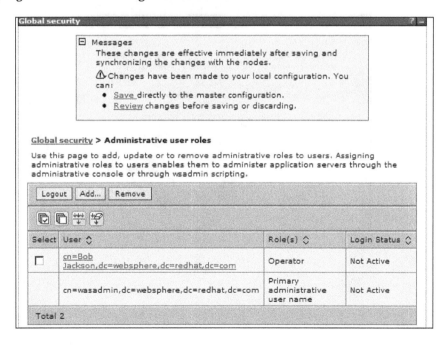

Bob Jackson can now log into the Administrative console as a user who has the ability to only start and stop applications as explained by the operator definition explained earlier in the *Administrative roles* section.

Click the **Logout** link located in the top section of the Admin console and log back in as Bob Jackson using the User ID Bob Jackson and the password password.

The login User ID in our examples uses the **Common Name** (CN) attribute as defined in our LDAP configuration. So for Bob, his CN is **Bob Jackson,** so this is his User ID to log into the Admin console. By using this know-how, you can configure your LDAP by adding your own custom objects and WebSphere LDAP settings to ensure the configuration filters use these settings and control what style of User ID are required for login names. Often large organizations employ a global directory, which is used for both desktop logins and email, it is possible to federate your organization's global directory if it supports LDAP to be used by WebSphere. However, it is recommended that you use a separate LDAP directory for administrative security of WebSphere Server.

Once logged in, the **Welcome** screen will show a message stating this user has limited administrative rights as shown in the following screenshot:

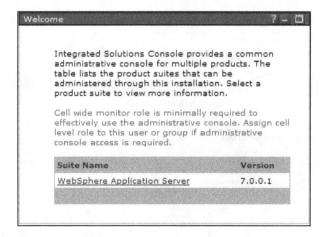

Navigate to the **WebSphere enterprise applications** screen and you will see that there are only three options available—**Start**, **Stop**, and **Rollout Update**, as shown in the following screenshot:

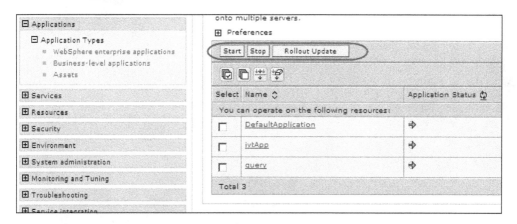

You can now log out Bob Jackson and log in again using `wasamdin` to gain full administration capabilities.

Summary

We learned that for global security to work, we need a repository of users and groups of users who are authorized to access the administrative console (admin console). WebSphere uses three main types of registries which can be used to store the users and groups which are given access to log in and configure the server. On large systems used by businesses and other organizations, there will likely be several system administrators and application servers dispersed across more than one machine, and if you use a Local OS user registry, each machine would have its own user registry and it would be hard to keep them all up-to-date and secure, and hence LDAP is a better option.

4
Administrative Scripting

As a WebSphere administrator, you will soon find that doing administration manually becomes laborious when you have a large number of administration tasks to perform. Whether you work for a large organization or not, you will also have to deploy many applications into your WebSphere environments. In Chapter 2, we learned how to manually deploy an EAR file using the administration console and we found that, depending on the type of application being deployed, there could be many configuration elements involved before the application is considered ready for runtime use. To speed up deployments and make them more consistent and controllable, we need to look at how we can automate our deployments. It is also important that we are able to automate the configuration of WebSphere which can save many hours of manual administrative efforts. WebSphere supports the use of the Jython language for administrative scripting. Jython is an implementation of the high-level, dynamic, object-oriented Python language written in 100% pure Java, and seamlessly integrated with the Java platform. By using Jython scripts, we can readily craft administrative tasks and run them in an automated fashion using the WebSphere administration tool called wsadamin.sh. By creating scripts, we can automate configurations and application deployments.

In this chapter, we will cover the following topics:

- Automated deployment
- ws_ant (Ant)
- wasadmin.sh
- Python/Jython
- Command line tools

Automation

Automation doesn't come for free; it requires some effort from the administrator, yet the rewards are great. Being able to automate an application deployment allows for the control of naming standards, ensures consistency each time the application is deployed or WAS configuration is required. Scripting lends to auditing and version control and the ability to do in minutes what could take a human hours - and without human-induced errors. As administrators, our key goals are to deploy new applications and update existing applications and Application Server configurations rapidly without error. IBM has provided administration tools that can run automation scripts. There are two main tools used for automation—one is called **wsadmin** which uses the Jython and **Java Application Control Language (JACL)** languages, and **ws_ant** which uses Ant which is an XML-based Java build language. The wsadmin tool can be used for both deployment and configuration of all areas of WebSphere, whereas ws_ant is mainly best used for application deployment. We will cover ws_ant first, the move on to wsadmin.

The ws_ant tool

ws_ant is based on Apache Ant. Ant is an interpreted language which is designed to sequentially run shell-based commands which can extend to use Java classes. If you wish to learn more about Ant, you can read up about it on the Apache web site located at `http://ant.apache.org/`.

Ant XML-based configuration files contain sequential commands as groups of tasks. These XML files reference a tree of task groups called targets, in which various tasks are specified to run. Each task is run by an object that implements a particular task interface. WebSphere utilizes Ant and the ws_ant utility provides specific Ant tasks which are designed to make application deployment easier for application developers. It is not recommended that ws_ant be used in production servers as it is strongly linked to development. In enterprise systems, developers will not have access to live systems. ws_ant is not scalable like wsadmin scripting, which is more suitable for enterprise WebSphere designs and production deployment.

The ws_ant tool can be found at the following location:

```
<was_root>/bin/ws_ant
```

The WebSphere Application Server ws_ant tool is based on the open source Apache Ant. However, it has some additional WebSphere Application Server specific Ant tasks. The main ws_ant tasks are listed in the following table:

ws_ant task name	Description
wsListApps	Lists all the applications installed on a WebSphere application
wsInstallApp	Allows you to deploy an existing application into a WebSphere Application Server
wsUninstallApp	Allows you to uninstall an existing application from a WebSphere Application Server.
wsStartServer	Allows you to start a standalone server instance
wsStopServer	Allows you to stop a standalone server instance

More ws_ant tasks exist and you can search the WebSphere 7 Information Centre for information on the other ws_ant tasks at the following URL:

```
http://publib.boulder.ibm.com/infocenter/wasinfo/v7r0/index.jsp
```

Before ws_ant can be used, an XML file must be created which will contain the tasks it will run. Traditionally, Ant-based utilities look for a default XML file called build. xml. However, any XML file name can be used as long as you pass the name of the file on the command line when you run ws_ant.

To demonstrate the ws_ant tool, we will automate a deployment of the HR application we manually installed in Chapter 2.

If the HR application EAR file is installed in WebSphere, please uninstall it. If you have not yet uninstalled an EAR file from WebSphere, go through the following steps.

- Log into the Admin console and navigate to the **Application Types** section of the **Applications** panel located on the left-hand side of the admin console and click the **WebSphere enterprise applications** link.

In the **Enterprises Applications** panel, which lists the current installed applications, select the **HRListerEAR** application and click **Uninstall**.

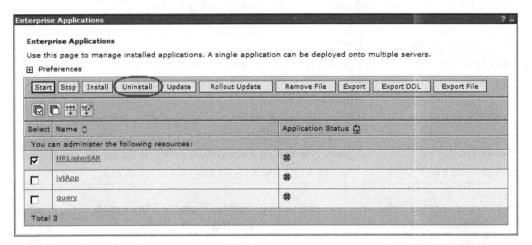

You will be prompted to confirm. Click **OK** to continue and once the application has been uninstalled, you will need to click **Save** to persist the configuration changes shown below.

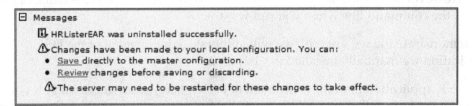

Deploying an application using ws_ant

We will now demonstrate the use of the ws_ant task called wsInstallApp. Before we can run a ws_ant automated application deployment, we need to create an XML file which will contain the ws_ant tasks we wish to run to deploy the application. We could use the name `build.xml` for the XML file to keep in line with common use of ant, but by using a different file we know what the script is for by just looking at its name.

1. Log into your Linux server using a secure shell.

2. Create a file called `deployHR.xml` in a folder called `/home/wasscripts/ws_ant/`

3. If the folder doesn't exist, you can run the following command:

    ```
    mkdir -p /home/wasscripts/ws_ant
    ```

4. Copy the following code into deployHR.xml and save the XML file:

```xml
<?xml version="1.0" encoding="UTF-8"?>

<project name="HR Lister Application Depoyment" default="build-all"
basedir=".">
    <!-- global properties -->
    <property name="hostName" value="localhost" />
    <property name="connType" value="SOAP" />
    <property name="port" value="8880" />
    <property name="userId" value="wasadmin" />
    <property name="password" value="wasadmin" />
    <property name="deployEar.dir" value="/home/deployments" />
    <property name="deployEar" value="HRListerEAR.ear" />
    <property name="wasHome.dir" value="/apps/was7" />

    <!-- mbean declaration" -->
    <taskdef name="wsInstallApp" classname="com.ibm.websphere.ant.
    tasks.InstallApplication" />

    <!-- installation Target-->
    <target name="installEar">
        <echo message="Deployable EAR File found at: ${deployEar.
    dir}/${deployEar}" />
        <wsInstallApp ear="${deployEar.dir}/${deployEar}"
        wasHome="${wasHome.dir}"
        conntype="${connType}"
        port="${port}"
        host="${hostName}"
        user="${userId}"
        password="${password}" />
    </target>

    <target name="build-all" depends="installEar">
        <!--Main Target-->
    </target>

</project>
```

5. To run the ws_ant script, we need to navigate to the `<was_root>/bin` folder and type the following command:

    ```
    ./ws_ant.sh -f /home/wasscripts/ws_ant/deployHR.xml
    ```

The result of running the `deployHR.xml` ws_ant script will be displayed to stdout (the shell scripts console). Below is a sample of the output you would expect to see.

```
root@websphere:/apps/was7/bin                                              _|□|×|
[root@websphere bin]# ./ws_ant.sh -f /home/wasscripts/ws_ant/deployHR.xml
WSVR0027I: The product will expire in 10 days.
Buildfile: /home/wasscripts/ws_ant/deployHR.xml

installEar:
     [echo] Deployable EAR File found at: /home/deployments/HRListerEAR.ear
[wsInstallApp] Installing Application [/home/deployments/HRListerEAR.ear]...
   [wsadmin] WSVR0027I: The product will expire in 10 days.
   [wsadmin] WASX7209I: Connected to process "server1" on node node01 using SOAP connector;  The typ
e of process is: UnManagedProcess
   [wsadmin] ADMA5016I: Installation of HRListerEAR started.
   [wsadmin] ADMA5058I: Application and module versions are validated with versions of deployment ta
rgets.
   [wsadmin] ADMA5005I: The application HRListerEAR is configured in the WebSphere Application Serve
r repository.
   [wsadmin] ADMA5053I: The library references for the installed optional package are created.
   [wsadmin] ADMA5005I: The application HRListerEAR is configured in the WebSphere Application Serve
r repository.
   [wsadmin] ADMA5001I: The application binaries are saved in /apps/was7/profiles/appsrv01/wstemp/Sc
ript120c1fd7a8b/workspace/cells/websphereNode01Cell/applications/HRListerEAR.ear/HRListerEAR.ear
   [wsadmin] ADMA5005I: The application HRListerEAR is configured in the WebSphere Application Serve
r repository.
   [wsadmin] SECJ0400I: Successfully updated the application HRListerEAR with the appContextIDForSec
urity information.
   [wsadmin] CWSAD0040I: The application HRListerEAR is configured in the Application Server reposit
ory.
   [wsadmin] ADMA5005I: The application HRListerEAR is configured in the WebSphere Application Serve
r repository.
   [wsadmin] ADMA5113I: Activation plan created successfully.
   [wsadmin] ADMA5011I: The cleanup of the temp directory for application HRListerEAR is complete.
   [wsadmin] ADMA5013I: Application HRListerEAR installed successfully.
[wsInstallApp] Installed Application [/home/deployments/HRListerEAR.ear]

build-all:

BUILD SUCCESSFUL
```

We have now seen how to use ws_ant to install an application. We will now create another script called `manageHR.xml` which will contain several ws_ant tasks. The `manageHR.xml` script is designed so we can call tasks individually or as a complete set from beginning to end. Create a file called `manageHR.xml` in the same folder you created earlier, for example:

`/home/wasscripts/ws_ant/manageHR.xml`

Copy the following code into the `manageHR.xml` file:

```
<?xml version="1.0" encoding="UTF-8"?>

<project name="Manage HR Lister Application Depoyment" default="build-
all" basedir=".">
    <!-- global properties -->
    <property name="hostName" value="localhost" />
    <property name="connType" value="SOAP" />
    <property name="port" value="8880" />
```

```
    <property name="userId" value="wasadmin" />
    <property name="password" value="wasadmin" />
    <property name="appName" value="HRLister" />
    <property name="deployEar.dir" value="/home/deployments" />
    <property name="deployEar" value="HRListerEAR.ear" />
    <property name="wasHome.dir" value="/apps/was7" />

    <!-- mbean declarations" -->
    <taskdef name="wsUninstallApp" classname="com.ibm.websphere.ant.
tasks.UninstallApplication" />
    <taskdef name="wsInstallApp" classname="com.ibm.websphere.ant.
tasks.InstallApplication" />
    <taskdef name="wsListApplications" classname="com.ibm.websphere.
ant.tasks.ListApplications" />

    <!-- List Target-->
    <target name="listApplications">
       <wsListApplications
       wasHome="${wasHome.dir}"
       conntype="${connType}"
       port="${port}"
       host="${hostName}"
       user="${userId}"
       password="${password}" />
    </target>

    <!-- Uninstall Target-->
    <target name="uninstallEAR">
       <wsUninstallApp application="${appName}"
       wasHome="${wasHome.dir}"
       conntype="${connType}"
       port="${port}"
       host="${hostName}"
       user="${userId}"
       password="${password}" />
    </target>

    <!-- installation Target-->
    <target name="installEAR">
       <echo message="Deployable EAR File found at: ${deployEar.
dir}/${deployEar}" />
       <wsInstallApp ear="${deployEar.dir}/${deployEar}"
       options="-appname ${appName}"
       wasHome="${wasHome.dir}"
       conntype="${connType}"
       port="${port}"
       host="${hostName}"
```

```
        user="${userId}"
        password="${password}" />
    </target>

    <target name="build-all" depends="listApplications, uninstallEAR,
listApplications, installEAR, listApplications">
        <!--Main Target-->
    </target>

</project>
```

The `manageHR.xml` build file contains several Ant targets that can be called individually by specifying a particular target to the `ws_ant` command line. By using the table below, you can see the syntax of the different types of command lines required to run the individual targets.

Target name to run	Command line syntax
`listApplications`	`<was_root>/bin/ws_ant.sh listApplications -f /home/wasscripts/ws_ant/manageHR.xml`
`uninstallEAR`	`<was_root>/bin/ws_ant.sh uninstallEAR -f /home/wasscripts/ws_ant/manageHR.xml`
`installEAR`	`<was_root>/bin/ws_ant.sh installEAR -f /home/wasscripts/ws_ant/manageHR.xml`
<No target specified>	`<was_root>/bin/ws_ant.sh install -f /home/wasscripts/ws_ant/manageHR.xml`

Feel free to experiment with the `manageHR.xml` file and try our different target combinations. If you chose to run the `manageHR.xml` file with no specific target mentioned, the `build-all` target shown below will be run which calls named targets in a particular order.

```
<target name="build-all" depends="listApplications, uninstallEAR,
listApplications, installEAR, listApplications">
        <!--Main Target-->
    </target>
```

Since the `manageHR.xml` file has a project declaration which specifies the default target being `build-all`, as shown below, the `build-all` target will be called if no target name is specified on the command line.

```
<project name="Manage HR Lister Application Deployment"
default="build-all" basedir=".">
```

ws_ant is a great tool for people with Java development experience as the concept of an Ant `build.xml` file is often used in building and packaging J2EE (Enterprise Edition) applications. You can learn the Ant syntax and idiosyncrasies from the Apache ant web site and by Googling for sample Ant projects to give you insights into the commands and the way in which Ant commands can be used in your ws_ant XML files. ws_ant is not designed for production system configuration and a better tool for administrative scripting in WAS is the wsadmin tool. ws_ant is in fact an Ant wrapper which calls some wsadmin commands internally.

The wsadmin tool

wsadmin acts as an interface to WebSphere Java objects for access by scripts. Internally, WAS employs special Java objects to communicate with internal MBeans (JMX management objects). If you wish to learn more about MBeans, go to the following URL: `http://java.sun.com/docs/books/tutorial/jmx/mbeans/index.html`.

WebSphere utilizes the JMX API to create MBeans that are exposed as an API of internal WebSphere objects, which wsadmin can utilize to configure WebSphere. In WAS 7, the wsadmin tool (`wsadmin.sh`) supports five top-level scripting objects, including the `AdminConfig`, `AdminControl`, `AdminApp`, `AdminTask`, and the `Help` object. Scripts use these objects for application management, configuration, control, and communicating with the internal MBeans that run in the WAS product. The following table explains the scripting objects.

Scripting Object	Description
AdminConfig	Communicates with the config service and used to modify, remove or display WebSphere internal configuration data. The object essentially supports making changes to the configuration WAS product.
AdminControl	Used to run commands which affect the server runtime. This object works with the running MBean objects within the WAS process. MBeans represent internal components of the runtime which can be manipulated by scripted calls.
AdminApp	Used to administer configurations and settings of deployed applications. Typical actions might include installing, modifying, and making administration changes to the application. AdminApp commands can also be run locally when the server is down.
AdminTask	Used to run administrative commands. Also has a local mode which, when invoked, allows AdminTask commands to be run locally when the server is down.
Help	Used to get help on available administrative commands from the other four main scripting objects.

The wsadmin tool can be run in different modes depending on the required use. The following table explains the different modes.

Mode	Description
Run scripting commands interactively	The wsadmin tool is run and commands are entered by the user interactive and are run inside the wsadmin interface.
Run individual scripting commands	Single commands are executed as command line parameters (arguments) to the main `wsadmin.sh` command.
Run scripting commands in a script file	The most common method is where commands are entered into a file and run by the wsadmin tool. Similar to running any batch file process or shell script.
Run scripting commands in a profile script	These scripts are run before the wsadmin script executes and can be used to set up environments or do pre-script actions.

For the purposes of this book, we will only refer to Jython as IBM has announced since WebSphere 6 that JACL is now deprecated and will be removed some time in the near future. The scripting interface for WebSphere is called the wsadmin tool. The tool is called by the `wsadmin.sh` script, which is located in the `bin` directory of an Application Server profile, that is `<was_profile_root>/bin`.

During the remaining chapters of the book, we will refer to this tool as wsadmin. wsadmin is run from a Linux command line and can also be called from other Linux shell scripts. In fact, any application that calls a Linux shell script can call wsadmin and this is what makes administering WebSphere much easier.

Interactive commands

To run the wsadmin tool, log on to your Linux machine where WebSphere is installed, and navigate to the `<was_profile_root>/bin` directory (for example, `/apps/was7/profiles/appsrv01/bin`) and type the following command

```
./wsadmin.sh -lang jython
```

 The first time you run wsadmin, there may be many lines containing ***sys-package-mgr*: processing modified jar...** reported. This is the tool preparing the Java files used by the wsadmin tool.

Once the wsadmin tool has loaded, you will see the following prompt:

```
root@localhost:/var/apps/was7/profiles/appsrv01/bin
[root@localhost bin]#
[root@localhost bin]#
[root@localhost bin]# ./wsadmin.sh -lang jython
WASX7209I: Connected to process "server1" on node nod01 using SOAP connector;  The type of process is: UnManagedProcess
WASX7031I: For help, enter: "print Help.help()"
wsadmin>
```

Type the following command and hit the *Enter* key:

print "Hello World"

You will see the text Hello World printed to the stdout (the shells screen).

Now, type the following command and hit *Enter*:

print Help.help()

You will see that help objects are listed on your screen as shown below:

```
wsadmin>print Help.help()
WASX7028I: The Help object has two purposes:

        First, provide general help information for the the objects
        supplied by wsadmin for scripting: Help, AdminApp, AdminConfig,
        and AdminControl.

        Second, provide a means to obtain interface information about
        MBeans running in the system.  For this purpose, a variety of
        commands are available to get information about the operations,
        attributes, and other interface information about particular
        MBeans.

        The following commands are supported by Help; more detailed
        information about each of these commands is available by using the
        "help" command of Help and supplying the name of the command
        as an argument.

attributes              given an MBean, returns help for attributes
operations              given an MBean, returns help for operations
constructors            given an MBean, returns help for constructors
description             given an MBean, returns help for description
notifications           given an MBean, returns help for notifications
classname               given an MBean, returns help for classname
all                     given an MBean, returns help for all the above
help                    returns this help text
AdminControl            returns general help text for the AdminControl object
AdminConfig             returns general help text for the AdminConfig object
AdminApp                returns general help text for the AdminApp object
AdminTask               returns general help text for the AdminTask object
wsadmin                 returns general help text for the wsadmin script
                        launcher
message                 given a message id, returns explanation and
                        user action message

wsadmin>
```

If we wish to drill down into more information on a particular scripting object, we can use the help command. To list more details for the AdminConfig object, we will type the following command:

print Help.AdminConfig()

Then you will get a detailed listing of the available commands supported by the AdminConfig object.

Type Exit to leave the wsadmin tool.

There are many commands listed for each of the main objects. We will not list them here, however; if you wish to see them for yourself, you can run the following four commands from an interactive wsadmin console to see the list of commands available.

- `print Help.AdminConfig()`
- `print Help.AdminControl()`
- `print Help.AdminApp()`
- `print Help.AdminTask()`

Individual commands

You can execute single wsadmin commands from the command line. This is an easy and effective way of making simple calls. It is not as useful as the interactive and command script option. However, there could be situations where you may want a shell script to call a single wsadmin method as a part of some administrative, monitoring, or reporting function.

To call wsadmin via the command line, you use the wsadmin tool with the -c option.

Ensure that you are in the <was_profile_root>/bin folder and type the following command:

./wsadmin.sh -lang jython -c 'AdminApp.list()'

The result will list the application on the server as shown in the sample below:

```
[root@websphere bin]# ./wsadmin.sh -lang jython -c 'AdminApp.list()'
WASX7209I: Connected to process "server1" on node websphereNode01 using SOAP connector;
  The type of process is: UnManagedProcess
'DefaultApplication\nHRListerEAR\nivtApp\nquery'
```

In the example above, you can see that a string of the current application is returned. You could use shell script commands to parse the line into a more readable format. An example could be that you want a shell script to call a wsadmin command and parse the results for a report. To demonstrate a Linux shell script that calls a wsadmin command, create a file called `listapps.sh` in a folder called `/home/wasscripts/linux` and copy the following code into it:

```
#!/bin/bash
export var=`/apps/was7/profiles/appsrv01/bin/wsadmin.sh -lang jython
-c 'AdminApp.list()'`
export raw_apps=$(echo $var|cut -f 2 -d \')
export parsed_apps=$(echo ${raw_apps} | sed 's/\\n/ /g')
for app in $parsed_apps
do
  echo $a
done
```

After saving the file, change permissions using the chmod linux command as follows:

./chmod 755 ./listapps.sh

Changing the permission to 755 will make the `listapps.sh` script executable.

Run the `listapps.sh` script by typing the following command:

/home/wasscripts/linux/listapps.sh

The results of the script will look similar to the following listing:

```
[root@websphere bin]# /home/wasscripts/linux/listapps.sh
DefaultApplication
HRListerEAR
ivtApp
query
```

As you can see from the example screenshot above, you can combine shell scripts and wsadmin commands to produce outputs which can be used to feed into other shell scripts.

Profile scripts

A profile script is a script that runs before the main Jython script, or before entering interactive mode. You can use profile scripts to set up a scripting environment that is customized for the user or the installation. For our example, we are going to create a profile script which gets the WebSphere call name before entering interactive mode.

Create a script called `/home/wasscripts/profilescript.py` and enter in the following code:

```
#Get cell name
cellName = AdminControl.getCell()
print "Cell name = " + cellName
```

Save the file and run it from `<was_profile_root>` using the following command:

`./wsadmin.sh -lang jython -profile /home/wasscripts/profilescript.py`

Before wsadmin enters the interactive mode, it will run the `profilescript.py` Jython script.

The results will be something similar to the following:

```
root@websphere:/apps/was7/profiles/appsrv01/bin                              _ □ ×
[root@websphere bin]# ./wsadmin.sh -lang jython -profile /home/wasscripts/profilescript.py
WSVR0027I: The product will expire in 10 days.
WASX7209I: Connected to process "server1" on node node01 using SOAP connector;  The type of process
 is: UnManagedProcess
Cell name = websphereNode01Cell
WASX7031I: For help, enter: "print Help.help()"
wsadmin>
```

Command script files

Using wsadmin with individual commands can be difficult when you want to run multiple commands and use variables to store transient data. Also, wsadmin doesn't have a history list of the previous command executed. It is recommended that you run all your scripts via a command file. A command file is just a text-based file containing the Jython commands you wish to execute. A scripted command file contains Jython commands and is passed to wsadmin via the command line. Using a command file is where we harness the power of wsadmin to run complex administrative scripts.

Listing installed applications with Jython

We will now demonstrate our first command file script. Create a folder called `wasscripts` in your `/home` folder and then take the following code and paste it into a new file called `listApplications.py` and save it within the `/home/wasscripts` folder.

```
#This Jython code will list all the applications installed on your
WebSphere server.
print AdminApp.list()
```

Run the script by typing the following command:

`<was_root>/bin/wsadmin.sh -lang jython -f /home/wasscripts/listApplications.py`

The result of running the script will be a listing of the installed applications in your WebSphere server. If you have not uninstalled any applications since Chapter 2, you will get the list shown in the following screenshot:

```
[root@websphere bin]# ./wsadmin.sh -lang jython -f /home/wasscripts/listApplications.py
WSVR0027I: The product will expire in 10 days.
WASX7209I: Connected to process "server1" on node node01 using SOAP connector;  The type of process
 is: UnManagedProcess
DefaultApplication.ear
HRListerEAR
ivtApp
query
```

Installing an application using Jython

We have now used the wsadmin tool a few times and have seen how it is used. What we will do now is cover how to deploy an application using Jython. We will create two Jython script files which we will call using the wsadmin tool. One script will install (deploy) an application and the other will uninstall it.

1. Create a file called `/home/wasscripts/uninstallApp.py`.

2. Copy in the following code:
   ```
   #Uninstall the application
   deployEAR="/home/deployments/HRListerEAR.ear"
   appName="HRListerEAR"
   AdminApp.uninstall(appName);
   #save
   AdminConfig.save();
   ```

3. Save the `uninstallApp.py` file.

4. To run the installation, type the following command:

```
<was_root>/bin/wsadmin.sh -lang jython -f /home/wasscripts/uninstallHR.py
```

The result of the above script will be similar to the following screenshot:

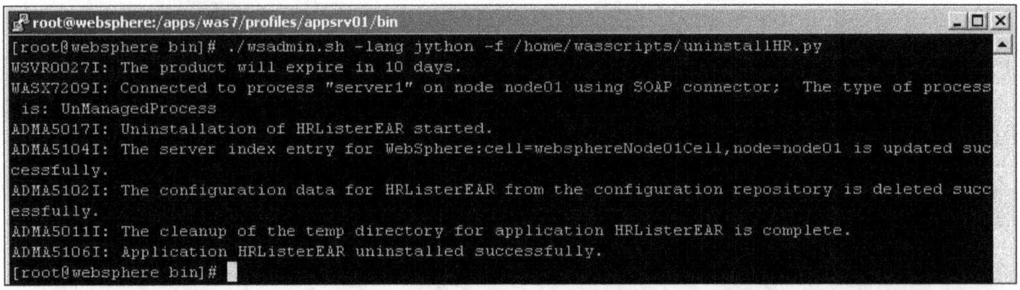

Now we have uninstalled the HRLister EAR file. We want to re-install it again using a different script containing the Jython to install an application.

1. Create a file called `/home/wasscripts/installApp.py`.

2. Copy in the following code:

```
#install the application
deployEAR="/home/deployments/HRListerEAR.ear"
appName="HRListerEAR"
attr="-appname " + appName + " "
AdminApp.install(deployEAR, "["+attr+"]" );
#save
AdminConfig.save();
```

3. Save the `installApp.py` file.

4. To run the installation, type the following command:

```
<was_root>/bin/wsadmin.sh -lang jython -f /home/wasscripts/
installHR.py
```

The result will be similar to the following screenshot:

```
root@websphere:/apps/was7/profiles/appsrv01/bin                                      _ □ ×
[root@websphere bin]# ./wsadmin.sh -lang jython -f /home/wasscripts/installHR.py
WSVR0027I: The product will expire in 10 days.
WASX7209I: Connected to process "server1" on node node01 using SOAP connector;  The type of process
is: UnManagedProcess
ADMA5016I: Installation of HRLister started.
ADMA5058I: Application and module versions are validated with versions of deployment targets.
ADMA5005I: The application HRLister is configured in the WebSphere Application Server repository.
ADMA5053I: The library references for the installed optional package are created.
ADMA5005I: The application HRLister is configured in the WebSphere Application Server repository.
ADMA5001I: The application binaries are saved in /apps/was7/profiles/appsrv01/wstemp/Script120c2163
46d/workspace/cells/websphereNode01Cell/applications/HRLister.ear/HRLister.ear
ADMA5005I: The application HRLister is configured in the WebSphere Application Server repository.
SECJ0400I: Successfully updated the application HRLister with the appContextIDForSecurity informati
on.
CWSAD0040I: The application HRLister is configured in the Application Server repository.
ADMA5005I: The application HRLister is configured in the WebSphere Application Server repository.
ADMA5113I: Activation plan created successfully.
ADMA5011I: The cleanup of the temp directory for application HRLister is complete.
ADMA5013I: Application HRLister installed successfully.
[root@websphere bin]#
```

The internal WebSphere MBeans available to wsadmin are extensive and powerful, which we will cover later in the chapter. Before we cover more advance scripting, we need to look at the Jython language so we can understand some of the typical constructs and uses of the core language, such as, if and for.

We know that WebSphere has employed the Jython language for use in administrative scripting, but how do we learn more about the Jython language? Well, we know that Jython is a Java implementation of the Python language which is often used in core Linux programming. By searching for it on Google, you will find many examples on how to use Jython. We are not going to go into every facet of the Jython language. You will gain experience over time. However, what we will do is cover some basic points which will help you in your WebSphere wsadmin scripting with Jython.

Helpful hint: If you are getting tired of typing -lang Jython to specify wsadmin to use the Jython language, you can change the wsadmin.properties file in WebSphere to make Jython the default language for scripting. The wsadmin.popreties file is located in the <was_profile_root>/properties/ folder. Edit the file and change the com.ibm.ws.scripting. defaultLang=jacl line to com.ibm.ws.scripting. defaultLang=jython and save to ensure that wsadmin defaults to use Jython.

Querying application status

Suppose you wanted to iterate through all the applications installed on your WebSphere server and query the installed applications to find their running status. We know from our previous interactive script that we can run `AdminApp.list()`. What we have not covered is that Jython returns list items. We can make calls to specific MBeans methods like the list method of AdminApp and can use the returned list object to iterate through elements of the list object. To demonstrate an iteration, we will create a file called `/home/wsscripts/iterateApps.py` and copy in the following code:

```
print "Getting Application Status..."
apps = AdminApp.list().splitlines();
for app in apps:
 #print app
 appObj=AdminControl.completeObjectName('type=Application,name='+a
pp+',*')
 if appObj != '' :
  appStatus = 'running';
 else :
  appStatus = 'stopped';
 print 'Application:'+app+'='+appStatus
```

The script above gets a list of applications installed, and for each application found, it queries the presence of the application's MBean to find out whether the application is running.

The following table explains key lines of the Jython code:

Code Element	Description
`apps = AdminApp.list().splitlines();`	The `apps` variable is assigned the Jython string as returned by the call to the `AdminApp.List()` function. However, the function returns a Jython string object which is essentially a list and we wish to separate the list into Individual string elements. By using the splitlines() method, we can convert the string list to an array of strings, which we can then iterate. Each element of the apps array contains one single application name.
`for app in apps:`	The `apps` variable is a Jython list, and since it is like an array of strings we can iterate through the list object. The `for` command allows us to move through the `apps` Jython list one element at a time, each time assigning the value to the app variable.

Code Element	Description
`appObj=AdminControl.compl eteObjectName('type=Appli cation,name='+app+',*')`	Now that we have an actual variable name as a string, we can make a call to the `AdminControl()` method called `completeObjectName` which queries WebSphere to return the application's internal MBean information.

`if appObj != '' :`
 	
 `  appStatus = 'running';`
	We use the `if` condition to evaluate the string and if it is not null, that is, if it is not an empty string, then the application has a running MBean, so we know the application has been started.

`else :`
 	
 `  appStatus = 'stopped';`
	The `else` condition evaluates the opposite of the `if` condition and sets the `appStatus` variable to the value of stopped, meaning that MBean is not running for the application.

`print 'Application:'+app+ '='+appStatus`	At the end of each iteration of the `for` loop, we print out a string response which contains the application name and its runtime status.

You will notice that certain lines are indented with one single space. Jython uses indentation to separate program elements. The amount of space is not important; as long as they are consistent indentations, Jython will be fine.

To run the Jython script, type the following:

`<was_root>/bin/wsadmin.sh -lang jython -f /home/wasscripts/iterateApps.py`

A typical result of running the script is shown in the following screenshot:

```
[root@websphere bin]# ./wsadmin.sh -lang jython -f /home/wasscripts/iterateApps.py
WSVR0027I: The product will expire in 10 days.
WASX7209I: Connected to process "server1" on node node01 using SOAP connector;  The type of process
 is: UnManagedProcess
Getting Application Status...
Application:DefaultApplication.ear=running
Application:HRListerEAR=stopped
Application:ivtApp=running
Application:query=running
[root@websphere bin]#
```

Now that we have covered the basics on how to use wsadmin with a command file, we will now look at how to create more advanced Jython and learn how to change the configuration of WAS. In Chapter 2, we created a J2C JAAS. To recap, a J2C JAAS is a Java authentication and authorization service alias which in simple terms is a database user name and password resource which can be changed independently from the actual data source itself. What we are going to do is look at how to write a script which will change the configuration of WebSphere using a script as opposed to manually configuring the J2C JAAS via the administrative console.

Create a file called /home/wasscripts/J2CManager.py and copy in the following code.

```
import sys
import java.util as util
import java.io as javaio
class JDBCUtil:
   def __init__(self,fullPropsPath):
      self.fullPropsPath=fullPropsPath

#-------------------------------------------------------------------
-----
### Create / Modify J2C Java Authentication and Authorization Service
(JAAS)
#-------------------------------------------------------------------
-----
   def J2CAuthentication(self,props1):
      appName = props1.get("AppName")
      updJAAS = props1.get("updJAAS")
      JAASAlias = props1.get("JAASAlias")
      JDBCName=props1.get("JDBCName")
      cellName = AdminControl.getCell()
      JAASConfigID = AdminConfig.getid("/Cell:"+cellName+"/Security:/
JAASAuthData:/" )
      JAASDescription = props1.get("JAASDescription")
      JAASUserId = props1.get("JAASUserId")
      JAASPassword =  props1.get("JAASPassword")
      JAASAttr = [["alias", JAASAlias], ["description",
JAASDescription], ["userId", JAASUserId], ["password", JAASPassword]]
      existingJAASList = AdminConfig.getid("/Cell:"+cellName+"/
Security:/JAASAuthData:/" )

      #Tidy up list and remove blank lines
      JAASItems=existingJAASList.splitlines();
      print "INFO: Looping through Existing JAAS Alias"
      updateJAASFlag="false"
      for JAASItem in JAASItems:
         print JAASItem
         existingJAASAlias = AdminConfig.
showAttribute(JAASItem,"alias")
         print "INFO: ExistingJAASAlias=%s" % existingJAASAlias
         if (cmp(existingJAASAlias, JAASAlias) == 0):
            print "INFO: JAASAuthInfo Exists, Updating
Alias:"+existingJAASAlias+" ......"
            AdminConfig.modify(JAASItem, JAASAttr )
            print "      Modified!"
            updateJAASFlag = "true"
            #Exit the foor loop, now we have updated our match
            break
```

```
            #end if
        #end For
        if (cmp(updateJAASFlag, "false") == 0):
            print "INFO: Creating new JAASAuthInfo Alias: "+JAASAlias+"
login/password ......"
            security = AdminConfig.getid("/Cell:"+cellName+"/Security:/"
)
            print "security=%s" % security
            AdminConfig.create("JAASAuthData", security, JAASAttr )
            print "INFO: J2C Authentication Created Successfully!"
        #end if
#---------------------------------------------------------------------
-----
# Save Configuration
#---------------------------------------------------------------------
-----

        print "Saving configuration..."
                AdminConfig.save()
                print "Complete!"
#---------------------------------------------------------------------
-----
# Load properties File
#---------------------------------------------------------------------
----

    def loadproperties(self):

        print "------load properties %s " % self.fullPropsPath
        properties = util.Properties()
        source = javaio.FileInputStream(fullPropsPath)
        bis = javaio.BufferedInputStream(source)
        props = util.Properties()
        props.load(bis)
        print "Properties file has been loaded"
        return props
#---------------------------------------------------------------------
-----
# Main entry point
#---------------------------------------------------------------------
----
fullPropsPath = sys.argv[0]
print "fullPropsPath=%s" % fullPropsPath
dsObj = JDBCUtil(fullPropsPath)
props1=dsObj.loadproperties()
dsObj.J2CAuthentication (props1)
```

Essentially, the code above uses a Jython class to create the main function which does the configuration work. In this example, we have used Java packages so we can use Java calls inside Jython for specific functions that Java provides to access a configuration file which contains configurable properties which are made available to the Jython code.

The following table explains the code line by line:

Code Element	Description
`import java.util as util`	Imports the `java.util` package which allows us to make use of the Java methods to work with external properties file.
`import java.io as javaio`	Imports the `java.io` package which gives Jython the ability to access the file system and read the properties file.
`class JDBCUtil:`	To demonstrate that Jython is an object-oriented language, we have declared a class called `JDBCUtil` which we will use to create a custom Jython object which has properties and methods.
`def __init__(self,fullPropsPath):`	Declare the constructor of the Jython class. A constructor is called when we create an instance of a class called an object. Essentially, this is the first method called when we instantiate an object of type `JDBCUtil` later in the main entry point of the code.
`def J2CAuthentication(self,props1):`	Defines a method (member function) of the `JDBCUtil` class. The `J2CAuthentication` method takes two variables.
	`self` passes in the object and `props1` passes in the props file object.
`appName = props1.get("AppName")` `updJAAS = props1.get("updJAAS")` `JAASAlias = props1.get("JAASAlias")` `JDBCName=props1.get("JDBCName")`	These lines get values from the properties file and assign them to local variables.

Code Element	Description
`cellName = AdminControl.` `getCell()`	This line uses the `AdminControl.` `getCell()` method to query WebSphere and get the `cellName`.

`JAASDescription = props1.`
`get("JAASDescription")`
 	
`     JAASUserId = props1.`
`get("JAASUserId")`
 	
`     JAASPassword =  props1.`
`get("JAASPassword")`
	These lines get values from the properties file and assign them to local variables.

`     JAASAttr = [["alias",`
`JAASAlias], ["description",`
`JAASDescription], ["userId",`
`JAASUserId], ["password",`
`JAASPassword]]`
	This line builds up an attribute string which we will use in the creation and modification of the JAAS alias.

`     existingJAASList`
`= AdminConfig.getid("/`
`Cell:"+cellName+"/Security:/`
`JAASAuthData:/" )`
	This line builds a configuration id of the `JAASAuthData` Mbeans which returns a string of the current `JAASAuthData` that exist in the WebSphere configuration.

`JAASItems=existingJAASList.` `splitlines();`	This line splits the string into a list which we can iterate through to query for `JAASAuthData` alias names.
`updateJAASFlag="false"`	Here, we set a flag which we will use to determine if the JAAS alias we are trying to create already exists.
`for JAASItem in JAASItems:`	Here, we loop through the list (array) of currently existing JAAS aliases and assign each one in turn to the variable called `JAASItem`.

`existingJAASAlias`
`= AdminConfig.`
`showAttribute(JAASItem,"alias")`
	This lines uses the `JAASItem` string and queries `JAASAuthData` to return the JAAS alias name which we will use for comparison.

`if (cmp(existingJAASAlias,` `JAASAlias) == 0):`	If we find a match between the alias name we wish to create and the one from the list of existing aliases, we will modify; otherwise, we will create a new one as it doesn't exist.
`AdminConfig.modify(JAASItem,` `JAASAttr )`	This line is executed when there is a match found, so we begin to set up the ability to update an existing alias.

Code Element	Description
`updateJAASFlag = "true"`	We set the flag so that the following code knows we have been modifying an existing alias, so we do not want to create a duplicate.
`if (cmp(updateJAASFlag, "false") == 0):`	If there was no match, it means we are creating the alias for the first time.
`security = AdminConfig.getid("/Cell:"+cellName+"/Security:/" )`	This line sets up the correct config id for the creation of a new `JAASAuthData` item.
`AdminConfig.create("JAASAuthData", security, JAASAttr )`	Here, we call `AdminConfig.create()`, passing the MBean configuration id.
`AdminConfig.save()`	We save the changes we have made in order to retain them in the internal WebSphere XML configuration files.
`def loadproperties(self):`	Defines the `loadproperties()` method and we pass in the instantiated `JDBCUtil` object so we can refer to internal properties.
`properties = util.Properties()`	This line creates a Java properties object which will contain our properties file information.
`source = javaio.FileInputStream(fullPropsPath)`	This line creates a `FileInputStream` which allows us to access the physical properties file.
`bis = javaio.BufferedInputStream(source)`	Here, we use a `BufferedInputStream` which makes efficient use of serializing the file into a usable string which we can assign to the in-memory `props` object which is of type `util.properties`.
`props = util.Properties()`	This line creates the `props` object, which contains the properties file.
`props.load(bis)`	Here, we load the file into the `props` object.
`return props`	This line returns the newly created `props` object which contains the values pairs of the properties file.

Code Element	Description
`fullPropsPath = sys.argv[0]`	This line gets the path to the properties file on disk. The path is passed as a command line argument to the `wsadmin.sh` tool and shows how Jython can use command line parameters for organization and configurability of your Jython variables.
`dsObj = JDBCUtil(fullPropsPath)`	This line creates an instant ion of the `JDBCUtil` class, creating an object called `dsObject`.
`props1=dsObj.loadproperties()`	This line calls the `dsObj`'s `loadproperties()` method to load the properties file into an object called `props1`.
`dsObj.J2CAuthentication (props1)`	This line calls the `dsObj`'s `J2CAuthentication` method, passing in the properties file as `props1` which then allows variables in the `J2CAuthentication` method to be assigned values by name from the properties file.

The script above contains several key concepts used in enterprise Jython scripting for WebSphere automation. We cannot cover all the various possibilities of what can be done with Jython; however the basic principles of using Jython have been covered to help you begin administrative scripting. Using scripts is the way forward and any investment on time spent developing automation scripts is well worth it.

Summary

In this chapter, we learned that WebSphere has several tools which allow automation. Scripts can be run which can either configure WebSphere or manage the runtime process, such as, stopping and starting servers and/or applications. We looked at the two most common tools used in WebSphere automation—wsadmin and ws_ant. We explained that ws_ant is based on Apache Ant and can be used to do basic deployments and installs, however it is really only suited for development environments. The wsadmin tool, however, can be used to configure all elements of WebSphere and provides an extensive set of methods which can configure the internals of WebSphere. Larger enterprises typically implement Jython using wsadmin as opposed to ws_ant. However, both tools have their uses, whereas wsadmin using Jython stretches across both development and production environments.

5
WebSphere Configuration

This chapter covers key areas important to the administration and functioning of WAS and deployed applications. We will cover the WebSphere file system and key XML configuration files which make up the core of the WebSphere configuration. We will also cover class loading and how WebSphere provides several levels of class-loader configuration for your application server and applications via the Admin console.

In this Chapter, we will cover the following topics:

- WebSphere file structure
- XML configuration files
- Logs
- Java Virtual Machine (JVM) settings
- Class loading

File structure

Thus far, we have installed WebSphere, deployed a few applications, and run some administrative scripts, and even changed some security options using the Administrative console. All configuration changes to WebSphere are saved in configuration files and it is important for the administrator to understand the WebSphere file system and where configuration files, repositories, and log files are located.

There are several main categories of files that we need to cover which are listed below.

- XML configuration files
- XML repositories
- Log files
- Properties files.

Before we delve into the types of files, we will first cover the WebSphere file system and explain the file structure and layout identifying key folders and file locations.

The WebSphere file system

Like almost any other software product, WebSphere uses a file system which contains both runtime files, that is, the product binaries and also configuration files. There are many folders and directories in the WebSphere folder structure. We will explain the structure in two sections. The first section will cover the key folders of the main product installation folders and the second section will cover the key folders within a profile.

 We cannot cover all the configurations of WebSphere in this chapter and so we have covered the most important folders. If you wish to investigate further, you can consult the online WebSphere Application Server Information Center located at the following URL: `http://publib.boulder.ibm.com/infocenter/wasinfo/v7r0/index.jsp`.

The product binaries file structure

The product folders contain the files and binaries which form the basis of the WebSphere product. All WebSphere profiles utilize and refer to these core files, so it is important to understand key folders and what they are used for. Below is a table of the key directories located on the WebSphere root path, which we have previously referred to as `<was_root>`.

Folder Name	Description
`bin`	Contains the core product runtime binaries, tools, and scripts which are used to run and administer WebSphere.
`logs`	Contains the main product installation and configuration logs. Very useful for debugging product installation issues and administrative tools when they are not working.
`samples`	If you opted to install samples, then this folder will exist and contain sample code and applications.

Folder Name	Description
scriptLibaries	This is a new feature of WebSphere 7 and contains a vast mount of re-usable Jython functions , which can be used to fully automate WebSphere configuration and application deployment.
profileTemplates	When you create a profile, WebSphere uses the XML files in this folder as templates. In WebSphere Application Server, we have two templates—the management template is used for creating a management profile and the default template is used to define an Application Server profile.
properties	Contains product-level configurations, for example, a registry of the current installed profile(s) and other product-level settings. This folder is often never changed by administrators.
uninstall	This folder contains the script and executables to cleanly uninstall WebSphere.

The profile file structure

As we have learned in Chapter 1, WebSphere uses profiles to determine the makeup of an application server. A WebSphere profile determines and controls the configuration of the actual application server. Most of the WebSphere Administration activities are centred on the profile and so understanding the underlying file system within a profile is very important. The table below outlines the key folders and subfolders of a profile.

Folder Name	Description
bin	Contains the scripts used to administer your application server from a command line. Most of the scripts in the `<was_profile_root>` call other scripts located in the `<was_root>` folder.
config	Contains the XML files which persist all the configurations made through the administrative console. We will cover these in detail later in this chapter.
firststeps	As we have seen in Chapter 1, this folder contains the first steps console that is available when using graphical installations. Not important for post-install administration.
installableApps	Contains default WebSphere applications which can be installed depending on the type of installation options used in the WebSphere install process. This is where `defaultApplication.ear` will be located which contains snoop, as seen in Chapter 2.

Folder Name	Description
installedApps	Contains the on-disk structure of the deployed applications as installed into WAS. This is a very important folder and is used extensively in administrative support of applications.
logs	Contains the log files pertinent to WAS runtime. Most debugging of administrative and application issues are achieved through the help of the logs contained in this folder.
properties	Contains key properties files which contain settings which can be used to change behaviours, for example, security for the wsadmin tool.
samples	Contains some portions of the sample applicationss required for runtime components – if samples have been installed.
temp	Contains runtime temporary files. For example, if JSPs within applications are converted to Java classes at runtime, then the temp folder will contain these Java classes.
tranlog	If an application contains distributed transactions then the tranlog folder will contain transactional logs which can be used for rollback. We will not be covering this topic in this book.
wstemp	Used by WebSphere during the deployment of applications as a temporary staging area and also contains in-transit configurations before console changes are saved.

XML configuration files

The entire WebSphere configuration is saved and persisted to XML files. When we use the Admin console to configure WebSphere, certain XML files are updated with the appropriate settings relating to each type of configuration. It is important that an administrator understands key XML files and understand what they are used for. When there are configuration or runtime issues, knowing these files and their locations can help with problem-solving. Below is a list of the most important configuration files that a WebSphere administrator should be aware of. It must be noted that some files exist more than once in different scopes, that is, cell level, node level, and server level.

Scope is more important for the WebSphere Network Deployment product, which is not covered in this book.

Cell level XML files

Below is a list of the key XML configuration files found at the scope of cell level.

- `resources.xml`
    - Defines operating cell scope environmental resources, including JDBC, JMS, JavaMail, URL end point configuration, and so on.
- `security.xml`
    - Contains security data , including all user ID and password information.
- `virtualhosts.xml`
    - Contains virtual host and Multipurpose Internet Mail Extensions (MIME)-type configurations.
- `variables.xml`
    - Contains cell level WebSphere variables
- `admin-authz.xml`
    - Contains the roles set for administration of the Admin console.
    - `/apps/was7/profiles/appsrv01/config/cells/<cell_name>/`
- `wimconfig.xml`
    - Contains the federated repository configurations for global security
    - `<was_profile_root>config/cells/<cell_name>/wim/config/`
- `profileRegistry.xml`
    - Contains a list of profiles and profile configuration data

Node level XML files

Below is a list of the key XML configuration files found at the scope of node level.

Located in: `/<was_profile_root>/config/cells/<cell_name>/nodes/<node_name>/`

- `variables.xml`
    - Contains node level WebSphere variables
- `resources.xml`
    - Defines node scope environmental resources, including JDBC, JMS, JavaMail, URL end point configuration, and so on
- `namestore.xml`
    - Provides persistent JNDI namespace binding data
- `serverindex.xml`
    - Specifies all the ports used by servers on this node

Server level XML files

Below is a list of the key XML configuration files found at the scope of server level.

Located in: `/<was_profile_root>/config/cells/<cell_name>nodes/<node_name>/servers/<server_name>/`

- `variables.xml`
    - Contains server level variables
- `server.xml`
    - Contains application server configuration data
- `resources.xml`
    - Contains the configuration of resources, such as, JDBC, JMS, JavaMail, and URL end points at server scope

An administrator should rarely ever have to edit these files, and if you do feel at some point that you need to, you must realize that you can seriously damage your WebSphere installation if you do not understand the influence of changes to these files. All administration should be done through the Admin console or with administrative scripts. It is not recommended that you edit these files directly. It is possible that configurations become corrupt; after all, WebSphere is essentially a software application and things can and do go wrong. Knowing about these files will also aid you in understanding the way WebSphere works and will prepare you for the WebSphere Network Deployment product, which is more commonly used in large enterprises.

Important properties files

As an administrator, it is important that you understand the `soap.client.props` and `sas.client.props` files located in the `<was_profile_root>/properties` folder. These files are required to be edited when you enable global security. If you enable security for a WebSphere Application Server cell, you will have to manually enter in the username and password every time you run the `wsadmin` tool. By editing the `sas.client.props` and the `soap.client.props` files, you can specify the username and password you have configured for global security so you are not prompted to enter the username and password every time you run administrative scripts.

The soap.client.props file

When global security is enabled in the cell and you use the `wsadmin` tool with the SOAP protocol (SOAP is the default connector protocol), you will need to update the following properties in the `soap.client.props` file with the appropriate values as shown below so that the wsadmin tool does not prompt for a username and password.

```
com.ibm.SOAP.securityEnabled=<true>
com.ibm.SOAP.loginUserid=<username>
com.ibm.SOAP.loginPassword=<password>
Optionally, set the following property:
com.ibm.SOAP.loginSource=none
```

The sas.client.props file

When global security is enabled in the cell and you change wsadmin to use a **Remote Method Invocation** (**RMI**) connector when using wsadmin (RMI is not the default protocol), you need to set the following properties in the `sas.client.props` file with the appropriate values as shown below so that the wsadmin tool does not prompt for a username and password.

```
com.ibm.CORBA.loginUserid=
com.ibm.CORBA.loginPassword=
Also, set the following property:
com.ibm.CORBA.loginSource=properties
```

The default value for this property is prompt in the sas.client.props file.

If you leave com.ibm.CORBA.loginSource and com.ibm.CORBA.
loginSource to the default values, a dialog box appears with a
password prompt. If the script is running unattended, it appears to hang;
this is quite a common issue when a WebSphere server has been set up
for the first time.

Logs

The WebSphere application server uses logs to log what is happening during server
runtime. Administrators can use the logs to determine application server runtime
status. Logs are also very useful during problem determination when there are
problems with WebSphere. The main log folder is the application server's logs
directory which is found in the <was_profile_root> folder. Below is a screenshot
of a typical logs directory.

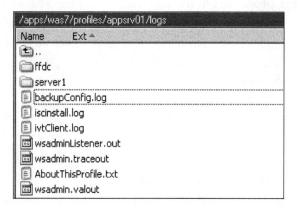

In the screenshot above, you will see that the application server is located in a profile
named appsrv01, which is located in the profiles directory. The logs folder
is located in the /apps/was7/profiles/appsrv01 folder which is referred to as
<was_profile_root>. The logs folder will always be here unless you override log
locations in the Administrative console.

JVM logs

The main logs for a WebSphere Application Server are contained in a folder with
the same name as the application server. In our example, our application is called
server1, so the log files are contained in the server1 directory located within
the logs directory, which is within the <was_profile_root> folder. Below is an
example of the logs that are typically generated by a WebSphere Application Server.

```
/apps/was7/profiles/appsrv01/logs/server1
Name          Ext ▲
📁 ..
📄 native_stderr.log
📄 native_stdout.log
📄 startServer.log
📄 stopServer.log
📄 SystemErr.log
📄 SystemOut.log
📄 SystemOut_09.01.28_18.34.44.log
📄 server1.pid
```

You can see in the screenshot above that it is typical for a running server to have generated several logs during server runtime. Not all the logs will exist immediately; some are spawned when certain conditions occur. The table below explains what each log is for and what you might expect to find in the log.

Log Name	Description
`native_stderr.log`, `native_stdout.log`	`stdout` and `stderr` streams are redirected to log files at application server startup, which contain text written to the `stdout` and `stderr` streams by native modules, that is, Linux Modules, and so on. In normal error-free operations, these logs files are typically empty.
`startServer.log`	This log file is named `startServer.log` and is created in your `logs` directory when the server starts up. This log is very useful to determine JVM parameters used in the start-up process, the server's process id, and also the date and time in which the server was started. If there are errors experienced during the start-up (for example, security configuration errors where the application server cannot start), then log information will exist for problem determination.
`stopServer.log`	This file logs the fact that the server was stopped via a command line. If the server has trouble stopping, then Java stack traces will be written to the log which can be used in determining why a given application server failed to stop.
`SystemErr.log`	This log file contains Java exceptions and stack traces. An empty `SystemErr.log` file does not necessarily indicate a successfully running application server JVM. You may need to consult the other logs in this directory.

Log Name	Description
`SystemOut.log`	This log file contains messages as generated by the JVM during runtime. Some messages are informational, some are warnings or status updates. Applications can be configured to write to the log and so it is very common for the `SystemOut.log` to be your first port of call in application debugging.
	Both this log file and the SystemErr.log file should be checked after starting an application server to confirm that both the server and applications have started correctly.

`SystemOut_`
`<date_time_stamp>.`
`log`
	This filename style is an example of a log file roll-over due to the log being full. WebSphere can be configured to roll over in different style and will be covered later in the chapter.

`<server_name>.pid`	This file contains the process id of the server. In Linux, this is the actual process id assigned to the JVM process.

Configuring logs

JVM logs can be configured in the administrative console. Log configuration is specific to each Application Server JVM. To change the JVM logs configuration, log in to the Admin console and navigate to the **Troubleshooting** section in the left-hand-side navigation panel and click on **Logs and trace** as shown below.

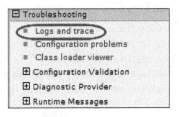

You will then be presented with a list of Application Server JVMs. In our example, we only have one. Click on the **server1** JVM (Application Server) and you will be presented with a list of options as shown below.

Logging and Tracing

Logging and Tracing > server1

Use this page to select a system log to configure, or to specify a log detail level for components and groups of components. Use log levels to control which events are processed by Java logging.

General Properties

- Diagnostic Trace
- JVM Logs
- Process Logs
- IBM Service Logs
- Change Log Detail Levels

Click on the **JVM Logs** option and you will be presented with a configuration form where we can change the location where the JVM will create logs and you can also change the style in which the application server JVM will log information.

Changing log file locations

To change the log file location, you can use the log configuration page as shown below and change the **File Name** field to specify the location within the file system where you want your logs located.

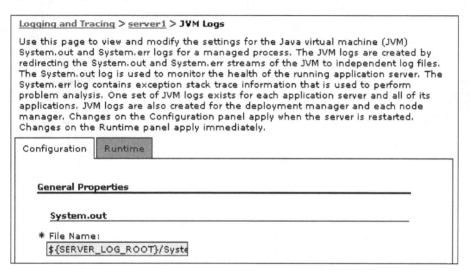

In the screenshot above, you will notice that there is a system variable called **${SERVER_LOG_ROOT}** which identifies the root location of the logs. You can override system variables by navigating to the **Environment** panel and selecting the **WebSphere variables** link.

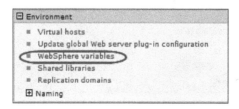

When you access the WebSphere variables page, you will see a list of configured WebSphere variables. For now, take a look at the following screenshot and you will see the variable called **LOG_ROOT**. This variable is used as part of the default file system path for the location of the JVM servers log files.

Select	Name ◇	Value ◇	Scope ◇
New Delete			
	You can administer the following resources:		
☐	APP_INSTALL_ROOT	${USER_INSTALL_ROOT}/installedApps	Node=node01
☐	CONNECTJDBC_JDBC_DRIVER_PATH		Node=node01
☐	CONNECTOR_INSTALL_ROOT	${USER_INSTALL_ROOT}/installedConnectors	Node=node01
☐	DB2390_JDBC_DRIVER_PATH		Node=node01
☐	DB2UNIVERSAL_JDBC_DRIVER_NATIVEPATH		Node=node01
☐	DB2UNIVERSAL_JDBC_DRIVER_PATH		Node=node01
☐	DB2_JCC_DRIVER_NATIVEPATH		Node=node01
☐	DB2_JCC_DRIVER_PATH		Node=node01
☐	DB2_JDBC_DRIVER_PATH		Node=node01
☐	DEPLOY_TOOL_ROOT	${WAS_INSTALL_ROOT}/deploytool/itp	Node=node01
☐	DERBY_JDBC_DRIVER_PATH	${WAS_INSTALL_ROOT}/derby/lib	Node=node01
☐	DRIVER_PATH	${WAS_INSTALL_ROOT}	Node=node01
☐	INFORMIX_JCC_DRIVER_PATH		Node=node01
☐	INFORMIX_JDBC_DRIVER_PATH		Node=node01
☐	JAVA_HOME	${WAS_INSTALL_ROOT}/java	Node=node01
☐	JVM_CACHE		Node=node01
☐	LOCALHOST_NAME	localhost	Node=node01
☐	LOG_ROOT	${USER_INSTALL_ROOT}/logs	Node=node01
☐	MICROSOFT_JDBC_DRIVER_NATIVEPATH		Node=node01
☐	MICROSOFT_JDBC_DRIVER_PATH		Node=node01
Page: 1 of 2 ▷ Total 38			

Changing log styles

As explained previously above, the **Logging and Tracing | server1 | JVM Logs** page is used to change log settings. In addition to log locations, we can also change the style in which logs are written. Often there may be several applications installed on one single JVM and so there could be loads of messages being generated by both WebSphere internal runtime processes and the application(s), and hence the log files will increase over time. It is important to not let your logs grow so large that they invariably fill up your operating system's disk space. Using the setting on the **JVM Logs** page, an administrator can control the size and style of logging. This is also very important during problem-solving, where application(s) are configured to write debug statements to SystemOut.log and thus they can generate very large log files. To make logs more manageable, we can change the log size and the number of log files. By using a combination of the **File Size**, **Time** and **Maximum Number of Historical Log Files** fields, we can control the sizes of our logs. The table below shows some typical log requirements and what settings you would use from this page to configure the logs.

Scenario	Settings required on the log configuration page
Ensure logs are no larger than 2MB in size.	In the **Log File Rotation** section, tick the **File Size** field and set the **Maximum Size** to **2**.
Roll the logs over every day.	Uncheck the **File Size** field and check the **Time** field.
Roll logs every 5MB and ensure we always have 100MB of historical log files at any time.	Check the **File Size** field, set the **Maximum Size** field to **5** and type **20** in the **Maximum Number of Historical Log Files** field.

During debug, it is very important that you configure log sizes to manageable sizes because if they get too large, then log files will become unmanageable for downloading for debugging purposes and will fill up your file system. If logs are left to rollover without control, then historical log information can be lost. It is critical that you think about logs and how you will manage logging in production systems.

FFDC logs

In the logs folder, you will see a folder representing the name of the application server JVM. In our example, the folder is called server1 as this is the default name given to our server in our initial installation in Chapter 1. You will also notice a folder called ffdc which stands for **First Failure Data Capture**; this folder contains detailed logs of exceptions found during the runtime of the WebSphere Application Server.

Viewing JVM logs

There are several ways in which we can view logs. We can view them via the admin console or via the file system.

Viewing logs in the admin console

To view the logs via the console, go to **Logging and Tracing | server1 | JVM Logs** in the admin console, and you will be presented wit the JVM logs configuration page as discussed earlier. Once you are in the **JVM Logs** page, click on the **Runtime** tab to see options to **View** the SystemOut.log and SystemErr.log files, as shown below,

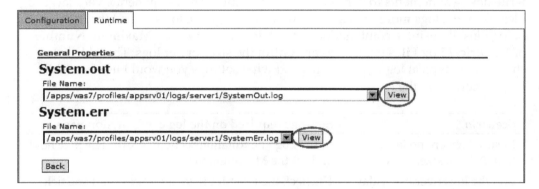

Viewing logs on the file system

The best way to view the JVM logs is via the operating system. Linux provides command line options which allow the administrator to find and view log files very quickly. Scanning log files can be arduous if there is lots of logs with verbose log information , that is, if the logs are large in size. A WebSphere administrator can use Linux commands to search log files for keywords, phrases, error codes, and so on.

We will demonstrate two Linux commands called grep and tail which are the most commonly used Linux commands when dealing with logs.

Linux tail command

The Linux tail command is very useful when you want to watch logs while the server is running and wish to watch the messages being written to the log as they happen in real time. To demonstrate using tail, we will watch an existing SystemOut.log using one SSH session as we start and stop the WebSphere server in a separate SSH session.

Open an SSH session to your Linux box and Navigate to <was_profile_root>/logs. Then change directory to your server's log folder, that is, cd server1

Type the following command:

```
tail -f ./SystemOut.log
```

You should now have an SSH window open looking something similar to the following screenshot:

```
root@websphere:/apps/was7/profiles/appsrv01/logs/server1
[root@websphere server1]# ls -ltr
total 2040
-rw-r--r--  1 root root 1048462 Jan 28 18:34 SystemOut_09.01.28_18.34.44.log
-rw-r--r--  1 root root   78771 Mar  1 00:48 stopServer.log
-rw-r--r--  1 root root  170650 Mar  1 00:49 SystemErr.log
-rw-r--r--  1 root root   26021 Mar  1 00:49 native_stdout.log
-rw-r--r--  1 root root   23755 Mar  1 00:49 native_stderr.log
-rw-r--r--  1 root root   88305 Mar  1 00:50 startServer.log
-rw-r--r--  1 root root       5 Mar  1 00:50 server1.pid
-rw-r--r--  1 root root  582156 Mar  9 11:46 SystemOut.log
[root@websphere server1]# tail -f SystemOut.log
```

Leave your existing PuTTY (SSH) session open. Open a second SSH session to your Linux box and navigate to the `<was_profile_root>/bin` folder.

Type the following command to stop `server1`:

```
./stopServer.sh server1
```

You will see in the original PuTTY window the messages informing that the JVM is being stopped, as shown in the screenshots below.

In this SSH session window we have used the `./stopServer.sh` command to stop the `server1` JVM. WebSphere reports that the server has stopped.

```
root@websphere:/apps/was7/profiles/appsrv01/bin                      _ □ ×
[root@websphere ~]# cdwb
[root@websphere bin]# ./stopServer.sh server1
ADMU0116I: Tool information is being logged in file
            /apps/was7/profiles/appsrv01/logs/server1/stopServer.log
ADMU3100I: Reading configuration for server: server1
ADMU3201I: Server stop request issued. Waiting for stop status.
ADMU4000I: Server server1 stop completed.

[root@websphere bin]# ./startServer server1
-bash: ./startServer: No such file or directory
[root@websphere bin]# ./startServer.sh server1
ADMU0116I: Tool information is being logged in file
            /apps/was7/profiles/appsrv01/logs/server1/startServer.log
ADMU3100I: Reading configuration for server: server1
ADMU3200I: Server launched. Waiting for initialization status.
ADMU3000I: Server server1 open for e-business; process id is 3013
[root@websphere bin]# ./stopServer.sh server1
ADMU0116I: Tool information is being logged in file
            /apps/was7/profiles/appsrv01/logs/server1/stopServer.log
ADMU3100I: Reading configuration for server: server1
ADMU3201I: Server stop request issued. Waiting for stop status.
ADMU4000I: Server server1 stop completed.

[root@websphere bin]#
```

In this SSH session below, we have used the `tail` command to watch the log. You can see that messages were being displayed as the server was stopping. The `tail` command keeps watching the log and displays the end of the file as the log file grows. The `tail` command keeps looking at the end of the file, hence the name **tail**.

```
root@websphere:/apps/was7/profiles/appsrv01/logs/server1                                    _|□|X|
[3/9/09 13:04:20:658 GMT] 00000007 EJBContainerI I   WSVR0059I: EJB jar stopped: Calendars.jar
[3/9/09 13:04:20:761 GMT] 00000007 ApplicationMg A   WSVR0220I: Application stopped: SchedulerCalendars
[3/9/09 13:04:20:763 GMT] 00000007 ApplicationMg A   WSVR0217I: Stopping application: filetransferSecured
[3/9/09 13:04:20:819 GMT] 00000007 servlet        I com.ibm.ws.webcontainer.servlet.ServletWrapper doDestroy SRVE0253I: [filetransferSe
cured] [/FileTransfer] [transfer]: Destroy successful.
[3/9/09 13:04:20:890 GMT] 00000007 ApplicationMg A   WSVR0220I: Application stopped: filetransferSecured
[3/9/09 13:04:20:892 GMT] 00000007 ApplicationMg A   WSVR0217I: Stopping application: ManagementEJB
[3/9/09 13:04:21:074 GMT] 00000007 EJBContainerI I   WSVR0041I: Stopping EJB jar: mejb.jar
[3/9/09 13:04:21:086 GMT] 00000007 EJBContainerI I   WSVR0059I: EJB jar stopped: mejb.jar
[3/9/09 13:04:21:196 GMT] 00000007 ApplicationMg A   WSVR0220I: Application stopped: ManagementEJB
[3/9/09 13:04:21:451 GMT] 00000007 SchedulerServ I   SCHD0040I: The Scheduler Service is stopping.
[3/9/09 13:04:21:454 GMT] 00000007 SchedulerServ I   SCHD0002I: The Scheduler Service has stopped.
[3/9/09 13:04:21:467 GMT] 00000007 AppProfileCom I   ACIN0009I: The application profiling service is stopping.
[3/9/09 13:04:21:469 GMT] 00000007 ActivitySessi I   WACS0049I: The ActivitySession service is stopping.
[3/9/09 13:04:21:652 GMT] 00000007 ObjectPoolSer I   OBPL0011I: The Object Pool service is stopping.
[3/9/09 13:04:21:656 GMT] 00000007 distSecurityC I   securityServiceStarted is false
[3/9/09 13:04:21:668 GMT] 00000007 CGBridgeSubsc I   CWRCB0104I: The core group bridge service has stopped the subscription router.
[3/9/09 13:04:21:670 GMT] 00000007 CGBridgeServi I   CWRCB0103I: The core group bridge service has stopped.
[3/9/09 13:04:21:699 GMT] 00000007 TCPChannel    I   TCPC0002I: TCP Channel TCPInboundChannel_ipcc.Default has stopped listening on ho
st localhost.localdomain (IPv4: 127.0.0.1) port 9633.
[3/9/09 13:04:22:029 GMT] 00000007 FailureScopeC A   WTRN0105I: The transaction service has shutdown successfully with no transactions
requiring recovery.
[3/9/09 13:04:22:075 GMT] 00000007 ServerCollabo A   WSVR0024I: Server server1 stopped
```

The `tail` command will continue to watch the file until the command is canceled with *Ctrl+C*.

> The `tail` command is one of the most common commands you will use during problem determination. It allows you to watch log files as the server is running so that you can identify error messages as they appear. It is recommended that you research the Internet to see more examples and command line options of the `tail` command.

Linux grep command

Another very useful command is the Linux `grep` command. The `grep` command allows you to search files to see if they contain certain combinations of characters. The characters could be certain keywords, error messages, status messages, or any other combinations of text strings that you could be looking for in a single log file or even a group of log files. To demonstrate the use of the `grep` command, we are going to look for the text string `WebSphere Platform` in all the log files in the JVM log directory.

Navigate to `<was_profile_root>/logs/server1`.

Type the following command:

```
grep -i "WebSphere Platform" *
```

`grep` will do a case-insensitive search of all the files in the current directory scanning for the text, listing all files which contain the text sub-string `WebSphere Platform` as seen below.

The image above shows many successful finds. The `grep` command lists all lines of the files and the file name of every file in which it finds the search string. This is a very powerful tool and can be used in a number of different ways. It is recommended that research is done to learn and understand all variants and uses of the `grep` command as it is one of the most powerful Linux command line tools in an administrator's arsenal.

JVM settings

An important part of configuring your application server JVM is through the use of JVM parameters. Since an application server is based on the Java Virtual Machine (JVM), we can pass certain parameters to the JVM to set specific runtime settings. To view and change the JVM configuration for an application server's process, use the Java virtual machine page of the administrative console. It is also possible to use the wsadmin tool with Jython to change JVM configuration through scripting. However, we will not cover configuration using scripting and the wsadmin tool.

Changing JVM settings using the admin console

In the administrative console, go to **Servers | Server Types | WebSphere application servers | <server_name>**. Then, under **Server Infrastructure**, go to **Java and process management | Process definition**, select **Java virtual machine** (application server) then set the field values for the JVM settings as required and click **OK**. Click **Save** to retain the changes. You must restart the application server for all JVM parameter changes to take effect.

Below is a table of common JVM settings that an administrator would want to set.

JVM Parameter	Description
Verbose class loading	Turns on verbose debug output for class loading. The default is to not enable verbose class loading.
Verbose garbage collection	Sets verbose debug output for garbage collection. The default is not to enable verbose garbage collection as it involves a performance hit on the application server.
Verbose JNI	Specifies verbose debug output for native method invocation. This is only used if you wish to understand what is happening with external libraries which your application may be calling.
Initial heap size	Size in Megabytes of the minimum memory allocated to the JVM's heap.
Maximum heap size	Size in Megabytes of the maximum JVM heap size.

Regarding memory management using the JVM setting above, you must understand that tuning a JVM is not easily discussed unless attention to detail is given and so we have not put in a recommended initial heapsize or recommended maximum heap size as this will depend on the nature of the application installed. For a rule of thumb, there should be no need to set your JVM maximum heap size greater than 1024 Megabytes, and if you are required to do so, it is most often due to inefficiencies in the application design. For more detailed recommendations for tuning your JVM, you can consult the Info Center at the following URL:

```
http://publib.boulder.ibm.com/infocenter/wasinfo/v7r0/index.
jsp?topic=/com.ibm.websphere.nd.iseries.doc/info/iseriesnd/ae/tprf_
tunejvm_v61.html.
```

If the URL above does not supply enough information, you can search the WebSphere 7 Information Center using the JVM keyword as your search word and many documents will be found, which will contain the information required to learn about tweaking WAS JVMs. It is also possible to use Google to search for information on the Java Virtual Machine and how it works, thus you will be able to learn the many of the facets of JVMs.

You can also set custom properties via the additional properties link found in **Application servers \<server_name> \Process definition \Java Virtual Machine**. Custom properties are often used by applications for externalizing configurations options. An example of using custom properties could be an application which implements Log4j which is an open source logging system. In an application which uses Log4j, a configuration file called log4j.xml file is required to allow configuration of log levels and log file locations. By using a custom property, you could make use of a JVM parameter which can be configured by an administrator at deployment time to specify the location where the Log4j log files will be written. This means that the location of the Log4j log file(s) are not hard-coded into the `log4j.xml` file and the location can be changed by the administrator, rather than making an application change which would be required due to the fact that the `log4j.xml` file is contained within the EAR and thus saves possible re-deployments.

Class loaders

Class loaders are an integral part of the JVM code and are responsible for finding and loading class files both for the application server itself and applications. It is important that an administrator understands class loaders and how they affect the JVM and deployed applications. Application developers and deployers must understand and consider the location of Java classes and Java resource files, and the class loaders used to access those files, must also be able to make available the appropriate class files to deployed applications. The configuration of class loaders also affects the packaging of applications and their runtime behavior. In this book, we cannot completely cover all the issue and intricacies of class loaders; however, we will attempt to explain class loading and what configuration elements an administrator can use in the administrative console to change class loading behavior.

Class loading basics

A simple and easy way to understand class loaders is to use the concept of a parent/child hierarchy. When a class loading request is presented to a class loader at whatever level, it first asks its parent class loader to fulfil the request. The parent class loader, in turn, asks its parent for the class until the request reaches the top of the hierarchy. If the class loader at the top of the hierarchy cannot fulfil the request to load a class, then the child class loader that called it is responsible for loading the class. If the child is also unable to load the class, the request continues back down the hierarchy until a class loader fulfils it or a `ClassNotFoundException` is produced by the last class loader at the bottom of the parent/child hierarchy. A simple diagram can be seen below which shows the class loading hierarchy of WebSphere.

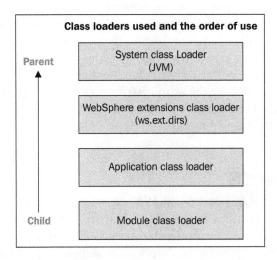

The design and packaging of an application will determine the behavior of class loading. What we mean is that each EAR file can have many Java Archives (JARs) and Web Archives (WARs) inside of it, which will influence the class loading requirements. It really comes down to what Java packages, custom or not, have been included in the applications code base. Because class loading can cause issues, WebSphere provides the ability to influence class loading behavior.

WebSphere class loaders

In WebSphere, there are several ways to configure class loaders for applications and modules to ensure that they access the Java classes and Java resources packaged within.

Below is a list of the three main class loaders which can be configured via the administration console:

- Application server class loader.
    - ° The application server class loader policy affects all applications that are deployed on the server.
- Enterprise application class loader.
    - ° An application class loader is the parent class of an Enterprise application (EAR) and all modules within it. An application class loader groups enterprise bean (EJB) modules, shared libraries, and dependency Java archive (JAR) files associated to an application. Dependency JAR files are JAR files that contain code which can be used by both enterprise beans and servlets.
- Web module class loader.
    - ° A web module has its own Web application archive (WAR) class loader to load the contents of the web module, which are in the `WEB-INF/classes` and `WEB-INF/lib` directories.

Application server class loader

Essentially, this option is setting a single class loader for all applications in the entire application server. The application class loader policy controls the isolation of applications that run in the system (on the server). An application class loader groups enterprise bean (EJB) modules, shared libraries, and JAR files that contain code which can be used by both enterprise beans and servlets. The application class loader policy controls whether an application class loader can be shared by multiple applications or is unique for each application.

Configuring server class loaders

To change an application server's class loader using the Admin console, click **Servers\ Server Types\WebSphere application servers\< server_name>** to open the application server settings page. Looking at the page, you can see the section labelled **Server-specific Application Settings** as shown below.

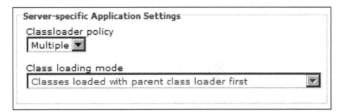

This image above shows two pick lists which are explained in the tables below.

Classloader policy

The table below explains the **Classloader policy** field as found in the **Server-specific Application Settings** section.

Option	Description
Single	Applications are not isolated from each other. Uses a single application class loader to load all of the EJB modules, shared libraries, and JAR files which are contained in all applications installed into the JVM.
Multiple	Applications are isolated from each other. Gives each application its own class loader to load the EJB modules, shared libraries, and JAR files.

Class loading mode

The table below explains the **Class loading mode** field as found in the **Server-specific Application Settings** section.

Option	Description
Classes loaded with parent class loader first	Sets the loading of classes to its parent class loader before attempting to load the class from its local class path. This is the default value for **Class loading mode** and is often referred to in discussion as "Parent first."
Classes loaded with local class loader first (parent last)	Tells the class loader to start with loading classes from its local class path before asking its parent. In simple terms, it means the application can use its own version of a class that its parent would normally have loaded. Often referred to as "Parent last".

Often you will leave the Class loading mode field as is. However, it could happen that several applications from different vendors installed on the same JVM might conflict with each other, or even WebSphere's own internal class loading could conflict with an application's class loading and so understanding this setting is important.

Application class loader

An enterprise application is a grouping of one or more web, EJB, or application client modules. Enterprise applications can also override settings within the contained modules deployment descriptors to combine or deploy them in a more useful way. By placing JAR files in the enterprise application instead of the global class path of an application server, they are also within the application and thus they get deployed along with the application. The idea is that an EAR file encapsulates all its required resources and hence it can be pre-configured using a manifest file to specify how it will load its internal classes. You can search Google to understand how manifest files work.

Configuring application class loaders

To configure an application's class loading settings, you need to look at the settings of an installed application. To look at an application class loading settings, click **Applications\Application Types\WebSphere enterprise applications\<application_name>\Class loading** and update detection to access the page for configuring an application class loader. Below is a screenshot of the relevant fields from an application class loader.

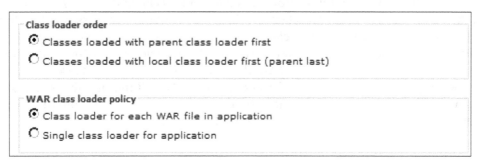

You can see in the screenshot above that there are two sections. One section defines the class loader order and the second the class loader policy. The following table explains these options.

Class loader order

The table below explains the **Class loading mode** field found in the **Server-specific Applications Settings** section.

Option	Description
Classes loaded with parent class loader first	Sets the loading of classes to its parent class loader before attempting to load the class from its local class path.
Classes loaded with local class loader first (parent last)	Tells the class loader to start with loading classes from its local class path before asking its parent.

WAR class loader policy

The table below explains the class loader options for a WAR file(s) in an EAR file.

Option	Description
Class loader for each WAR file in application	A separate class loader is assigned to each WAR file.
Single class loader for application	One class loader is assigned to all WAR files.

Web module class loader

Each web module has two folders for Java code—one is called WEB-INF/classes and the other WEB-INF/lib. The classes' folder may contain Java classes within the web application. We can specify a class loader which looks at this folder, so that if changes are made to the classes, they are automatically reloaded by the application server. The lib folder may contain JAR files that the web application also uses. You should place third-party JAR files and other utility JAR files in this folder. However, if other Web or EJB modules use the JAR files, move them into the **Enterprise Application's** class path which is global to the application.

Configuring module class loading

Within an EAR file, we know that we can have more then one WAR file module. WebSphere allows each module to be configured for class loading. To configure a WAR class loader, you need to drill down into EAR files modules. To do this, follow the following sequence in the Admin console. Click **Enterprise Applications\<application name>\Manage Modules\<module_name>** and you will then be able to see the **Class loader order** field in the **Manage Module** page.

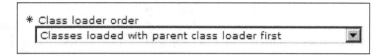

Class loader order

The table below explains the options of the `Class loader order` field shown above.

Option	Description
Classes loaded with parent class loader first	If set, the class loader searches the application's class loader for the class.
Classes loaded with local class loader first (parent last)	If set, the class loader searches within the WAR class loader first to load a class.

Class loading isolation

Essentially, we can group class loading into three isolation types. By using combinations of the settings in the application server and application class loader configurations, we can produce three different class loading isolations. Below is a table which explains the three types of isolation which are achieved by combinations of the previously explained class loading types.

Isolation Type	Application sever class loader policy	WAR class loader policy
Full	Multiple	WAR (Module)
Partial	Multiple	Single (Application)
Minimal	Single	Single (Application)

When the application server policy is **Single**, it indicates a single class loader for all applications installed in the application server. **Multiple** indicates multiple class loaders. A class loader is assigned for each application so each application becomes isolated from all other applications installed in the same JVM. The WAR class loader policy is simply either **WAR (Module)** or **Single (Application)**. **Single (Application)** indicates a single class loader for the entire application no matter how many WAR files are included. **WAR (Module)** indicates a class loader for each web module.

 Choosing **Single** for the application server policy and **WAR (Module)** for the WAR module policy is essentially ignored as, once you set a server to use a Single class loader, there is only one class loader for the entire application server.

Summary

In this chapter, we learned that all configurations done in the administrative console are ultimately saved into XML files in the underlying WebSphere file structure. There are key XML files which an administrator should be familiar with to help problem-solve WebSphere configuration and runtime issues. We learned that there is also a key properties file which is required to be edited if global security is turned on. We covered WebSphere logging and that all that WebSphere administrators need to be familiar with is where application logs are located and how to read them and search them using Linux commands. We also covered the dark art of class loaders, which is very important in the running of applications. Often developers do not understand class loading and so, when applications are deployed, it is up to the WebSphere administrator to configure WebSphere to ensure that all the applications' required classes load correctly.

6
WebSphere Messaging

Messaging in a large enterprise is common and a WebSphere administrator needs to understand what WebSphere Application Server can do for Java Messaging and/or **WebSphere Message Queuing (WMQ)** based messaging. Here, we will learn how to create **Queue Connection Factories (QCF)** and **Queue Destinations (QD)** which we will use in a demonstration application where we will demonstrate the **Java Message Service (JMS)** and also show how WMQ can be used as part of a messaging implementation.

In this chapter, we will cover the following topics:

- Java messaging
- Java Messaging Service (JMS)
- WebSphere messaging
- Service integration bus (SIB)
- WebSphere MQ
- Message providers
- Queue connection factories
- Queue destinations

Java messaging

Messaging is a method of communication between software components or applications. A messaging system is often peer-to-peer, meaning that a messaging client can send messages to, and receive messages from, any other client. Each client connects to a messaging service that provides a system for creating, sending, receiving, and reading messages. So why do we have Java messaging? Messaging enables distributed communication that is loosely-coupled. What this means is that a client sends a message to a destination, and the recipient can retrieve the message from the destination. A key point of Java messaging is that the sender and the receiver do not have to be available at the same time in order to communicate. The term **communication** can be understood as an exchange of messages between software components. In fact, the sender does not need to know anything about the receiver; nor does the receiver need to know anything about the sender. The sender and the receiver need to know only what message format and what destination to use. Messaging also differs from electronic mail (email), which is a method of communication between people or between software applications and people. Messaging is used for communication between software applications or software components. Java messaging attempts to relax tightly-coupled communication (such as, TCP network sockets, CORBA, or RMI), allowing software components to communicate **indirectly** with each other.

Java Message Service

Java Message Service (JMS) is an application program interface (API) from Sun. JMS provides a common interface to standard messaging protocols and also to special messaging services in support of Java programs. Messages can involve the exchange of crucial data between systems and contain information such as event notification and service requests. Messaging is often used to coordinate programs in dissimilar systems or written in different programming languages. By using the JMS interface, a programmer can invoke the messaging services like IBM's WebSphere MQ (WMQ) formerly known as MQSeries, and other popular messaging products. In addition, JMS supports messages that contain serialized Java objects and messages that contain XML-based data.

A JMS application is made up of the following parts, as shown in the following diagram:

- A **JMS provider** is a messaging system that implements the JMS interfaces and provides administrative and control features.

- JMS clients are the programs or components, written in the Java programming language, that produce and consume messages.

- Messages are the objects that communicate information between JMS clients.

- Administered objects are preconfigured JMS objects created by an administrator for the use of clients. The two kinds of objects are destinations and **Connection Factories (CF)**.

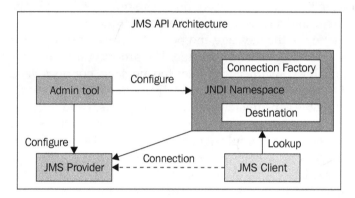

As shown in the diagram above, administrative tools allow you to create destinations and connection factories resources and bind them into a **Java Naming and Directory Interface (JNDI)** API namespace. A JMS client can then look up the administered objects in the namespace and establish a logical connection to the same objects through the JMS provider.

JMS features

Application clients, Enterprise Java Beans (EJB), and Web components can send or synchronously receive JMS messages. Application clients can, in addition, receive JMS messages asynchronously. A special kind of enterprise bean, the message-driven bean, enables the asynchronous consumption of messages. A JMS message can also participate in distributed transactions.

JMS concepts

The JMS API supports two models:

Point-to-point or queuing model

As shown below, in the point-to-point or queueing model, the sender posts messages to a particular queue and a receiver reads messages from the queue. Here, the sender knows the destination of the message and posts the message directly to the receiver's queue. Only one consumer gets the message. The producer does not have to be running at the time the consumer consumes the message, nor does the consumer need to be running at the time the message is sent. Every message successfully processed is acknowledged by the consumer. Multiple queue senders and queue receivers can be associated with a single queue, but an individual message can be delivered to only one queue receiver. If multiple queue receivers are listening for messages on a queue, Java Message Service determines which one will receive the next message on a first-come-first-serve basis. If no queue receivers are listening on the queue, messages remain in the queue until a queue receiver attaches to the queue.

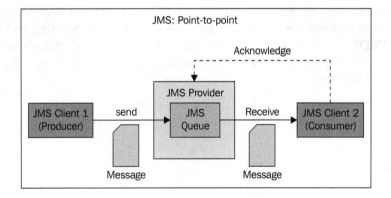

Publish and subscribe model

As shown by the above diagram, the publish/subscribe model supports publishing messages to a particular message topic. Unlike the point-to-point messaging model, the publish/subscribe messaging model allows multiple topic subscribers to receive the same message. JMS retains the message until all topic subscribers have received it. The Publish & Subscribe messaging model supports durable subscribers, allowing you to assign a name to a topic subscriber and associate it with a user or application. Subscribers may register interest in receiving messages on a particular message topic. In this model, neither the publisher nor the subscriber knows about each other.

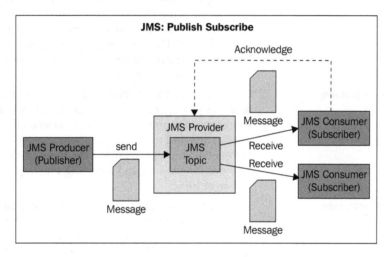

By using Java, JMS provides a way of separating the application from the transport layer of providing data. The same Java classes can be used to communicate with different JMS providers by using the JNDI information for the desired provider. The classes first use a connection factory to connect to the queue or topic, and then populate and send or publish the messages. On the receiving side, the clients then receive or subscribe to the messages.

JMS API

The JMS API is provided in the Java package `javax.jms`. Below are the main interfaces provided in the `javax.jms` package:

Interface	Description
ConnectionFactory interface	A WebSphere configured resource object that a client uses to create a connection to the JMS provider. JMS clients access the connection factory through interfaces so the application code does not need to be changed if the underlying JMS implementation changes. Administrators configure the connection factories which have JNDI names so that JMS clients can look them up. These resources in WebSphere are known as JMS Resource references.
Connection interface	Once a connection factory is obtained, a connection to a JMS provider can be created. A connection represents a communication link between the application and the messaging system. Depending on the connection type, connections allow users to create sessions for sending and receiving messages from a queue or topic.
Destination interface	A WebSphere-configured resource object that serves as the identity of a message destination, which is where messages are delivered and consumed. It is either a queue or a topic. The WebSphere administrator creates these resource references, and client applications discover them using JNDI lookups.
MessageConsumer interface	A Java object created by a session. It receives messages sent from a destination. The consumer can receive messages synchronously or asynchronously for both queue- and topic-type messaging.
MessageProducer interface	A Java object created by a session that sends messages to a destination. The user can create a sender to a specific destination or create a generic sender that specifies the destination at the time the message is sent.

Messaging applications use the above listed interfaces in the Java code to implement JMS. The demo JMS Test Tool application contains code which you can look into to see how the above interfaces are used. We will cover the JMS Test Tool later in the chapter when we demonstrate how to deploy an application which uses messaging.

WebSphere messaging

WebSphere Application Server implements two main messaging sub-systems. The default-messaging-provider is internal to WebSphere and the WebSphere MQ messaging provider which uses WebSphere MQ. First, we will cover the default messaging provider which is implemented by using a SIB. Then, we will move onto the WebSphere MQ messaging provider. To demonstrate use of the SIB and the default Messaging provider, we will deploy an application which will use JMS via the SIB. Before we deploy the application, we will need to set up the JMS resources required for the application to implement Java messaging using the **Java Message Service (JMS)**.

Default JMS provider

WebSphere Application Server comes with a default JMS provider as part of its installation and supports messaging through the use of the JMS. The default JMS provider allows applications deployed to WAS to perform asynchronous messaging without the need to install a third-party JMS provider. This is a very useful feature which runs as part of the WebSphere Application Server. The default JMS provider is utilized via the SIB and you can use the Administrative console to configure the SIB and JMS resources.

Enterprise applications use JMS CF to connect to a service integration bus. Applications use queues within the SIB to send and receive messages. An application sends messages to a specific queue and those messages are retrieved and processed by another application listening to that queue. In WebSphere, JMS queues are assigned to queue destinations on a given SIB. A queue destination is where messages can be persisted over time within the SIB. Applications can also use topics for messages. Applications publish messages to the topics. To receive messages, applications subscribe to topics. JMS topics are assigned to topic spaces on the bus. The JMS topics are persisted in the SIB and accessed via appropriate connection factories which applications use to gain access to the bus.

The following table gives a quick overview of the types of resource available for configuring JMS resources for the Default JMS provider running in the SIB.

JMS Resource Type	Description
JMS provider	A JMS provider enables messaging based on the **Java Messaging Service (JMS)**. It provides J2EE (Enterprise Edition) connection factories to create connections for JMS destinations.
JMS activation specification	A JMS activation specification is associated with one or more message-driven beans and provides the configuration necessary for them to receive messages and is specific to SIB implementation.
JMS connection factory	A JMS connection factory is used to create connections to the associated JMS provider of JMS destinations, for both point-to-point and publish/subscribe messaging.
JMS queue connection factory	A JMS queue connection factory is used to create connections to the associated JMS provider of JMS queues, for point-to-point messaging.
JMS queue	A JMS queue is used as a destination for point-to-point messaging.
JMS topic connection factory	A JMS topic connection factory is used to create connections to the associated JMS provider of JMS topics, for publish/subscribe messaging.
JMS topic	A JMS topic is used as a destination for publish/subscribe messaging.

WebSphere SIB

Before our applications can be installed and set up to use the default messaging provider, we must create a service integration bus. In a way, the SIB provides the backbone for JMS messaging when you are using the default provider. The default provider is internal to WebSphere Application Server and no third-party software is required utilize it.

A service integration bus supports applications using message-based and service-oriented architectures. A bus is a group of interconnected servers and clusters that have been added as members of the bus. Applications connect to a bus at one of the messaging engines associated with its bus members.

Creating a SIB

To create a **Service Integration Bus** (**SIB**), log into the admin console and navigate to the **Service integration** section within the lefthand side panel and click on **Buses**, as shown in the following screenshot:

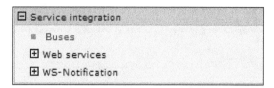

Click **New** to enter the **Create a new Service Integration Bus** page where we will begin our SIB creation. Type **InternalJMS** in the **Enter the name of your new bus** field and uncheck the **Bus security** checkbox as shown below and then click **Next**.

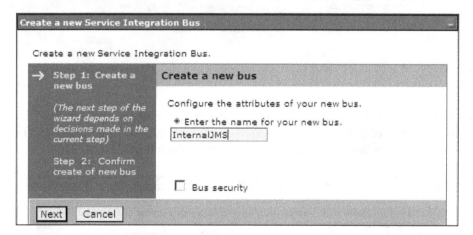

On the next screen, you will be prompted to confirm your SIB settings. Click **Finish** to complete the creation of the SIB. Once the wizard has completed, click **Save** to retain your configuration change. You will be returned to a screen which lists the available SIBs installed in your WebSphere configuration. Now that the SIB has been created, you can click on the SIB name to configure settings and operation of the SIB. We will not be covering managing a SIB in this book as it is beyond our scope. All we need to do is create a SIB so we can demonstrate an application using the default JMS provider which requires a SIB to operate.

To complete the configuration, we must add an existing server as a member to the SIB so that we have a facility for message persistence. The SIB is just a service integration bus, almost like a connecting conduit, however we need and actual members, which in our case will be our application server called **server1**, which contain the actual implementation for the message store.

To add a server as a bus member, click on the bus name called **InternalJMS** in the SIB list and then navigate to the **Topology** section and click **Bus members** as shown below.

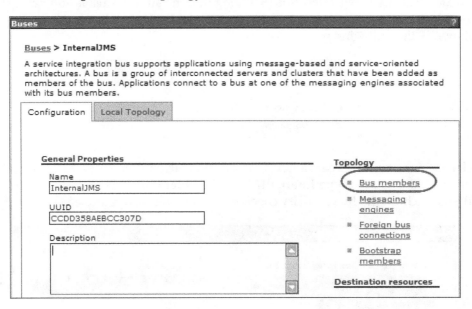

You will now be presented with a screen where you can add bus members. Click **Add** and you will be able to select the server you wish to add as a member to the bus. You will notice that the server is already pre-selected as shown below.

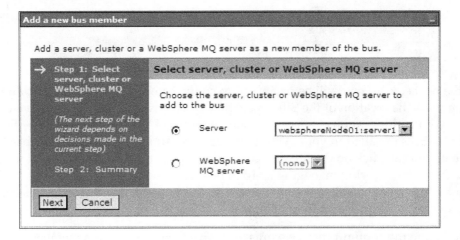

Click **Next** to the final screen, where you will select the **File store** option from the option group field labeled **Choose type of message store for the persistence of message state**. Click **Next** to view the next configuration page where we will use the page defaults. Click **Next** to enter the **Tune performance parameters** page where we will also use the defaults. Clicking **Next** again will take you to the final summary page where you will click **Finish** to finalize adding the application server as a bus member. Click **Save** to retain the changes. You will now see the application server called server1 listed as a bus member. Now we can move on to configure the JMS resources.

Configuring JMS

Once we have created a SIB, we can configure JMS resources. The types of resources we need to create depend entirely upon the application you are deploying. In our demo JMS application, we are going to demonstrate putting a message on a queue using a sending Servlet which places messages on a queue, known as the sender, and then demonstrate receiving a message on the receiving Servlet, known as the receiver. This exercise will give you a detailed enough overview of a simple implementation of JMS. To continue, we will need to set up a queue connection factory which the application will use to connect to a message queue and an actual queue which the application will send messages to and receive messages from.

Creating queue connection factories

To create a queue connection factory, navigate to the **Resources** section of the left-hand-side panel in the Administrative console and click **Queue connection factories** from the **JMS** category as shown below.

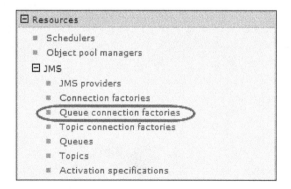

Select a scope of cell from the cell-scope pick-list and then click **New** to create a new QCF. In the **Select JMS resource provider** screen as shown below, select **Default messaging provider** from the available provider options and click **OK**.

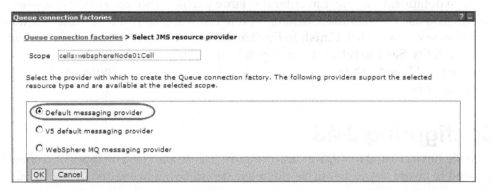

On the next page, you will be asked to fill in configuration settings for the QCF. We will only need to fill in a few fields. As shown below, type **QCF.Test** in the **Name** field, **jms/QCF.Test** in the **JNDI name** field and select the bus called **InternalJMS** from the **Bus name** field.

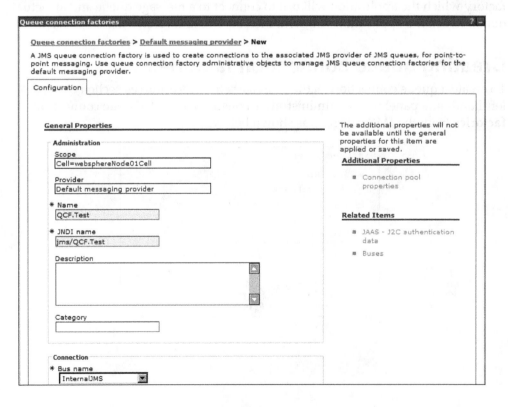

Click **Apply** and then **Save** when prompted to do so in order to retain the changes. You will now see the QCF listed in the list of configured QCF.

Creating queue destinations

To create a queue, we will follow a similar process to creating a QCF. Select **Queues** from the JMS category located in the **Resources** section found in the left-hand-side panel of the Admin console.

Select **Default messaging provider** from the list of messaging providers and then click on **OK** to enter the queue configuration page.

On the queue configuration page, enter **Q.Test** in the **Name** field and **jms/Q.Test** in the **JNDI name** field.

Select **InternalJMS** from the **Bus name** field found in the **Connection** section and select **Create Service Bus destination** from the **Queue name** field and click **Apply**. You will then be prompted to create a queue destination.

In the **Create a new queue for point-to-point messaging** screen, type **QD.Test** in the **identifier** field and click **Next**.

In the following screen of the wizard labelled **Assign the queue to a bus member**, you will see that **server1** sis already pre-selected in the field called Bus member. The bus mentioned in the **Bus member** field is where the actual queue destination will be created Clicking **Next** will present you with the final step, a summary screen where you can click **Finish** and then **Save** to retain your queue configuration.

To view your queue destination, you need to select the bus called InternalJMS from the list of buses found by navigating to the **Service integration** section of the left-hand-side panel from the Admin console and then click **Buses**. You will recognize this screen as the main bus configuration page we used when we created the SIB. Click the **Destinations** link located in the **Destination resources** section shown in the **Destinations** page as shown in the screenshot below.

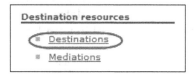

You will then be presented with a list of queue destinations in the SIB.

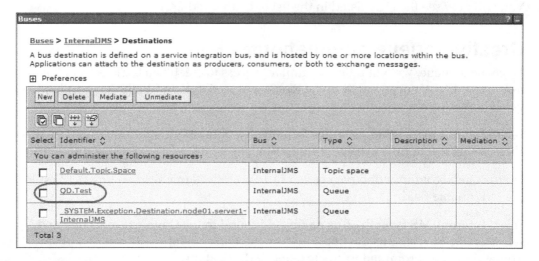

To create **Topics Connection Factories (TCF)** and **Topic Destinations (TD)** for publish/subscribe messaging, you can follow a similar process. Publish/subscribe messaging will not be demonstrated in this book; however, you can use the process defined for creating QCF and QD as an example of how to create TCF and TD.

Installing the JMS demo application

To demonstrate the use of QCF and QD in the SIB, we will manually deploy an EAR file which contains two servlets that can be used to test JMS configurations.

The JMS Test Tool application is a web application which provides a controller Servlet, which will process requests from an input page, which allows a user to put a simple message on a queue then get the message. The application is not industrial strength; however, it goes a long way to demonstrating the basics of JMS. The application can be downloaded from www.packtpub.com and it also contains all the source code, so you can look into the mechanics of simple JMS programming. We will not explain the code in this chapter as it detracts from administration; however, feel free to change the code and experiment in your learning of JMS.

After you have downloaded the `JMSTester.ear` file to your local machine, use the Admin console to deploy it using the instructions in Chapter 2 as a guide. We will take you through some screens to ensure you correctly configure the appropriate resources as part of the installation.

When you start the installation (deployment) of the EAR file, ensure you select the option called **Detailed** from the **How do you want to install the application?** section on the **Preparing for the application installation** screen as shown below to expose the configuration steps required by the EAR file, otherwise you will be given the default JMS configuration and you might not understand how JMS has been configured in the application. Another good reason for selecting the Detailed option is that the wizard will present extra screens which will allow you to optionally override the JNDI mappings for resource references.

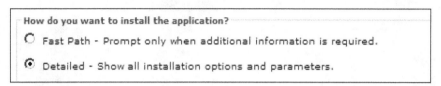

On the **Install New Application** screen, change the application name to **JMS Test Tool**, and then keep clicking **Next** until you come to Step 6, the **Bind message destination references to administered objects** page. When you get to this page, type `jms/Q.Test` in the **Target Resource JNDI Name** field, which means you want to bind the application's internal resource reference called `jms/Queue` to the WebSphere configured JMS queue destination called `jms/Q.Test` (which we created earlier) as shown below.

Bind message destination references to administered objects

Each message destination reference that is defined in your application must map to an enterprise bean.

⊞ Apply Multiple Mappings

Select	Module	EJB	URI	Message destination object	Type	Target Resource JNDI Name
☐	JMSTester		JMSTester.war, WEB-INF/web.xml	jms/Queue	Link	jms/Q.Test

Using this level of JNDI abstraction means that the application does not need to know the actual JMS implementation technology, which in this case happens to be the internal WebSphere Default JMS provider. Click **Next** to proceed to the next step of the wizard. The next screen of the wizard will be the **Map resource references to resources** screen where you will be given the option of binding the applications JNDI resource declarations to the actual JNDI implementation as configured in WebSphere. In the image below you can see that the application has been configured to point to a QCF called jms/QCF, however in our configuration of WebSphere we have called our connection factory jms/QCF.Test. Type jms/QCF.Test into the **Target Resource JNDI Name** field.

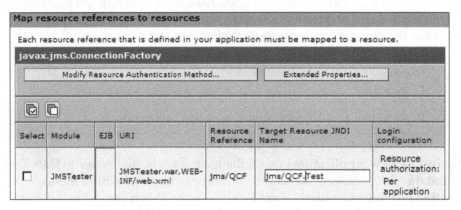

This concept of abstraction which WebSphere offers to J2EE applications which utilize indirect JNDI naming is a very powerful and very important part of configuring enterprise applications. Using indirect JNDI allows for the decoupling of the application from the application server actual implementation of JMS. The application is then pointed to the JNDI which it will use to look up the actual resource reference that has been configured in WebSphere. So, in simple words, the administrator decides what messaging sub-system the application will be using and is transparent to the application.

We have now completed the configuration elements that require user intervention, so we can keep clicking **Next** until the application wizard is complete. If you get any warning as shown below, you can ignore it; the warnings come up due to WebSphere telling you that you have configured the QCF and queue destinations at cell level, and that other applications could be referencing them as well. Just click **Continue** to move on to the next steps.

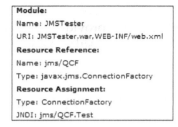

When you come to the Context root page, take note that the EAR file has been configured to use JMSTester as the web applications context root. We will leave this as defaulted for our demonstration; however, you could override it by typing in another context root. When you get to the **Summary** page of the wizard, click on **Finish** and **Save** to retain the applications deployment.

JMS Test Tool application

The JMS Test Tool application provides a simple test harness to send and receive messages to and from queues. The application can be downloaded from `http://www.packtpub.com`. To launch the deployed application, you can use the following URL:

`http://<host_name>:9080/JMSTester/`.

If the application is deployed and has started error-free, you will be presented with the JMS Test Tool interface, which is a set of three HTML frames, as shown below.

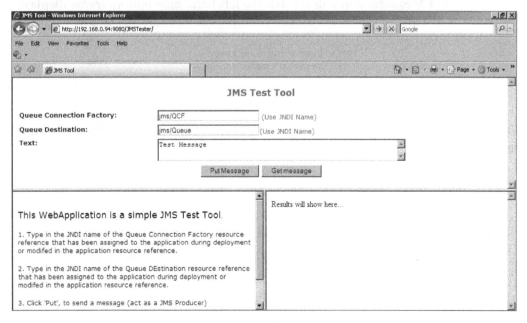

The main frame is the top-most frame where you enter a test message as shown below. The left-hand-side bottom frame provides help on how to use the tool, and the right-hand-side frame will show the results of a send or get message action.

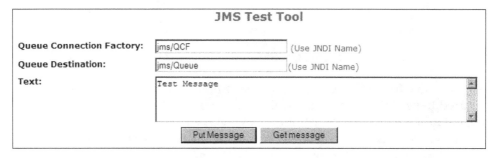

If you click **Put Message**, you will see that the left-hand-side bottom frame displays the status of the message being sent as shown below. Each time you click **Put Message**, a new message will be put on the queue.

```
INFO: Producing a message
MESSAGE:
Test Message

INFO: Message put on queue.

JMS Message ID=ID:414d5120545354444144513120202020d7c5db4920012f11
```

If you click **Get Message**, you will see that the left-hand-side bottom frame displays the contents of a given message retrieved from the queue as shown below.

```
INFO: Consuming a message
INFO: Message found on queue.
MESSAGE:
Test Message
```

Each time you click **Get Message**, the next message will be read from the queue until there are no more messages.

```
INFO: Consuming a message
INFO: No message found on queue!
```

You can use this application to test both JMS and local MQ queue managers. This concludes our overview of using JMS and the default messaging provider.

WebSphere MQ overview

WebSphere MQ formerly known as MQ Series is IBM's enterprise messaging solution. In a nutshell, MQ provides the mechanisms for messaging both in point-to-point and publish-subscribe. However, it guarantees to deliver a message only once. This is important for critical business applications which implement messaging. An example of a critical system could be a banking payments system where messages contain messages pertaining to money transfer between banking systems, so guaranteeing delivery of a debit/credit is paramount in this context. Aside from guaranteed delivery, WMQ is often used for messaging between dissimilar systems and the WMQ software provides programming interfaces in most of the common languages, such as Java, C, C++, and so on. If you are using WebSphere, then it is common to find that WMQ is often used with WebSphere when WebSphere is hosting message-enabled applications. It is important that the WebSphere administrator understands how to configure WebSphere resources so that application can be coupled to the MQ queues.

Overview of WebSphere MQ example

To demonstrate messaging using WebSphere MQ, we are going to re-configure the previously deployed JMS Tester application so that it will use a connection factory which communicates with a queue on a WMQ queue manager as opposed to using the default provider which we demonstrated earlier.

Installing WebSphere MQ

Before we can install our demo messaging application, we will need to download and install WebSphere MQ 7.0. A free 90-day trial can be found at the following URL:

`http://www.ibm.com/developerworks/downloads/ws/wmq/.`

Click the download link as shown below.

Operating system	Version	Size *	Download method
Download now AIX, HP-UX Itanium, iSeries, Linux®, Sun Solaris x86-64, Sun Solaris/SPARC, Windows	V7.0	186MB to 600MB	HTTP | Download Director

Similar to Chapter 1, you will be prompted to register as an IBM website user before you can download the WebSphere MQ Trial. Once you have registered and logged in, the download link above will take you to a page which lists download for different operating systems.

Select **WebSphere MQ 7.0 90-day trial** from the list of available options as shown below.

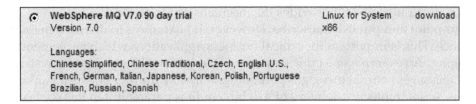

Click **continue** to go to the download page. You may be asked to fill out a questionnaire detailing why you are evaluating **WebSphere MQ (WMQ)**. Fill out the question as you see fit and submit to move to the download page.

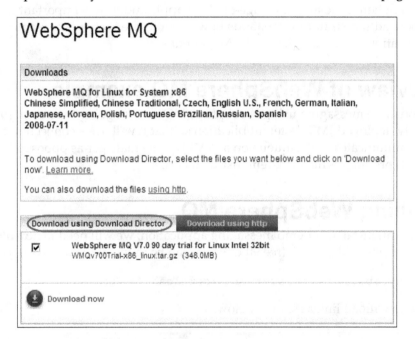

As shown above, make sure you use the IBM HTTP Download director as it will ensure that your download will resume, even if your Internet loses a connection.

 If you do not have a high-speed Internet connection, you can try downloading a free 90-day trial of WebSphere MQ 7.0 overnight while you are asleep.

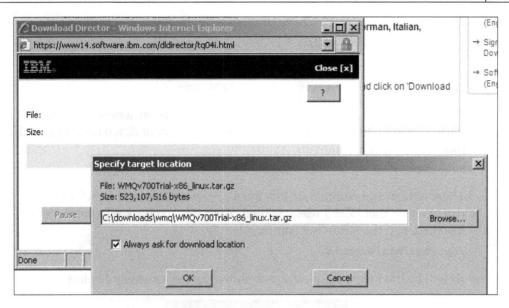

Download the trial to a `temp` folder, for example `c:\temp`, on your local machine. The screenshot above shows how the IBM HTTP Downloader will prompt for a location where you want to download it to. Once the WMQ install file has been downloaded, you can then upload the file using an appropriate secure copy utility like Winscp to an appropriate folder like `/apps/wmq_install` on your Linux machine. Once you have the file uploaded to Linux, you can then decompress the file and run the installer to install WebSphere MQ.

Running the WMQ installer

Now that you have uploaded the `WMQv700Trial-x86_linux.tar` file on your Linux machine, and follow these steps:

1. You can decompress the file using the following command:

    gunzip ./WMQv700Trial-x86_linux.tar.gz

2. Then run the `un-tar` command:

    tar -xvf ./ WMQv700Trial-x86_linux.tar

3. Before we can run the WMQ installations, we need to accept the license agreement by running the following command:

    ./mqlicense.sh -accept

4. To run the WebSphere MQ installation, type the following commands:

```
rpm -ivh MQSeriesRuntime-7.0.0-0.i386.rpm

rpm -ivh MQSeriesServer-7.0.0-0.i386.rpm

rpm -ivh MQSeriesSamples-7.0.0-0.i386.rpm
```

5. As a result of running the MQSeriesServer installation, a new user called **mqm** was created. Before running any WMQ command, we need to switch to this user using the following command:

```
su - mqm
```

6. Then, we can run commands like the `dspmqver` command which can be run to check that WMQ was installed correctly. To check whether WMQ is installed, run the following command:

```
/opt/mqm/bin/dspmqver
```

The result will be the following message as shown in the screenshot below:

Creating a queue manager

Before we can complete our WebSphere configuration, we need to create a WMQ queue manager and a queue, then we will use some MQ command line tools to put a test message on an MQ queue and get a message from an MQ queue.

1. To create a new queue manager called **TSTDADQ1**, use the following command:

```
crtmqm TSTDADQ1
```

2. The result will be as shown in the image below.

```
-bash-3.00$ crtmqm TSTDADQ1
There are 89 days left in the trial period for this copy of WebSphere MQ.
WebSphere MQ queue manager created.
Creating or replacing default objects for TSTDADQ1.
Default objects statistics : 58 created. 0 replaced. 0 failed.
Completing setup.
Setup completed.
```

3. We can now type the following command to list queue managers:

```
dspmq
```

4. The result of running the **dspmq** command is shown in the image below.

```
-bash-3.00$ dspmq
QMNAME(TSTDADQ1)                                       STATUS(Ended immediately)
-bash-3.00$
```

5. To start the queue manager (QM), type the following command:

   strmqm

6. The result of starting the QM will be similar to the image below.

```
-bash-3.00$ strmqm TSTDADQ1
There are 89 days left in the trial period for this copy of WebSphere MQ.
WebSphere MQ queue manager 'TSTDADQ1' starting.
5 log records accessed on queue manager 'TSTDADQ1' during the log replay phase.
Log replay for queue manager 'TSTDADQ1' complete.
Transaction manager state recovered for queue manager 'TSTDADQ1'.
WebSphere MQ queue manager 'TSTDADQ1' started.
```

7. Now that we have successfully created a QM, we now need to add a queue called LQ.Test where we can put and get messages.

8. To create a local queue on the TSTDADQ1 QM, type the following commands in order:

   runmqsc TSTDADQ1

9. You are now running the MQ scripting command line, where you can issue MQ commands to configure the QM.

10. To create the queue, type the following command and hit *Enter*:

    define qlocal(LQ.TEST)

11. Then immediately type the following command:

    end

12. Hit *Enter* to complete the QM configuration, as shown by the following screenshot.

```
-bash-3.00$ runmqsc TSTDADQ1
5724-H72 (C) Copyright IBM Corp. 1994, 2008.  ALL RIGHTS RESERVED.
Starting MQSC for queue manager TSTDADQ1.


define qlocal(LQ.Test)
     1 : define qlocal(LQ.Test)
AMQ8006: WebSphere MQ queue created.
end
     2 : end
One MQSC command read.
No commands have a syntax error.
All valid MQSC commands were processed.
```

You can use the following command to see if your `LQ.TEST` queue exists.

```
echo "dis QLOCAL(*)" | runmqsc TSTDADQ1 | grep -i test
```

You have now added a local queue called `Q.Test` to the TSTDADQ1 queue manager.

```
runmqsc TSTDADQ1
DEFINE LISTENER(TSTDADQ1.listener) TRPTYPE (TCP) PORT(1414)
START LISTENER(TSTDADQ1.listener)
End
```

```
-bash-3.00$ runmqsc TSTDADQ1
5724-H72 (C) Copyright IBM Corp. 1994, 2008.  ALL RIGHTS RESERVED.
Starting MQSC for queue manager TSTDADQ1.


DEFINE LISTENER(TSTDADQ1.listener) TRPTYPE (TCP) PORT(1414)
     1 : DEFINE LISTENER(TSTDADQ1.listener) TRPTYPE (TCP) PORT(1414)
AMQ8626: WebSphere MQ listener created.
start listener(TSTDADQ1.listener)
     2 : start listener(TSTDADQ1.listener)
AMQ8021: Request to start WebSphere MQ Listener accepted.
 end
     3 : end
2 MQSC commands read.
No commands have a syntax error.
All valid MQSC commands were processed.
```

You can type the following command to ensure that your QM listener is running.

```
ps -ef | grep mqlsr
```

The result will be similar to the image below.

```
-bash-3.00$ ps -ef | grep mqlsr
mqm      29039 28666  0 18:22 ?        00:00:00 /opt/mqm/bin/runmqlsr -r -m TSTDADQ1 -t TCP -p 1414
```

To create a default channel, you can run the following command.

```
runmqsc TSTDADQ1
DEFINE CHANNEL(SYSTEM.ADMIN.SVRCONN) CHLTYPE(SVRCONN)
End
```

```
-bash-3.00$ runmqsc TSTDADQ1
5724-H72 (C) Copyright IBM Corp. 1994, 2008.  ALL RIGHTS RESERVED.
Starting MQSC for queue manager TSTDADQ1.


DEFINE CHANNEL(SYSTEM.ADMIN.SVRCONN) CHLTYPE(SVRCONN)
     1 : DEFINE CHANNEL(SYSTEM.ADMIN.SVRCONN) CHLTYPE(SVRCONN)
AMQ8014: WebSphere MQ channel created.
end
     2 : end
One MQSC command read.
No commands have a syntax error.
All valid MQSC commands were processed.
```

We can now use a sample MQ program called amqsput which we can use to put and get a test message from a queue to ensure that our MQ configuration is working before we continue to configure WebSphere.

Type the following command to put a test message on the LQ.Test queue:

```
/opt/mqm/samp/bin/amqsput LQ.TEST TSTDADQ1
```

Then you can type a test message: **Test Message** and hit *Enter*; this will put a message on the LQ.Test queue and will exit you from the **AMQSPUTQ** command tool.

```
-bash-3.00$ /opt/mqm/samp/bin/amqsput LQ.TEST TSTDADQ1
Sample AMQSPUT0 start
target queue is LQ.TEST
Test message

Sample AMQSPUT0 end
```

Now that we have put a message on the queue, we can read the message by using the MQ Sample command tool called amqsget. Type the following command to get the message you posted earlier:

```
/opt/mqm/samp/bin/amqsget LQ.TEST TSTDADQ1
```

The result will be that all messages on the LQ.TEST queue will be listed and then the tool will timeout after a few seconds as shown below.

```
-bash-3.00$ /opt/mqm/samp/bin/amqsget LQ.TEST TSTDADQ1
Sample AMQSGET0 start
message <Test Message>
no more messages
Sample AMQSGET0 end
```

We need to do two final steps to complete and that is to add the root user to the mqm group. This is not a standard practice in an enterprise, but we have to do this because our WebSphere installation is running as root. If we did not do this, we would have to reconfigure the user which the WebSphere process is running under and then add the new user to MQ security. To keep things simple, ensure that root is a member of the mqm group, by typing the following command:

```
usermod -a -G mqm root
```

We also need to change WMQ security to ensure that all users of the mqm group have access to all the objects of the TSTDADQ1 queue manager. To change WMQ security to give access to all objects in the QM, type the following command:

```
setmqaut -m TSTDADQ1 -t qmgr -g mqm +all
```

Now, we are ready to re-continue our configuring WebSphere and create the appropriate QCF and queue destinations to access WMQ from WebSphere.

Creating a WMQ connection factory

Creating a WMQ connection factory is very similar to creating a JMS QCF. However, there are a few differences which will be explained in the following steps. To create a WMQ QCF, log in to the Admin console and navigate to the **JMS** category of the **Resources** section found in the left-hand-side panel of the Admin console and click on **Queue connection factories.** Select the **Cell** scope and click on **New.** You will be presented with an option to select a message provider. Select **WebSphere MQ messaging provider** as shown below and click **OK.**

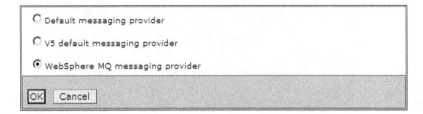

You will then be presented with a wizard which will first ask you for the name of the QCF. Type **QCF.LQTest** in the **Name** field and type **jms/QCF.LQTest** in the **JNDI name** field, as shown below.

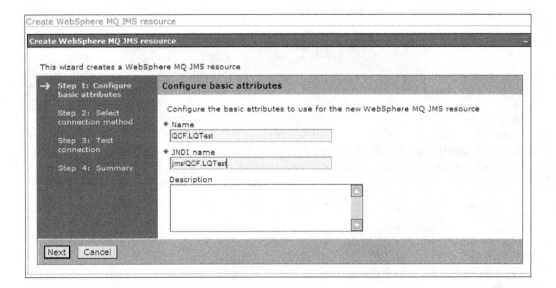

Click on **Next** to progress to the next step of the wizard, where you will decide on how to connect to WMQ. As shown in the following screenshot, select the **Enter all the required information into this wizard** option and then click on **Next.**

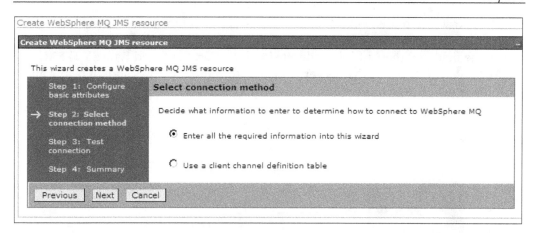

In the **Supply queue connection details** screen, you will need to type **TSTDADQ1** into the **Queue manager or queue sharing group name** field and click on **Next**.

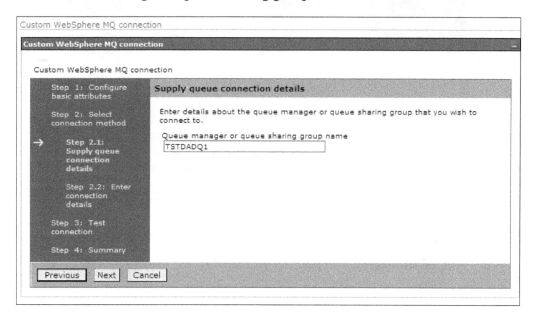

On the next screen of the wizard, you will be asked to fill in some connection details. Ensure that the **Transport** field is set to **Bindings then client**. Type **localhost** in the **hostname** field and then add the value **1414** to the **Port** field, and type **SYSTEM. ADMIN.SVRCONN** into the **Server connection channel** field as shown below and then click on **Next** to move on to the next step of the wizard.

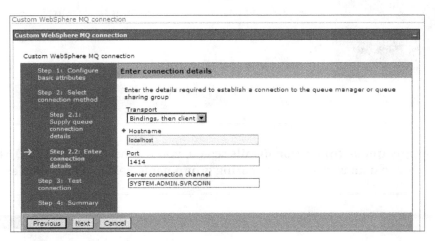

On the next page, you will be presented with a button to test your connection to WMQ. If you have set up WMQ correctly, then you will be able to connect and a results page will be displayed confirming a successful connection to WMQ. If you cannot connect at this stage, then you will need to check your MQ setup. Most often it is security that is the problem. If you find you have an issue with security, you can search Google for answers on how to change WMQ security. Once your test is successful, click on **Next** to move on to the final **Summary** page which will list your QCF configuration. On the final page of the wizard, click **Finish** to complete the WMQ QCF configuration and click **Save** to retain your changes. You will now see two QCF configurations, one for JMS and one for WMQ, as shown below:

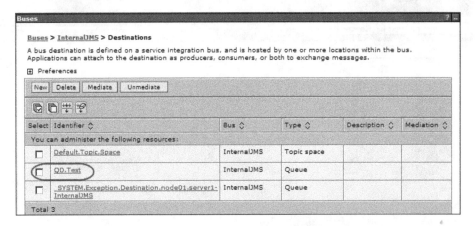

Creating a WMQ queue destination

The next step after creating a QCF is to create a queue destination. We will use the queue named LQ.Test which we created on the TSTDADQ1 queue manager. To create a new queue, navigate to the **JMS** category of the **Resources** section in the left-hand-side panel of the admin console and click **Queues**. Click on **New** to start the queue creation wizard. In the provider selector screen, select **WebSphere MQ messaging provider** and click on **Next**. You will then be presented with a page that allows you to specify settings for the queue. In the **Name** field, type **LQ.Test** and then type **jms/LQ.Test** in the **JNDI name** field. In the **Queue name** field, type **LQ.TEST** which is the actual name for the underlying queue, as shown below.

 Useful tip: Optionally, you can type the Queue Manager name, for example, **TSTDADQ1** into the **Queue manager or queue sharing group name** field, but if you ever use WMQ clustering, it is not required and will stop MQ clustering from working correctly.

Queues > LQ.Test

Queue destinations provided for point-to-point messaging by the W
queue destination administrative objects to manage queue destina

Configuration

General Properties

Administration

Scope
Cell=websphereNode01Cell

Provider
WebSphere MQ messaging
provider

* Name
LQ.Test

* JNDI name
jms/LQ.Test

Description

WebSphere MQ Queue
* Queue name
LQ.TEST

Click on **Apply** to submit the changes, and then click on **Save** to retain the changes to the WebSphere configuration repository. You will then be presented with a list of queues as shown below:

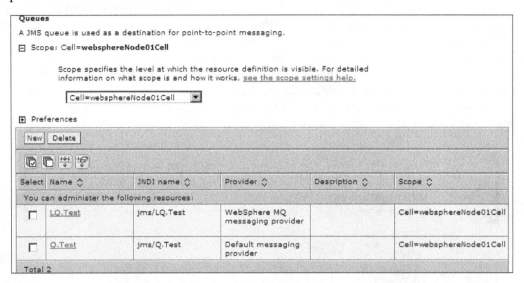

We have now configured a WebSphere MQ queue connection factory and a WebSphere MQ queue destination which our test application will use to send and receive messages from WMQ.

Reconfiguring the JMS demo application

Now that we have created a QCF and queue destination using WMQ as the message provider, we will need to reconfigure the JMS Test Tool application to point to the WMQ JNDI names as opposed to the Default Provider JNDI names. When we deployed the application, the installation wizard allowed us the option of re-pointing of the JNDI names. This was because the application's deployment descriptor declared resource references, which the installation wizard picked up and presented as configurable options in the installation wizard. Even after a deployment is complete, it is possible to reconfigure an application at any time by drilling down into the application configuration. We want to change the JNDI names the application is using for the QCF and queue destination. We are going to change jms/QCF.Test to jms/QCF.LQTest and jms/Q.Test to jms/LQ.Test. This re-mapping of the applications JNDI will allow the application to use WMQ instead of JMS via the SIB. To change the application's resource references, click **Applications** in the left-hand-side panel of the Admin console, and then expand the **Application Types** section and click **WebSphere enterprise applications**. Click on the JMS Test Tool from the application list. You will then be presented with the main application configuration panel. Look for a section called **References** as shown in the following screenshot:

References

- Resource references
- Message destination references
- Shared library references
- Shared library relationships

Click on the **Resource references** link and change the **Target Resource JNDI Name** field to **jms/QCF.LQTest** as shown below and then click on **OK** to return back to the previous page.

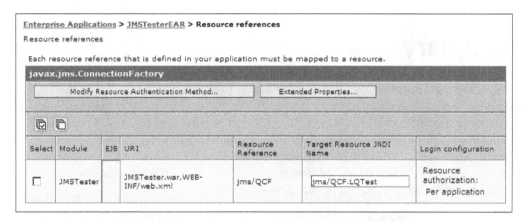

Click on **Continue** if you get any warnings. We have now re-pointed the application's QCF reference to the new WMQ QCF configuration.

To change the queue destination, we click on the **Message destination references** link and change the **Target Resource JNDI Name** field to **jms/LQ.Test** as shown below.

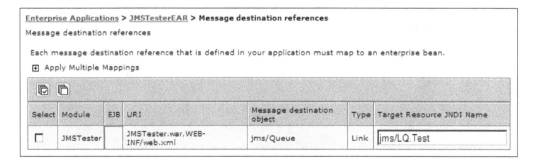

We have now completed the re-mapping of resources. Click on **Save** to make the changes permanent and restart the application server. When you next use the JMS Test Tool application, the sending and receiving of messages will be using WMQ instead of the Default Messaging Provider.

 You can use the following command to show the messages sitting on the LQ.TEST queue if you wish to see the queue depth (how many messages are on the queue):

```
echo "dis ql(*) curdepth where (curdepth gt 0)" |
runmqsc TSTDADQ1
```

Summary

In this chapter, we learned that WebSphere provides a level of abstraction to messaging configuration by allowing resources to be referenced by JNDI. We deployed a message-enabled application which required a queue connection factory and queue destination which it used to send and receive messages. We configured two different implementations of JMS. One implementation used the internal Default Messaging Provider, which required a SIB to be created, and we covered how to create the QCF and queue destinations and bound the applications resource references to those configured in WebSphere.

We then covered how to install WebSphere MQ and learned how to create a queue manager and a queue. Then, in WebSphere, we created a QCF and queue destination using the WebSphere MQ provider and demonstrated how to to re-map our applications resource references to re-point the application to use MQ messaging subsystem as opposed to the internal messaging subsystem.

There are many uses of messaging in enterprise applications and we have essentially covered the key areas for configuring WebSphere to facilitate resources for message-enabled applications.

7
Monitoring and Tuning

Keeping your WebSphere system well-oiled is paramount in keeping your environment as trouble-free as possible. In a software world, for some strange reason, things break and they stop running. This can be due to software bugs, network traffic, server load, and so on. By tuning your environment, you will ensure your applications perform as best as possible and by monitoring them you will be able to keep an eye on your systems to ensure that they run error-free.

In this chapter, we will cover the following topics:

- Using **Tivoli Performance Viewer (TPV)**
- Request metrics and PMI
- Dynamic caching
- Java Virtual Machine (JVM) parameters
- Java core dumps
- Java heap dumps
- Basic JVM tuning

Before we look at how to tune WebSphere's configuration, we will need to look at some of the tools that are provided within WebSphere itself, which can be used to view runtime metrics and monitor the state of application running within WebSphere Application Server (WAS). We will then discuss some of the key JVM, and configuration settings which can be used to improve performance.

Tivoli Performance Viewer

IBM WebSphere provides a tool to help with tuning and it is called TPV. This tool is embedded in the Administration console. For a quick recap of history, for Version 4.0 of WebSphere, TPV was originally named the Resource Analyzer. For Version 5.0, TPV was implemented as a standalone Java application. In Versions 6.0.x and onwards, TPV is embedded in the Administrative console and provides a graphical display for showing live activity using a **Scalable Vector Graphics (SVG)** viewer from Adobe.

By using TPV, you can view summary reports, or log **Performance Monitoring Infrastructure (PMI)** performance data in real time. You can also save logging data as XML files. You can later play-back the logged data (saved XML files) through the TPV viewer to see what happened during a recorded logging session over a particular time period.

It must be said that JVM tuning, in general, is a bit of a black art; however, by applying common sense and using the monitors that TPV provides you can monitor the health of your WebSphere Application Server and identify areas where simple tuning can improve performance. TPV provides metrics which can be selected for a given report and the data logged can be view graphically or as a table.

It must be noted that you can not only view current activity or log PMI performance data from WAS, but can also log PMI data for other installed products or applications that have implemented PMI.

TPV monitoring can be broken down into three main categories, as shown below:

- System resources
    - ° Monitor JVM memory usage
    - ° CPU utilization
    - ° Monitor sessions
    - ° Server response time
    - ° Monitor PMI metrics
    - ° Custom Application MBeans (Java Management Extensions [JMX]) attributes

- WebSphere pools and queues
    - ° Monitor thread pools
    - ° Monitor DB (JDBC) connection pools

- Application data
  - ° User sessions and details
  - ° Enterprise JavaBeans (EJBs)
  - ° Metrics of all web applications
  - ° Servlet response times

Enabling Tivoli Performance Viewer

To access Tivoli Performance Viewer, navigate to the **Monitoring and Tuning** section located in the lefthand side navigation panel of the administrative console as shown below:

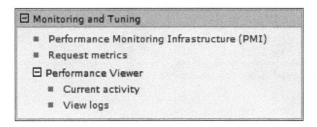

Now expand the **Performance Viewer** category and click on the **Current activity** link located underneath which will take you to a page which lists available servers to be monitored, as shown below:

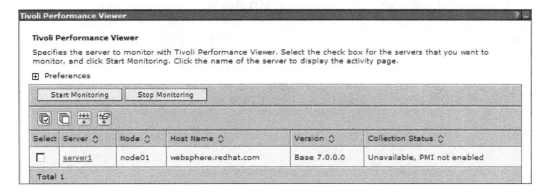

You will notice in the screenshot above that the **Collection Status** column is telling us that for **server1**, PMI is not enabled. Before we can use TPV, we must enable PMI and restart the server.

To enable PMI, click on the **Performance Monitoring Infrastructure (PMI)** link located in the **Monitoring and Tuning** section of the lefthand side panel in the Administrative console, which will take you to a page which lists the servers which can be configured for PMI. We are using WebSphere base, so we only have one server. Click on **server1** to enter the PMI configuration page as shown below.

General Properties

☐ Enable Performance Monitoring Infrastructure (PMI)

☐ Use sequential counter updates

Currently monitored statistic set

○ None

    No statistics are enabled.

◉ Basic

    ⊞ Provides basic monitoring, including Java EE and the top 38 statistics.

○ Extended

    ⊞ Provides extended monitoring, including the basic level of monitoring plus workload monitor, performance advisor, and Tivoli resource models.

○ All

    ⊞ All statistics are enabled.

○ Custom

    Provides fine-grained control to selectively enable statistics.

In the PMI configuration page, you will see several options. Check the **Enable Performance Monitoring Infrastructure (PMI)** checkbox to turn on PMI. You can opt to select the **Use sequential counter updates** checkbox for more precise monitoring, but you might find that there is a performance hit if this option is used.

In the next section called **Currently monitored statistic set,** you will see that the **Basic** option is the default selection. We will change this to **Extended** which will give us more reporting modules to use in our TPV reports.

 Often external monitoring tools like the full IBM Tivoli product and third-party tools like HP SiteScope will require the **Extended** option to be turned on to allow full monitoring of WebSphere.

Click on **Apply** and then **Save** and restart the application server to start PMI.

If you tail the application server's SystemOut.log located in the <was_profile_root>/logs/<server_name> folder, you will notice that PMI is now enabled as shown by the screenshot below:

`[8/3/09 10:33:59:484 BST] 00000000 PMIImpl        A   CWPMI1001I: PMI is enabled`

Before we continue on to TPV, we should also remove any applications that we do not need as this will ensure TPV is not listing too many modules, especially servlets which can make the summary report pages very long. In our example, we have removed two applications called **ivtApp** and **query** which were installed by the WebSphere install wizard by default and are used by the **First Steps** wizard as seen in Chapter1. We also remove the **DefaultApplication** which we installed in Chapter 2. We do not need these applications. If you have not already removed these applications, please remove these now by going to the **WebSphere enterprise applications** Link of the **Applications** section on the left-hand-side panel of the administrative console and following the process to uninstall these applications. Ensure you save the configuration and restart your Application Server as required. Once you have completed this exercise of removing applications, you should only have the HR Lister and JMS Tester applications remaining.

We will now go to the **Current activity** link and this time we will click on **server1** and enter the **Tivoli Performance Viewer** main page.

The main TVP page is split into two sections: the lefthand side contains a tree-based control from which you select objects to monitor and the righthand side shows a reporting panel which is currently defaulted to the summary report called **Servlets Summary Report**.

Let's walk through the options available on the lefthand panel. The panel lists a number of **Performance Modules**, as shown in the following screenshot:

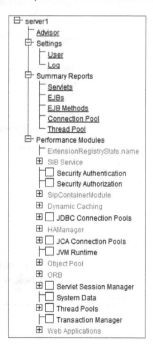

Key TPV categories

The table below describes the TPV categories as seen in the previous screenshot.

Module section	Description
Advisor	You can use **Advisor** to examine data while your application is running and it also provides advice to help tune systems for optimal performance using the PMI data collected. There are several tables listed in the **Advisor** panel:
	The first table represents the number of requests per second and the response time in milliseconds for the web container. You will also notice that there is a pie graph in the left-hand-side of the **Advisor** panel displaying the CPU activity.
	Another table displays average thread activity for the different resources like the web container. Data is shown as number of threads busy or idle.
	The last table is an advice table where WebSphere will list messages suggestion tuning. Select the message you want to view to determine if you wish to follow the advice.
Settings	This section allows you to adjust several settings:
	The **refresh rate** of how frequently TPV gathers statistics. The default is 30 seconds.
	The in-memory **buffer size** of data being collected
	The view data, which controls how stats are displayed. The options are: <ul><li>Raw Value<ul><li>Displays the actual value.</li></ul></li><li>Change in Value<ul><li>Displays the change in the current value from the previous value.</li></ul></li><li>Rate of Change<ul><li>Displays the result of calculation determining the rate of change between value changes.</li></ul></li></ul>
Log Settings	The **Log Settings** control what happens when Start Logging is clicked such as: Duration, Maximum File Size, Maximum Number of Historical Files, and so on.
Summary Reports	Summary reports are available for each application server. This list of reports is covered below in a separate table titled **Summary Reports**.
Performance Modules	Performance modules provide graphics and charts of various performance data on system resources, such as CPU utilization, database connection pools and other custom PMI as set by applications. The types of modules are covered below in a separate table titled **Key Performance Modules**.

Summary Reports

The table below describes the types of reports available in the **Summary Reports** section of TPV.

Servlets	The **Servlets** report shows the total number of requests, average response time, and multiplication of total requests by average response time for all the servlets in a table layout. The **Servlets** option provides a table column sorting feature to help you find which servlet is the slowest or fastest and which servlet is called most frequently.
EJBs	Enterprise JavaBeans (**EJBs**) show the total number of method calls, average response time, and multiplication of total method calls by the average response times for all the enterprise beans , and the data is presented in a table layout. The **EJBs** table provides a sorting feature to help you find which EJB is the slowest or fastest and which EJB is called most frequently.
EJB Methods	The **EJB Methods** report shows the total number of method calls, average response time, and multiplication of total method calls by average response time for the individual EJB methods and the data is displayed in a table layout. **EJB Methods** provide a table column sorting feature; for example, you can sort by average response time to help you find which EJB method is the slowest or fastest and which EJB method is called most frequently.
Connection pool	**Connection Pool** shows a chart of pool size and a pool in use for each data source.
Thread pool	**Thread Pool** shows charts of pool size, active threads, average response time, and throughput in the thread pool.

Key performance modules

Each performance module has several counters associated with it and these counters are displayed in a table underneath the data chart or table. Selected counters are displayed in the chart or table on the righthand side of the TPV screen. You can add or remove counters from the chart or table by selecting or deselecting the checkbox displayed next to each counter from the list of available counters as listed in the navigation tree. Depending on your WebSphere configuration, the number of applications and actual application design, you will be able to view different counters. Some counters are always available and these can be considered the default counters. However, if your application incorporates custom PMI counters these will also be listed. Since there are numerous performance counters which can be used, for the purpose of this article we will name a few of the most common counters, which you will invariably use in most tuning exercises.

- JDBC connection pools
- JVM runtime

- Servlet session manager
- System data
- Thread pools
- Transaction manager
- Web applications

When you wish to perform monitoring of your server or applications, you will most probably use the above listed counters to help you determine the success or failure of tuning WebSphere or applications. Tuning for performance is a relative event, meaning that there are no hard and fast rules. Using the tools presented here will give you an arsenal of possible areas to look within the admin console to change settings and options and to help you determine the effect of changes you make when you are debugging slow performance or making changes to enhance performance. A key point for tuning is to start from a known reference. There is often a misunderstanding that if you know all of the settings of WebSphere Application Server, then you can use them all to gain best performance. Yes, it is true that particular settings can be recommended for certain situations, however, it depends on the Operating System (OS), the version of WebSphere, fix pack levels, application design, code design, and server load. It is important to note that there is no magic answer, just knowledge and experience from trial and error and hopefully every time you go through performance testing and analysis, you will document lessons learned which can be applied to known issues or configurations in your environments over time. Often these experiences can be used as a baseline for other situations in other environments in the future.

 Helpful hint: If you experience an error similar to **Data Not Available** being displayed when trying to access the TPV graphing utility and you are prompted to download the Adobe SVG dll, and still the graphical interface fails to work after the download, then visit the Adobe SVG Zone web site at `http://www.adobe.com/svg/main.html` to test your Adobe SVG Viewer. You can also download the most recent version of the Adobe SVG Viewer, view the release notes, and report any bugs with the Adobe SVG Viewer from this web site.

Starting Tivoli Performance Viewer

What we will do now is look at how to start monitoring and look at some of the ways we can use TPV. Ensure that you have opened the **current activity** screen in the Administrative console. You can do this by clicking **Monitoring and Tuning | Performance Viewer | Current activity** from the left-hand-side panel of the Admin console. The TPV current activity collection page is displayed. Click on **Start Monitoring** to start logging the current activity of the server you want to monitor, as shown below:

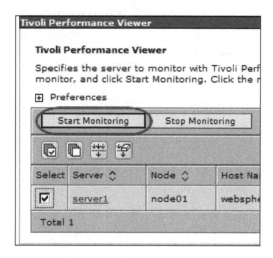

The **Collection Status** column will be updated to **monitoring**.

Click on the server name, in our case it is **server1**, and then the TPV console panel will be displayed, providing a navigation tree on the left and a view of real-time data for the server you have selected. We now can select which parts of the server activity data that we want to view by checking options from the navigation tree. We wish to find out the state of the JBDC connection pools in our server. To do this, check the **JDBC Connection Pools** performance module as shown below and we are be presented with a graph and a table underneath showing the counters which can be added to the graph. The default refresh internal is 30 seconds, so the graph will refresh after every 30 seconds.

The righthand panel contains two sections. The top section is the graph and the table in the bottom section contains the list of possible counters for the currently selected performance modules. Back when we set PMI to be use extended data, it was so that we could see more counters displayed in the left-hand tree than if we had set PMI to basic. For **JDBC Connection Pools**, there are three counters enabled for display viz, **CreateCount**, **CloseCount**, and **AllocateCount**. These counters refer to the number of created connections, how many have been created and closed and how many are currently allocated. If we open a browser to the HR Lister application using the URL `http://<host_name>:9080/hrlister`. We will see that the counters will increase over time. Below is a sample graph before we open any sessions to the HR Lister application.

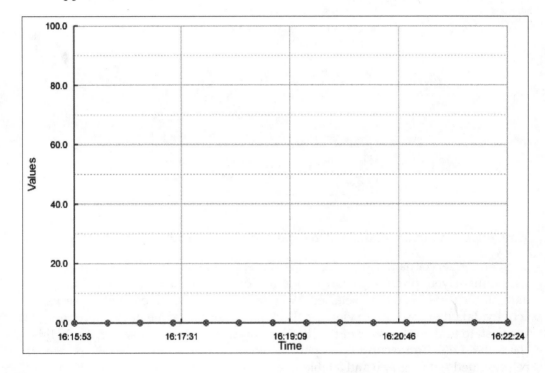

After opening a session to the HR Lister application using a browser, we will see the graph update over time. However, to see the change more clearly, we may need to change the scale of the counters by a factor of 10, so that we can see the single connection more clearly. The image below is the graph updated just over two minutes later.

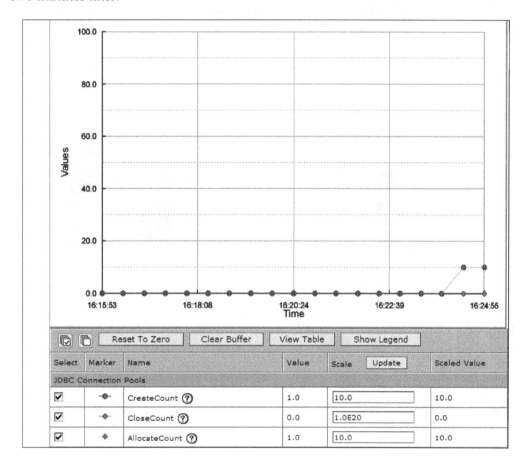

If you now open a second browser session to the same URL, you will see that another connection is established. If you refresh your browser several times, thus making more database calls, thus making more database calls, you will see that TPV shows the counters increasing as more JDBC connections are opened. In our example, we continued and opened four browser sessions to the HR Lister application over a period of a few seconds and the screenshot below shows the allocated count increasing as we opened more sessions, creating more database connections.

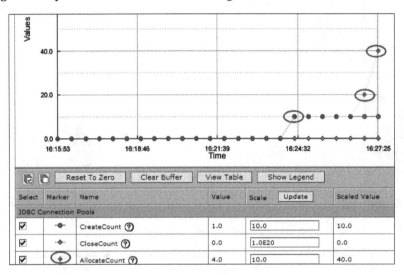

If you click on **Show Legend**, you will see labels appear on the graph for each counter you have chosen to display, as shown below:

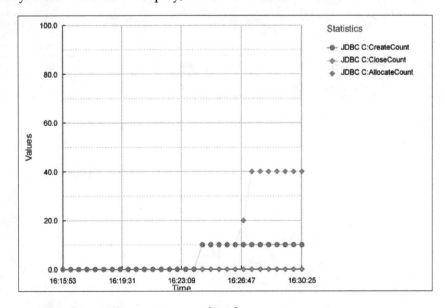

Closing the browser sessions will not necessarily relinquish all the DB connections; this will depend on your code and the underlying DB. When testing a DB connection, you will need to understand what connection timeouts will be for your particular JDBC data source configuration.

We can review the default properties of our data source which we created in Chapter 2. We do this by navigating to **JDBC providers | MyJDBCDriver | Data sources | MyDataSource | Connection pools**. We can see that the **unusedTimeout** field is set to **1800** seconds which specifies the maximum number of seconds that an idle connection can remain in the pool before being discarded by the maintenance thread. This means that if we close all our browser sessions, after 30 minutes the connections in the connection pool will be discarded. Thus, it might take time for your graph to report no connections we don't really want to go into discussing the ins and outs of tuning database connections as it is beyond the scope of this book, but we can see by the simple demonstration that we can use TPV to monitor PMI metrics and can use the intelligence gathered to help us adjust configuration settings for optimal performance.

Before we finish discussing TPV, we must mention that by clicking on the **Start Logging** button at the top of the graph, the counter metrics will be saved to an XML file which can be played back later. You can set the location of the log files by clicking the **Log** link in the **Settings** category in the righthand side navigation panel of the TPV page as shown in the screenshot below:

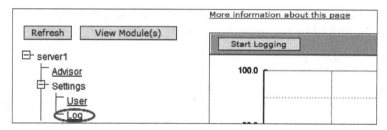

You can set several settings such as duration of logging, maximum file size, how many times the log file will roll over, and even the name for the file.

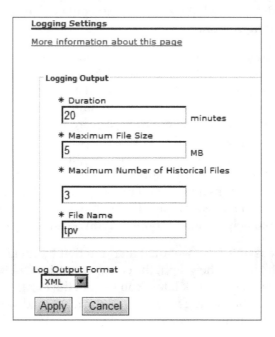

The log files will be saved to the `<was_profile_root>/ logs/tpv` folder and a typical log file would be named as follows:

```
tpv_server1_1238601424024_1.xml
```

To view logged data, navigate to the **Monitoring and Tuning | Performance Viewer** section of the lefthand side panel in the Admin console and click **View logs**. You will then be able to browse for a previously logged XML file and play back the recorded data through the viewer. You can browse the server's file system and look for the XML file you wish to play back as shown below:

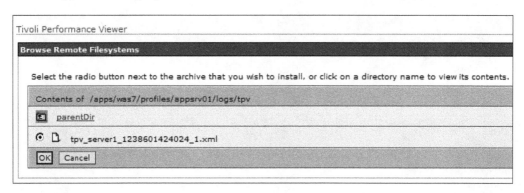

Once you have selected the file you want, you can then select **View Log**, as shown below:

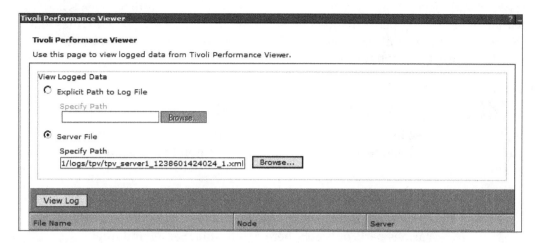

The result of clicking on the **View Log** button is the TPV player, which is shown in the following screenshot:

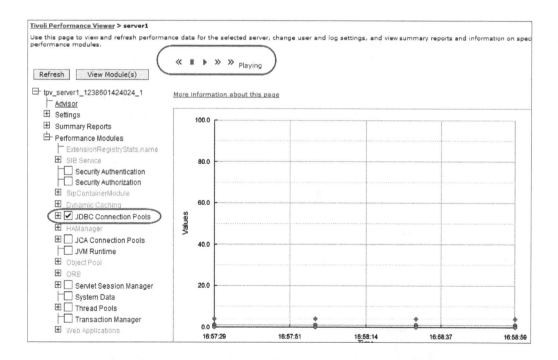

As shown in the preceding screenshot, you can select the counters you wish to review and the graph will display the data by time sequences and by using the forward and reverse buttons, you can review the metrics as required. This is a great feature to use during performance analysis as you can build a log of XML files that can be saved as an audit trail that analysis was done and can serve as a baseline of results of particular configurations.

PMI for external monitoring

If you decide to use third-party tools to monitor WebSphere, then the following list will serve as a quick guide to the PMI you should be monitoring to ensure the health of your system.

- Average response time
  - Response time statistics indicate how much time is spent in various parts of WebSphere Application Server and might quickly indicate where the problem is

- Number of requests (transactions)
  - Enables you to look at how much traffic is processed by WebSphere Application Server, helping you to determine the capacity that you have to manage

- Number of HTTP sessions
  - The number of live HTTP sessions reflects the concurrent usage of your site

- Web server and EJB thread pools
  - Thread pools might constrain performance due to their size

- Database and connection pool size
  - The thread pools setting can be too small or too large, therefore causing performance problems

- Java Virtual Memory (JVM)
  - Use the JVM metric to understand the JVM heap dynamics, including the frequency of garbage collection

- CPU, I/O, System paging
  - CPU, I/O, and paging, to handle the workload capacity

Request metrics

WebSphere Application Sever also provides a request metrics facility that allows you to track the processing time of transactions, and key WAS components. Once enabled, the metrics can be sent to third-party monitoring agents like **Application Response Measurement (ARM)** Agents, and can also be saved to log files.

ARM is an industry-standard API that is used to monitor the availability and performance of applications. This monitoring is done from the perspective of the application itself, so it reflects those units of work (transactions) that are important from the perspective of measuring. We cannot cover how third-party tools like Tivoli which use this information via ARM as it is beyond the scope of this book; however, we can show how to configure WebSphere for products which use ARM.

Once enabled in WebSphere, the request metrics subsystem tracks individual transactions in a given piece or work, that is, a transaction as it is flowing through WebSphere. The information logged can be used to map a picture of what happened during the transaction. This is often used to track timings of individual components when you want to monitor your system is running within performance thresholds and it is also a great way to help find bottlenecks in throughput during performance trouble shooting exercises. Some reasons why metrics are useful are listed below. This is not a comprehensive list; however, it will serve as a guide to why request metrics may be considered important to your WebSphere service.

- Hung transactions
  - The application may be hanging in certain situations and you may wish to monitor when and for how long a transaction hangs.

- Falling transactions
  - You may wish to monitor when key transactions fail which may mean other subsystems have also failed.

- Response times
  - Often an application or service will need to meet a service-level commitment like number of transactions per second.

- Application usage
  - Sometimes application usage may need to be monitored to justify features or provide feedback for improvements and removal of redundant code or processes.

Enabling request metrics

To turn on request metrics, navigate to the **Monitoring and Tuning** section of the lefthand side of the Administrative console and click on the **Request Metrics** link to open the **Request Metrics** configuration page, as shown below:

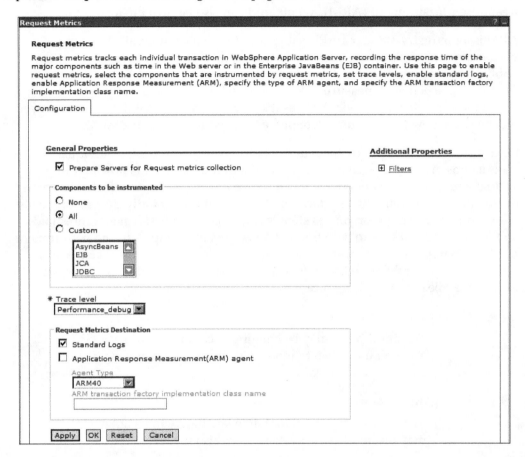

Components to be instrumented

By default, request metrics is enabled. However, there may not be any actual logging of component metrics. You have three options to choose the appropriate components to be measured viz, **None**, **All**, or **Custom**. To enable all request metrics, choose **All** from the **Components to be instrumented** field. You also have a choice to select specific components by selecting **Custom**. The components that can be measured are listed below.

- EJB
- JCA

- JDBC
- JMS
- JNDI
- Portlet
- SIB
- Servlet
- Servlet filter
- WebServices

For our demonstration, we are going to select **All**.

Trace level

The **Trace level** field is used to specify how much trace data to accumulate for a given transaction. Please select **Performance_debug.**

Request metrics destination

There are two possible destinations; you can select them all or just one. As mentioned above, we can allow the request metrics to be sent to an ARM Agent, or a log file or both. For the purpose of our exercise, we are going to send the metrics to the standard log files, which means the metrics will be sent to the SystemOut.log file.

Click on **Apply** and **Save** your reconfiguration and restart the application server.

When the application restarts, you will see extra metrics information written out to the standard JVM logs, for example, SystemOut.log.

Request metrics in SystemOut.log

Once you have enabled request metrics and have restarted your application server, you can then open the HR Lister program. To run the HR Lister program, use the URL mentioned above when we discussed TPV to open the HR Lister application in a browser. Once the application has opened in a browser and generated some log information, we can use the view command on Linux to view the on-disk log file. Use the following commands to view the SystemOut.log file:

```
cd \<was_profile_root>\logs\server1
view ./SystemOutlog
```

Once inside the `view` tool, type `:$` to go to the end of the `SystemOut.log` file, then use CTRL-B to navigate back through the log to look for log entries that contain `PmiRmArmWrapp` which identify request metrics showing up in the log for specific application transactions. To exit `view`, use the `:q!` command to close and exit without saving.

Below is an example of request metrics found in `SystemOut.log` when the HR Lister application has been opened in a browser. The actual numbers are not important in this list below; it is only to show you what kind of data you get when RM is enabled.

Example log messages and meanings

The entry below shows how long it took to get a JDBC connection factory, in this case it was instantaneous as it says 0 milliseconds.

Note: Due to connection pooling, the first connection always takes longer and subsequent connections come form the pool. In this example, the application had previously made a connection so a connection was already open so it re-used an existing connection.

```
[4/3/09 7:41:04:334 BST] 00000028 PmiRmArmWrapp I   PMRM0003I:  pa
rent:ver=1,ip=192.168.0.94,time=1238738901071,pid=8712,reqid=41
19,event=1 - current:ver=1,ip=192.168.0.94,time=1238738901071,p
id=8712,reqid=4120,event=1 type=JDBC detail=javax.resource.spi.
ManagedConnectionFactory.createConnectionFactory(ConnectionManager)
elapsed=0
```

The entry below shows it took a lot longer to actually create a connection to the Oracle Database. In this line, it took 1 millisecond.

```
[4/3/09 7:41:04:346 BST] 00000028 PmiRmArmWrapp I   PMRM0003I:  pa
rent:ver=1,ip=192.168.0.94,time=1238738901071,pid=8712,reqid=41
19,event=1 - current:ver=1,ip=192.168.0.94,time=1238738901071,p
id=8712,reqid=4122,event=1 type=JDBC detail=javax.resource.spi.
ManagedConnection.getConnection(Subject, ConnectionRequestInfo)
elapsed=1
```

The entry below shows that it took 12 ms to run the query to get the list of tables.

```
[4/3/09 7:41:04:361 BST] 00000028 PmiRmArmWrapp I   PMRM0003I:  pa
rent:ver=1,ip=192.168.0.94,time=1238738901071,pid=8712,reqid=41
19,event=1 - current:ver=1,ip=192.168.0.94,time=1238738901071,p
id=8712,reqid=4123,event=1 type=JDBC detail=java.sql.Statement.
executeQuery(String) elapsed=12
```

As you can see above, when request metrics are enabled, there will be request metrics information in the log which is very useful to help you tune performance by analyzing intervals and durations.

Retrieving performance data with PerfServlet

WebSphere provides an EAR file called `PerfServletApp.ear` located in the `<was_root>/installableApps` directory. You can install this application and a servlet contained within the application called PerfServlet allows HTTP access to performance metrics across an entire server. The servlet provides the data in XML format and, since it is served via HTTP, it can be accessed across firewalls. The XML data is provided in an industry format known as the Java Platform, Enterprise Edition (Java EE) 1.4 Performance Data Framework.

To install the PerfServlet, follow the instructions we learned in Chapter 2 and deploy the `PerfServletApp.ear` file. After you have deployed the application, you will need to configure security within the servlet as it has a role which needs to be mapped to users to allow access to the applications. To set security on the PerfServletApp application, you need to navigate to the **Applications | Application Types | WebSphere enterprise applications** link and click to get the list of installed applications. Look for the name of your application (it will be **perfServletApp** if you have not changed the name) and click to enter the applications configuration page. Click on the **Security role to user/group mapping** link to enter the map security roles screen. Select the **monitor** role and click the **Map Users** button as shown next.

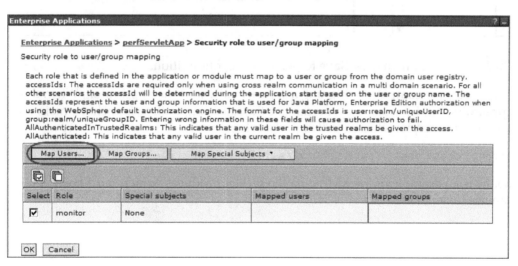

In the **Search and Select Users** section, type **wasadmin** in the **Search string** field and click on the **Search** button. Then, when you see the LDAP name of wasadmin appear, you can click the right arrow to move the wasadmin user to the selected field, as shown below:

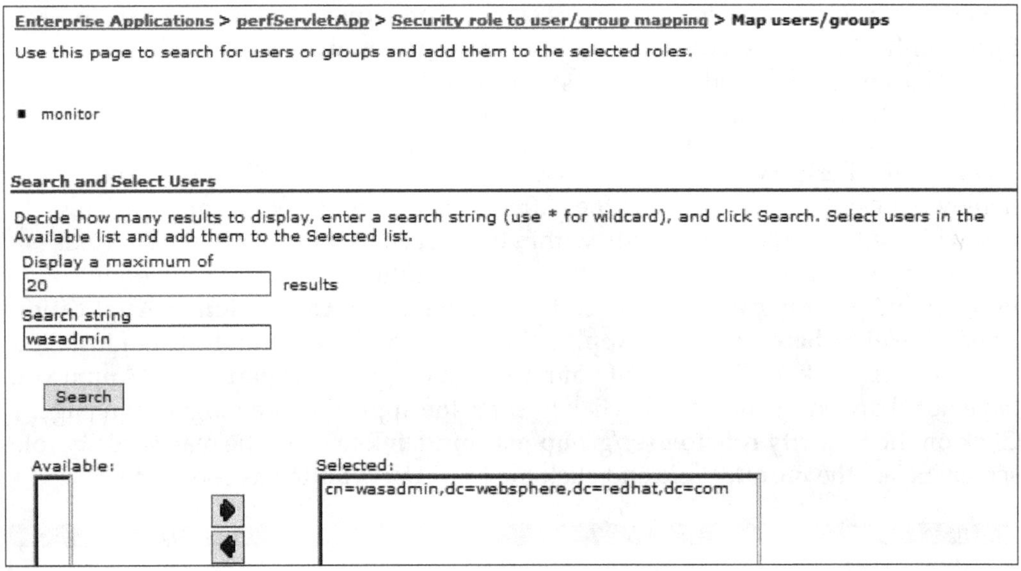

Enterprise Applications > perfServletApp > Security role to user/group mapping > Map users/groups

Use this page to search for users or groups and add them to the selected roles.

■ monitor

Search and Select Users

Decide how many results to display, enter a search string (use * for wildcard), and click Search. Select users in the Available list and add them to the Selected list.

Display a maximum of

20   results

Search string

wasadmin

Search

Available:

Selected:

cn=wasadmin,dc=websphere,dc=redhat,dc=com

Click on **OK** and then click **Save** to persist the configuration.

Once you have competed assigning a security role, start the application. When the application has been started, you can use the following URL to launch the main data presentation servlet which is called perfservlet.

```
http://<host_name>/wasPerfTool/servlet/perfservlet
```

Below is an example of the XML data the servlet produces, which third-party tools can use to get to metrics via HTTP.

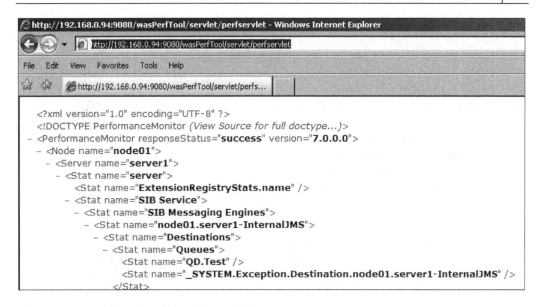

```
<?xml version="1.0" encoding="UTF-8" ?>
<!DOCTYPE PerformanceMonitor (View Source for full doctype...)>
- <PerformanceMonitor responseStatus="success" version="7.0.0.0">
 - <Node name="node01">
   - <Server name="server1">
     - <Stat name="server">
         <Stat name="ExtensionRegistryStats.name" />
       - <Stat name="SIB Service">
         - <Stat name="SIB Messaging Engines">
           - <Stat name="node01.server1-InternalJMS">
             - <Stat name="Destinations">
               - <Stat name="Queues">
                   <Stat name="QD.Test" />
                   <Stat name="_SYSTEM.Exception.Destination.node01.server1-InternalJMS" />
                 </Stat>
```

Dynamic caching

By enabling the dynamic cache service, you can improve performance. The dynamic cache service improves performance by caching the output of servlets, commands, web services, and JavaServer Pages (JSP) files. The dynamic cache service works within the application server JVM, intercepting calls to cacheable objects. For example, it intercepts calls to a servlet and serves the response (Java objects) either from the cache or it caches the object once it has been created allowing the cached version to be called on the next call.

To enable the dynamic cache service, open the Administrative console and click **Servers | Application Servers | server | Container Services | Dynamic cache service** as shown below.

There is a penalty associated with caching, as the first time an object is cached it can take some time to store the object in the cache. During first use, the application might suffer performance degradation, until all objects are cached. It is recommended that during performance-tuning exercises, tests should be performed to determine whether this option offers benefit to application performance and ultimate end-user experience.

JVM tuning

Tuning the application server is recommended as opposed to just sticking with the default values assigned during an application server install. If the heap size is not managed or tuned, you may see the symptoms of poor memory management which can vary from intermittent performance problems to the periodic failure and automatic restarts of the JVM which may not generate a core dump or error. What we can do is set JVM arguments to ensure that Java core dumps are executed when the JVM crashes. A Java core dump is similar to a Linux core dump, which contains processes and state of the OS system; however, a Java core dump only contains the processes and state of the JVM itself. A JVM may crash due to hung threads or other internal JVM issues; it could be faulty code, that is, a bug, or many other scenarios like deadlocked code. A Java core dump is essentially a set of Java stack traces at the moment the error occurs, or if a core dump is manually issued. We cannot cover all the scenarios which can cause a JVM crash, but we can show you some configurations to help you catch debug information which you can use in your investigations to find the root cause of a JVM crash. If we set the JVM to core dump, we will get a core dump file which we can review. If the JVM crashed because it did not have enough memory, the core dump would say so. It is important that every administrator knows how to use settings and debug the resulting core dump file. First, we will look at how to generate a Java core dump, and then we will look at how to analyze core dumps.

JVM core and heap dumps

There are several ways in which core dumps can be initiated. Core dumps and heap dumps can be generated by the JVM when it gets to a point where the JVM crashes; for example, when a memory leak is detected and heap dumps are generated. However, we can also set up the JVM to generate core and heap dumps on request, a feature of JVMs.

Requesting a Java core dump using Jython

There are several ways to generate core dumps. First, we will create a simple Jython script which we can run to generate Java core dump information.

1. Create a file on your Linux system called `threadDump.py` and paste in the following code:

    ```
    jvmObject = AdminControl.completeObjectName("type=JVM,process=s
    erver1,*" )

    AdminControl.invoke(jvmObject, "dumpThreads" )
    ```

2. Save the file and run the file using the following command:

```
<was_profile_root>/wsadmin.sh -lang jython -f <path_to_file>/
threadDump.py
```

The result of running this Jython script is shown in the screenshot below:

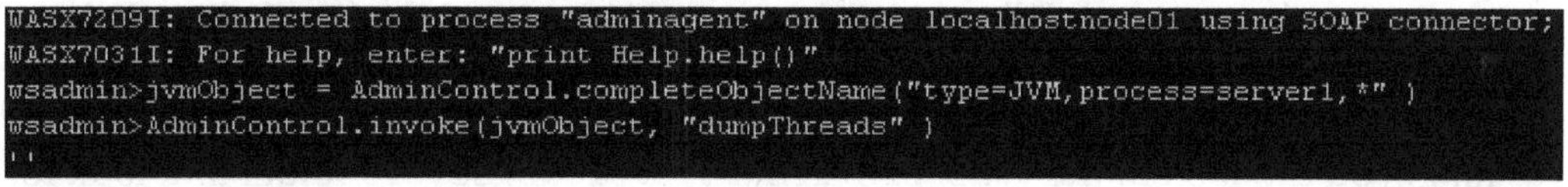

```
WASX7209I: Connected to process "adminagent" on node localhostnode01 using SOAP connector;
WASX7031I: For help, enter: "print Help.help()"
wsadmin>jvmObject = AdminControl.completeObjectName("type=JVM,process=server1,*" )
wsadmin>AdminControl.invoke(jvmObject, "dumpThreads" )
```

As we can see in the screenshot above, a thread core dump file with thread information has been requested. The actual core dump will be located in the <was_profile_root> directory and will be named something similar to the following:

```
javacore.20090403.221606.8712.0001.txt
```

Requesting a heap dump using Jython

By changing the script to the following, we can get the heap dump instead:

```
jvmObject = AdminControl.completeObjectName("type=JVM,process=serv
er1,*" )
AdminControl.invoke(jvmObject, "generateHeapDump" )
```

The result of running this Jython script is shown in the screenshot below:

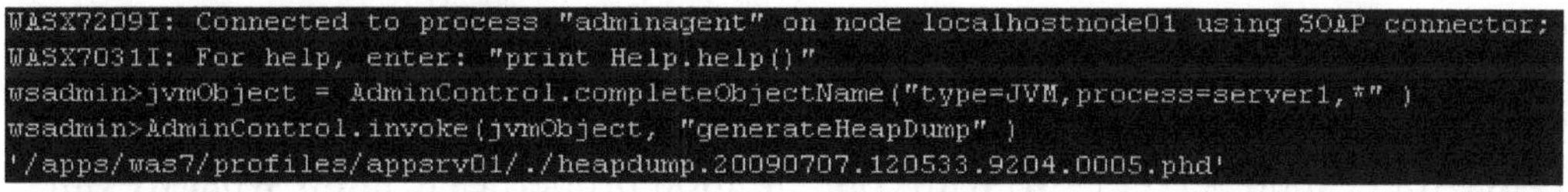

```
WASX7209I: Connected to process "adminagent" on node localhostnode01 using SOAP connector;
WASX7031I: For help, enter: "print Help.help()"
wsadmin>jvmObject = AdminControl.completeObjectName("type=JVM,process=server1,*" )
wsadmin>AdminControl.invoke(jvmObject, "generateHeapDump" )
'/apps/was7/profiles/appsrv01/./heapdump.20090707.120533.9204.0005.phd'
```

The actual heap dump will be located in the <was_profile_root> directory and will be named something similar to the following:
```
heapdump.20090403.222239.8712.0002.phd
```

Requesting a Java core dump using the kill command

We can also use the Linux `kill` command to request a core dump. We can send a signal called SIGQUIT by using the command line to send a user-signalled trigger to generate various dumps. What we are going to do is signal the WebSphere JVM to generate a Java core dump. Before generating a core dump, we need to know the Linux process id of our WebSphere server. If your application server **server1** is running, you can look in the `<was_profile_root>/logs/sever1` folder and look for a file called `server1.pid`. You can then type the following command to see what is in the file:

```
cat <was_profile_root>/logs/server/server1.pid
```

The result will show the WAS process id. We can then use the following command to send a SIGQUIT signal to the JVM to request a core dump.

```
kill -3 <pid>
```

The result will be a core dump file similar the Java core file generate by the Jython `dumpThreads` command used in the Jython example above.

JVM-triggered heap dump

By default, heap dumps cannot be requested from the JVM by using `kill -3` option; they only occur during explicit generation which is often due to situations when the Java heap is exhausted (an OutOfMemory condition is encountered and the resulting exception is not caught or handled by the application) and the JVM core dumps. It is possible to set up a JVM to allow for triggered heap dumps. WebSphere Application Servers are essentially IBM Java Virtual Machines and so we can configure the IBM JVM (Application Server JVM) with configuration properties to allow what we call **user signal heap dump generation**. To generate the Java core dump, heap dump, system core dump and a snap dump at user signal, the following options must be supplied to JVM. The following table is a list of some valid custom JVM properties which can be set for an Application Server JVM.

Custom JVM property	Value
IBM_HEAP_DUMP	<any_value>

When the Java heap OutOfMemory condition is encountered and the resulting exception is not caught or handled by the application, JVM-triggered generation is enabled by default, as are Heapdumps that are generated by other programming methods. To enable signal-based Heapdumps, set the IBM_HEAPDUMP or IBM_HEAP_DUMP environment variable to any value.

| IBM_HEAPDUMPDIR | <user_defined_path> |

The JVM checks each of the following locations for existence and write-permission, then stores the Heapdump in the first one that is available.

- The location that is specified by the IBM_HEAPDUMPDIR environment variable, if set.

- The current working directory of the JVM processes .

- The location that is specified by the TMPDIR environment variable, if set.

- The /tmp directory (X:\tmp for Windows, where X is the current working drive).

| IBM_HEAPDUMP_OUTOFMEMORY | True / False |

IBM_JAVADUMP_OUTOFMEMORY

By default, you get Heapdumps only when no more heap space is available; you do not get Heapdumps in crashes or through a signal to the JVM. You can disable this feature, and a similar one for Javadumps, by using IBM_HEAPDUMP_OUTOFMEMORY=FALSE and IBM_JAVADUMP_OUTOFMEMORY=FALSE respectively.

| IBM_JAVA_HEAPDUMP_TXT | <any_value> |

The generated Heapdump is by default in the binary, platform-independent, phd format, which can be examined using the available. However, it is sometimes useful to have an immediately readable view of the heap.

Custom JVM property	Value
IBM_JAVACOREDIR	<user_defined_path>

The JVM checks each of the following locations for existence and write-permission, and stores the Javadump in the first one available. Note that you must have enough free disk space (possibly up to 2.5 MB) for the Javadump file to be written correctly.

- The location specified by the IBM_JAVACOREDIR environment variable, if set.
- The current working directory of the JVM processes.
- The location specified by the TMPDIR environment variable, if set.
- The /tmp directory or, on Windows, C:\temp.
- If the Javadump cannot be stored in any of the above, it is put to STDERR.

For more information on JVM settings, you can refer to the IBM Developer Kit and Runtime Environment, Java 2 Technology Edition guides. An example guide can be found at the following URL:

http://publib.boulder.ibm.com/infocenter/javasdk/v1r4m2/index.jsp.

 It is also possible to turn off core dumps so the JVM does not write our dump files. To do this, you can set the custom properties that have Boolean options to false as opposed to true.

To demonstrate adding custom to the above JVM properties, we are going to set all of the above custom JVM properties manually. However, they could also be programmed via a Jython script. To add a JVM custom property, navigate to the servers view in the Admin console; for example, **Servers | Server Types | WebSphere application servers** and click on **server1**. Once you are in the server's main configuration page, navigate to the **Server Infrastructure** section and click **Process definition** from the **Java and Process Management** category, which will take you to the server configuration page where you can click on **Java Virtual Machine** as shown in the following screenshot:

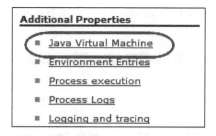

When you enter the Java Virtual Machine configuration page, you can click on the **Custom properties** link in the **Additional Properties** section, as shown below.

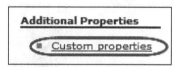

We can now add our custom JVM properties by clicking **New** and adding the properties one by one, as shown below.

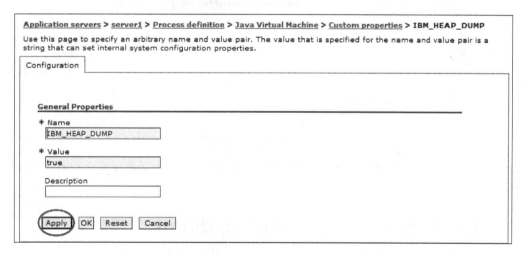

When you have added the custom properties, click **Save** to retain your changes, as shown below.

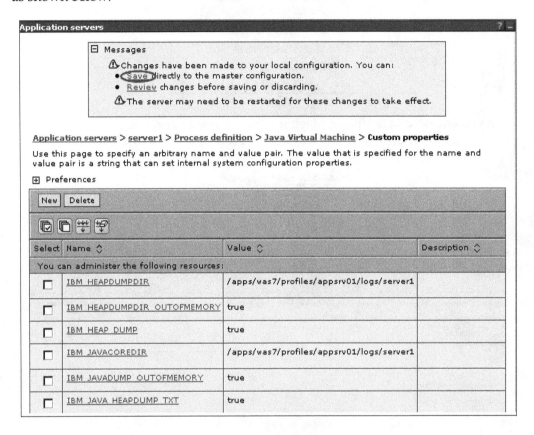

Once you have saved the new custom JVM properties, restart the application server for the properties to take effect.

Analysing a Java core (thread) dump

In this section, we are going to use a custom EAR file called `ThreadLock.ear`. The ThreadLock application contains a single servlet which we can call to create a thread lock. Once we have triggered a thread lock situation, we can then use `kill -3` to generate a Java core (thread) dump and demonstrate the usefulness of the free IBM monitor dump analyzer tool to diagnose the problem.

Download the `ThreadLock.ear` file from `http://www.packtpub.com` and manually deploy the application. The default to call the thread locking servlet will be as follows:

```
http://<host_name>:9080/threadlocker/DoThreadLock
```

Once the servlet has been loaded, it will report two locks which will cause a thread deadlock situation. After the servlet has been loaded, you can use `kill -3 <pid>` to tell the WAS JVM to generate a Java core (thread) dump, which we will analyze with the IBM tool.

IBM Thread and Monitor Dump Analyzer for Java

IBM provides a tool called IBM Thread and Monitor Dump Analyzer for Java (JCA) which allows you to analyze core dump files. You can download the tool from the IBM alpha works web site at the following URL:

`http://www.alphaworks.ibm.com/tech/jca/download.`

 Helpful hint: A Java thread dump is one of the traces/dumps that the JVM provides to help diagnosis of a hang, deadlock, that is, a contention issue. A resulting thread dump contains diagnostic information related to the JVM and the Java application captured at a point during runtime execution.

Installing the JCA tool

To install the JCA tool, follow the instruction as listed on the download page mentioned above. Essentially, all you have to do is unzip the ZIP file into an appropriate location like `C:\temp`. Ensure that you have JRE installed and listed in the Windows path, as the application is a Java application and requires JRE to run.

Generate a Java core dump to view the thread lock

If you have not already deployed the ThreadLock application to WebSphere, do so using the instructions mentioned previously in the *Analysing a Java core (thread) dump* section above. When you have loaded the servlet and created the thread lock situation, you can generate a thread dump using the Jython code as discussed in the *Requesting a Java core dump* section above. Once the core dump has been requested, run the JCA tool, which is shown below, to view the thread dump. Download the generated thread dump to your Windows desktop machine into the `C:\temp` folder for analysis.

Run the JCA tool by double-clicking on the `jca37.jar` (or later version) file and once loaded, you can open the generated thread dump file as shown in the image below:

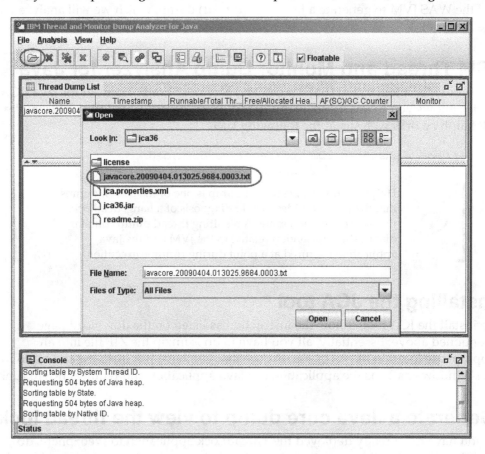

Once the thread dump has been loaded, you can double-click on an actual thread dump entry and an information window will load detailing the thread dump, as shown below:

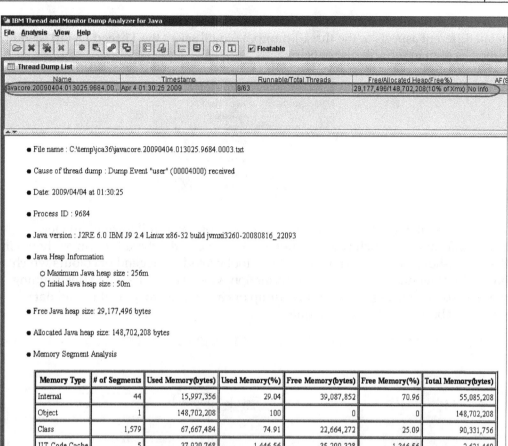

Memory Segment Analysis

By using the **Analysis** menu option, you can open separate windows which detail different aspects of the thread dump. We will select the **Thread Detail** menu option as seen in the screenshot below:

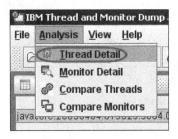

A new thread detail window will appear which you can scroll through to view thread information which was generated at the time of the thread dump as shown in the screenshot below. You can see that this tool provides a legend of colours which highlight different types of thread information which is very useful in determining the cause of a system-generated core dump or can be used to look at thread data which has been dumped upon request.

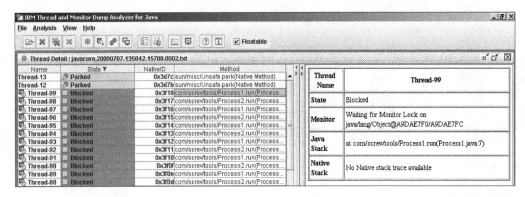

In the example above, threads have been sorted by state. What we can see is that there are many threads which have been blocked. What we can do is click on a particular thread and find out what thread is blocking the current selected thread.

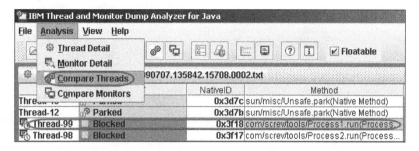

In our example, we identified **Thread-99**, as shown in the screenshot above, and then we selected **Compare Threads** from the **Analysis** menu. We chose to sort the Thread column as shown below to find Thread-99. Once **Thread-99** was located, we then clicked on the **Thread-99** line in the left-hand panel and thread information was loaded into the right-hand panel, as shown below.

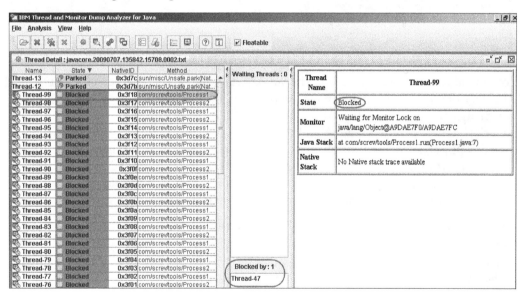

In the screenshot above, we can see that **Thread-99** is blocked by **Thread-47**. If we locate **Thread-47** and click on the thread row in the left-hand-side panel, we can see that Java stack information has been displayed in the right-hand panel, as shown below.

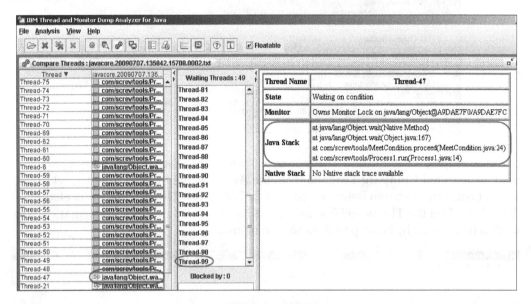

Looking at the Java stack trace for Thread-47, as shown above, we can see that the code has a Java object which is most probably in a mutual lock with other threads which also have a lock on the same object, and so these threads are in a deadlock situation. To fully understand what the problem is, you would then speak to a Java developer, and using the stack trace above, you can see that it is most probably due to an error related to code in either the `com.screv.tool.MeetCondition` or `com.screv.tools.Process1.class` files and so the developer could use this information to help track down the root cause in the actual code.

We cannot give thread dumps the full attention they deserve because they are beyond the scope for this book. However, using this tool is very simple and you can see by the basic example above that this tool from IBM is very useful in problem determination when your JVM unrepentantly core dumps.

Other analysis tools

There are many more tools available to help you with troubleshooting and problem analysis. Below is a table of tools which IBM makes available on `http://www.alphaworks.ibm.com`.

Tool	Description and download URL
Web Services Validation Tool for WSDL and SOAP	An analysis tool for Web services artifacts, including WSDL and SOAP messages. Download URL: `http://www.alphaworks.ibm.com/tech/wsvt`

HeapAnalyzer	A graphical tool for discovering possible Java heap leaks.
	
	Download URL:
	
	`http://www.alphaworks.ibm.com/tech/`
	`heapanalyzer`

IBM Pattern Modelling and Analysis Tool for Java Garbage Collector	A tool that parses verbose GC trace, analyzes Java heap usage, and recommends key configurations based on pattern modelling of Java heap usage. Download URL: `http://www.alphaworks.ibm.com/tech/pmat`
IBM Trace and Request Analyzer for WebSphere Application Server	A tool that detects delays and hangs in WebSphere(R) trace and HTTP plug-in trace. Download URL: `http://www.alphaworks.ibm.com/tech/tra`
IBM Web Server Plug-in Analyzer for WebSphere Application Server	A tool that detects improper or ill-advised WebSphere Application Server plug-in configurations and corresponding HTTP request/response failures. Download URL: `http://www.alphaworks.ibm.com/tech/wspa`
Database Connection Pool Analyzer for IBM WebSphere Application Server	A tool that analyzes problems in JDBC connection pools on WebSphere Application Server. Download URL: `http://www.alphaworks.ibm.com/tech/jcp`
Performance Analysis Tool for Java	A tool that automatically detects Java threads that consume unanticipated large amounts of system resources. Download URL: `http://www.alphaworks.ibm.com/tech/pat4j`
Processor Time Analysis Tool for Linux	A tool to detect Java threads that consume most of the processor resources on Linux. Download URL: `http://www.alphaworks.ibm.com/tech/ptat`

Setting the initial and maximum heap sizes

By default, an application server will take as much memory as it needs. A good tip to know is that you should start up your application with the minimum heap size that it needs to function. When the application starts up, the Garbage Collector will often run efficiently due to the heap being small. The first time the Garbage Collector runs it will become more efficient due to the heap initially being small. By implementing a maximum heap size, you limit the amount of memory the application can take. If you set the minimum heap size to be too large, the heap is most likely to be very fragmented when a need to do a heap compaction occurs. Compacting the heap is a very expensive operation, so it is important to help prevent heap fragmentation to maximize your JVM performance.

Tuning your heap size

Remember that we covered JVM settings in Chapter 5 where we learned we can use the Administration console to change the JVM Initial heap size and Maximum heap size using the field in the JVM configuration page. It is important to realize that these settings are in fact really just JVM arguments called –Xms and –Xmx respectively. To tune JVM memory, review the following guide.

- Start with a small heap. Set -Xms far lower than -Xmx.

- The default -Xms size is 256MB in WebSphere and since it is a low value it is a good starting point.

- To tune your JVM memory, increase the maximum heap size (-Xmx) over time to see how the application behaves.

- You can use TPV to monitor the JVM memory usage and by using verbose garbage collection settings you can monitor the JVM memory to help in your tuning.

Helpful hint: Note that the tuning recommendations above might not avoid fragmentation in all cases. It is recommended that you use Google to research JVMs to understand what other experts do to tune JVMs. IBM also offers advice in the WebSphere Application Server, Version 7.0 Information Center located at the following URL:

http://publib.boulder.ibm.com/infocenter/wasinfo/v7r0/index.jsp.

Summary

Often WebSphere administrators are asked questions like **what is the best configuration for performance and tracking so WebSphere and the applications installed within are tuned to perform, along with an optimal configuration?** The answer to this question is much like the classic answer **how long is a piece of a string**. However, using the tools and options explained in this chapter you will be able to apply different techniques by using the facilities provided by the administrative console, so you can, over time, tune your system for best performance. TPV can be used to watch an application during runtime, and along with request metrics, you can see what is happening and measure transaction durations so that you can create baselines which can be used to compare the best settings required for each situation. Once you have found key areas where there is a degradation in a particular component, you can then tune that component by altering WAS settings which influence the underlying JVM, whether it be by allowing more threads, more memory, better connection pooling, etc. This subject is a hands-on subject, not a theoretical exercise. You need to ensure that your applications go through performance testing, where you test your applications against known configurations and which allow you to determine the best configuration for your applications. It is important to realize that performance tuning involves a triangular relationship between the following three activities:

- Measuring system performance and collecting performance data
- Locating a bottleneck
- Eliminating a bottleneck

Enterprise application architecture can be challenging on most days. Often application development loses sight of the bottom-line that applications need to perform. Performance and response times are critical factors to the real-world success of application deployment. By using the tools provided by WebSphere Application Server, you can help developers ensure that applications and WebSphere are tuned for best performance.

8
Administrative Features

WebSphere 7 comes with a new feature called the administrative agent, which provides a single interface to administer multiple standalone application servers. The administrative agent can manage multiple nodes (an application server which is federated into a WebSphere cell is called a node) and provides a common Administrative console to administer the nodes, thus reducing the need to have separate Administrative consoles for each application server. In this chapter, we will also cover IBM HTTP Server and the WebSphere plugin. The plugin allows **IBM HTTP Server (IHS)** to be used in web application architecture designs where you may want server static content to be served by the web server and requests for dynamic context, such as servlets, to route to the application server.

In this chapter, we will cover the following topics:

- Administration agent
- Registration of nodes
- De-registration of nodes
- IBM HTTP Server (IHS)
- WebSphere plug-in

The administrative agent

In WebSphere 7, you can use the administrative agent to remotely install applications on application servers, change application server configurations, stop and restart application servers, and create additional application servers from a single Administrative console. This is a similar concept to the approach that WebSphere 7 Network Deployment (ND) takes, however, WebSphere 7 provides some of the some of the WebSphere ND administrative features without the cost and complexity associated with WebSphere ND.

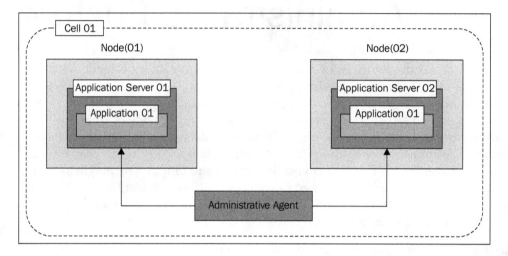

Before we continue, we will need to reconfigure our current WebSphere installation to create an administration agent profile and another application server profile. Then, we will be able to use a single Administrative console to manage two application servers.

Before we can demonstrate the administrative agent, we need to complete the following actions:

- Create a management profile for the administrative agent
- Use the `registerNode` command to register at least one application server node with the administrative agent

Creating an administration profile

Just like we created an application server profile in Chapter 1, we have two options here: we can either install manually using the graphical installer, or we can use a response file. To ensure you grasp the concepts of the confirmation process, we are going to use the manual method.

Profile Management Tool

As in Chapter 1, we are going to use the Profile Management Tool (PMT) to create our profiles.

To start the PMT, `ssh2` to your Linux box and navigate to the following folder:

```
<was_root>\bin\ProfileManagement
```

Ensure that you have a Xming running so that the X-Windows-based graphical installer will display. Remember, you can refer to Chapter 1 for instructions on how to use Xming with puTTy.

Type the following command:

```
./pmt.sh
```

The installer will load. Click on the **Launch Profile Management Tool** button, as shown below.

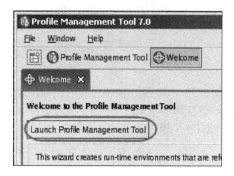

You will notice our current application server profile, which we created in Chapter 1, as shown below.

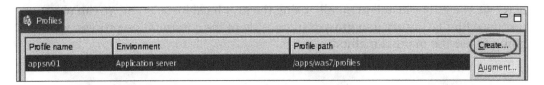

What we are going to do now is create a new administrative agent profile. Click on the **Create** button to start the creation of the new profile. Select **Management** from the list of profile types as seen below and click **Next**. On the next screen, click **Advanced Profile Creation**, which will allow us to specify our own values for the following wizards steps. Then, click **Next** to proceed to the next screen. On the next screen, you will be asked if you wish to install an Administrative console; we are going to accept the default as shown below:

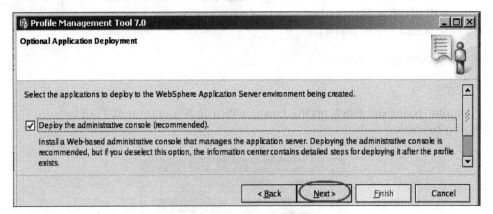

Click **Next** to continue to the **Profile Name and Location** screen. Type **adminagent01** in the **Profile name** field and type **/apps/was7/profiles/adminagent01** in the **Profile directory** field, as shown in the following screenshot:

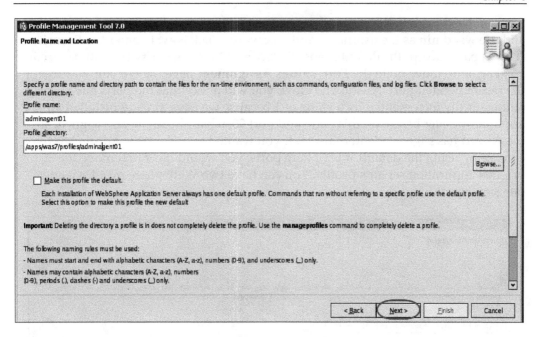

On the next screen, you will be given the opportunity to change the cell and node names. We are going to leave the defaults as shown below.

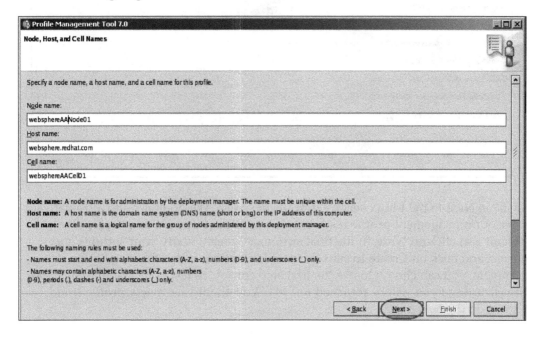

Click on **Next** to go to the security pages. We will turn on administrative security and use **wsadmin** as the username and password. Click **Next** to enter the **Security (Part 1)** page, accept the defaults, and click **Next**. On the **Security (Part 2)** page, click **Next** again to move on to the **Port Values Assignment** page, where you will accept the recommended port. As shown below, you will notice that the ports have been automatically incremented by a value of 1 because we have already installed an application sever before on this node and port **9060** has already been assigned, so the wizard has suggested alternatives. If you wanted to make your Administrative console by using the default WebSphere ports, you would have to remove the original application server's profile. You can have two WebSphere profiles using one single port.

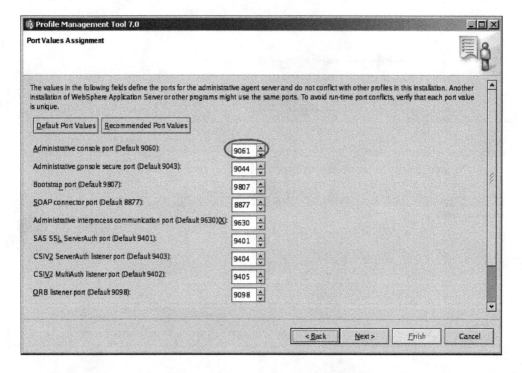

Click on **Next** to the **Linux service definition** screen. We don't need to automatically have our management profile restarted on server boot-up so we can accept the default and click on **Next**. In the final summary screen, verify your settings are correct and click on **Create** to start the profile creation. When the installation is complete, you can choose to use the first step console to test your installation. Close the wizardand you will be returned to PMT. You should see a new profile listed, shown on the next page.

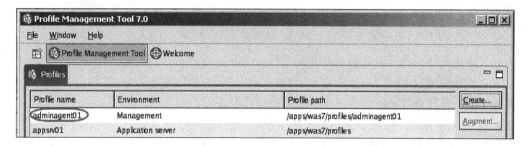

 You may notice that our application sever shown in the screenshot above is stored directly in the profiles folder. When you start to use the administrative agent, it is recommended that you use a separate folder for each profile so that you can clearly identify them at the file-system level and navigate between them.

Close the PMT tool.

Starting the administrative agent

To start the administrative agent, navigate to the following folder:

`<was_root>/profiles/adminagent01/bin`

Then type the following command:

`./startServer.sh adminagent`

You can also stop the administrative agent by using the following command:

`./stopServer.sh adminagent`

One the administrative agent (**adminagent**) has started, we can log in to the console of the adminagent. The URL for the adminagent's console will be:

`http://<host_name>:9061/ibm/console`

 If you find you cannot log in to the console, it's because you need to adjust your firewall settings to allow ports 9061 and 9044. 9061 will be the non-secure HTTP port for the admin console of the admin agent, and port 9044 will be the secure HTTPs port. If you decided to use Red Hat, then you can run the `/usr/bin/setup` command to add the appropriate ports to our firewall configuration.

If you access the non-secure 9061 port, the console will redirect you to the secure URL, as follows: `https://<host_name>:9044/ibm/console/logon.jsp`.

Log in to the console using **wasadmin** as your username and password.

Administrative agent console

When you log in to the admin console of the administrative agent, you will notice that it is similar to the admin console for an application server. There are fewer options available, however. The way the adminagent console works is that you can federate (register) nodes (standalone application server profiles) to be administered from a central interface. We will briefly look at the **Administrative agent** section. Navigate to the **System administration section** of the lefthand side main navigation panel and click **Administrative agent**, as shown below.

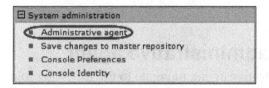

The **Administrative agent** page is very similar to that of a standalone application server configuration page. Here, you can view ports information, and JVM settings pertaining to the actual administration agent itself.

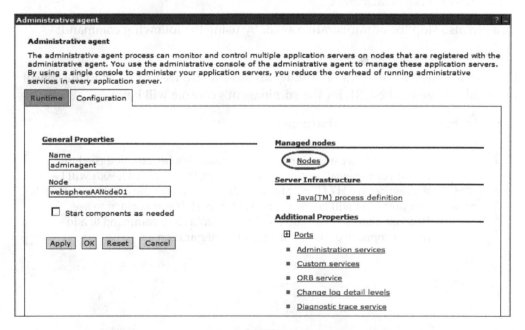

Click on the **Nodes** link in the **Managed Nodes** section to view the nodes which have been federated into the cell for administration. As shown below, you can see that we have not yet federated any application server nodes.

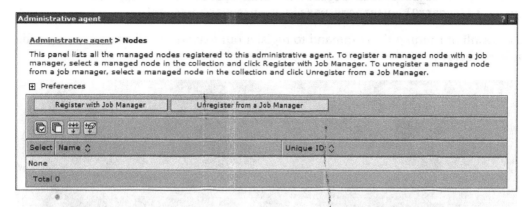

Registering an application server node

To register nodes to be administered centrally by the admin agent, we need to go to the application server profile which we created in Chapter 1 and run the `<admin_ profile_root>registerNode.sh` command. An example path for the admin agents profile root would be something like `/apps/was7/profiles/adminagent01/bin`.

The syntax of `regsiterNode.sh` is as follows:

```
Usage: registerNode -profilePath <path to the base profile to be
registered>
          [-host <adminagent host>] [-connType <SOAP | RMI | JSR160RMI |
IPC>]
          [-port <adminagent JMX port>] [-name <managed node name>]
          [-openConnectors <SOAP,IPC,...>] [-username <adminagent user
name>]
          [-password <adminagent password>] [-nodeusername <base node
user
          name>] [-nodepassword <base node password>] [-profileName
          <adminagent profile name>] [-portsFile <jmx ports filename>]
          [-trace] [-help]
```

To register our application server and federate into the admin agent's cell, type the following command:

```
<admin_profile_root>/bin/registerNode.sh -profilePath /apps/was7/
profiles/appsrv01 -username wasadmin -password wasadmin
```

The result of running the command to register our existing application server profile is listed below:

```
[root@localhost bin]#
[root@localhost bin]#
[root@localhost bin]# /apps/was7/profiles/adminagent01/bin/registerNode.sh -profilePath /apps/was7/profiles/appsrv01 -username
 wasadmin -password wasadmin
ADMU0116I: Tool information is being logged in file
           /apps/was7/profiles/adminagent01/logs/registerNode.log
ADMU0128I: Starting tool with the adminagent01 profile
ADMU8053I: Successfully connected to AdminAgent Server: localhost:8877
ADMU8002I: Exchanging signers between adminagent and node with path
           /apps/was7/profiles/appsrv01
ADMU8007I: Exchanged signers successfully.
ADMU0505I: Servers found in configuration:
ADMU0506I: Server name: server1
ADMU2010I: Stopping all server processes for node localhostnode01
ADMU0512I: Server server1 cannot be reached. It appears to be stopped.
ADMU8010I: Begin registration of Application Server with path
           /apps/was7/profiles/appsrv01
ADMU0024I: Deleting the old backup directory.
ADMU8004I: Backing up the original config directory of the node will be
           registered.
ADMU8037I: Backing up the original wsadmin.properties file of the node will be
           registered.
ADMU8036I: Registering the node with an AdminAgent.
ADMU8042I: Node has been successfully registered.
ADMU8040I: The administrative agent is initializing the administrative
           subsystem for the registered node.
ADMU8014I: The administrative subsystem for registered node has been
           successfully initialized.
ADMU8041I: The administrative agent is starting the administrative subsystem
           for the registered node.
ADMU8015I: The administrative subsystem for registered node has been
           successfully started.
ADMU8012I: Application Server with path /apps/was7/profiles/appsrv01 has been
           successfully registered.
```

Now that we have successfully registered the application server defined by the appsrv01 profile which contains our JVM called **server1**, we now need to restart the admin agent server's profile and then log back in to the admin agent's admin console.

Type the following commands to bounce the admin agent.

```
./stopServer.sh adminagent
```

```
./startServer.sh adminagent
```

If Xming is running, you will be presented with an X Windows popup like the one below:

The prompt as shown above is because the `soap.client.props` file has not been set with the new security details since we created the admin agent's profile. Refer to Chapter 3 to learn how to edit the `soap.client.props` file to stop the security prompt occurring during server starting and stopping. If X Windows is not running, you may also get an error, so what you can do is pass the `-username` and `-password` options via the command line, for example, `./stopServer.sh adminagent -username wasadmin -password wasadmin`.

Once the admin agent server has restarted, then log back in to the console using the following URL:

```
https://<host_name>:9044/ibm/console/
```

You will now see that the login page of the admin console has changed, as shown below:

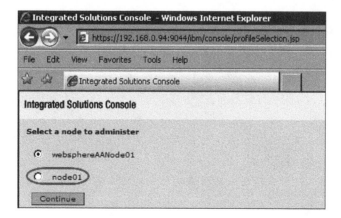

You will notice that we now have two nodes. The first node is the new admin agent node that we created earlier, and **node01** is the node name of our application server, which we created in Chapter 1.

It is now time to suggest that naming conventions be used in your use of the admin agent, so that you can clearly see at a glance which profile is being administered.

Select **node01** for the **Select a node to administer** radio options and click on **Continue**. You will be presented with a login screen to log in to the application server's admin console. It is now important to note that you can now start and stop your application server and still maintain access to an administrative console. Since the application server is now registered with the admin agent, the application is no longer connected to the admin console. The application servers admin console is now de-coupled from the application server. You can no longer log in to the application server's admin console directly. At any time, you can also de-register the application server from the admin agent by using the ./ deregisterNode.sh command found in the <agent_profile_root>/bin directory.

Using the administration agent is a very powerful administration feature of WebSphere 7. We will now create a second application server profile so we demonstrate how to administer two application servers independently of each other, using the same common administration console.

Creating a second application server node

Now, we are using the administration agent and so we can register as many application server profiles we like and administer them all from a common interface. We will now create a new application server profile using PMT.

Navigate to the <was_root>/bin/ ProfileManagement folder. Ensure that you have sarted Xming, and type the following command:

```
./pmt.sh
```

Create another profile called **appsrv02** by selecting **Application server** from the create profile wizard, as shown below.

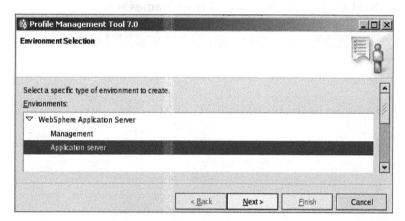

Click **Next** and select the **Advanced profile creation** option when asked. Then click **Next** again to enter the **Optional Application Deployment** screen. On this screen, as shown below, please make sure that all radio options are deselected. We do not need sample applications. We also don't want the default application at this stage and we don't require an admin console as we will be registering this application server with the admin agent.

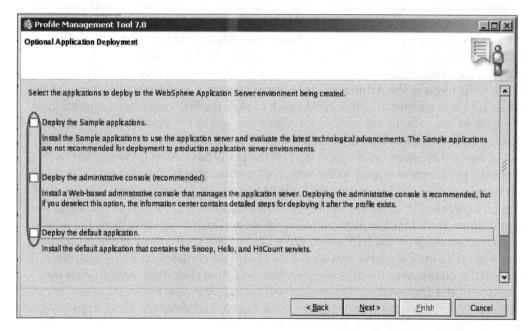

Click on **Next** to go to the **Profile and Location** screen. Type **appsrv02** in the **Profile name** field and type **<was_root>/profiles/appsrv02** in the **Profile location** field and then click on **Next** to go to the **Nodes and Host Names** screen.

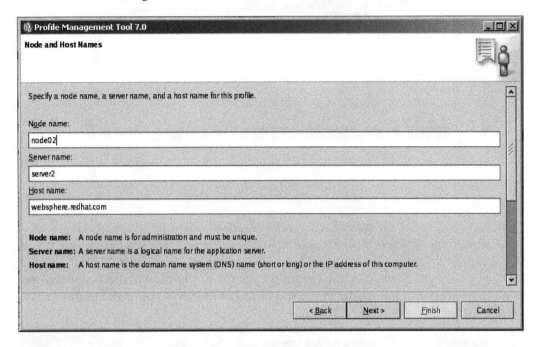

As shown above, type **node02** in the **Node name** field and type **server2** for the **Server name**. The **Host name field** will automatically be filled in with the <host_name> you entered last time you used the PMT and you can change this as required. Click **Next** to go to the **Administrative Security** screen and enter **wasadmin** as the username and password. Click **Next** twice to skip the SSL certificate generation as we wish to use self-signed certificates. Once you get to the **Port Values Assignment** screen, you will notice that the admin console ports are grayed out as we are not using them. Also note, once again, that all the ports have been incremented by 1 from the port numbers used in the appsrv01 profile, that is, the server1 JVM. Click on **Next** and skip the **Linux service definition** page. You will be presented with a screen to create a Web Server definition. If we had IBM HTTP Server installed, we could allow the wizard to automatically create a Web Server definition; the admin agent can administer the IHS sever. We will skip this section as we will be creating this manually once we have installed IBM HTTP Server later on in the chapter. Click on **Next** to continue to the summary screen, and then click on **Create** to start the creation of the **appsrv02** profile, which will contain the new application server called server2. When the wizard is complete, click **Finish** and close the **First steps** console window. In the PMT screen, you will now see that there are three profiles listed, as shown in the following screenshot:

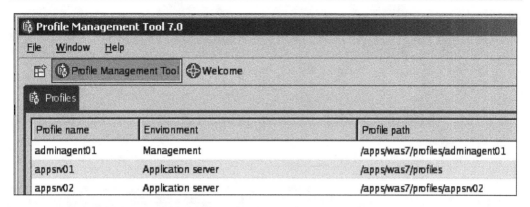

You can now close the PMT.

We now have to register the new profile with the admin agent. Type the following command to register the **appsrv02** profile:

```
<admin_profile_root>/bin/registerNode.sh -profilePath /apps/was7/
profiles/appsrv02 -username wasadmin -password wasadmin
```

Once the registration has finished, restart the admin agent using the stop and start commands which we learned earlier. When you next log in to the admin agent console, you will see that there are now two servers you can administer, as shown below.

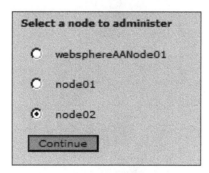

Select **node02** from the **Select a node to administer**, log in using **wasadmin** as the username and password and navigate to the **Servers | Server Types** section and click **WebSphere application servers**. You can now start server2 by selecting **server2** from the list and clicking **Start**, as shown below.

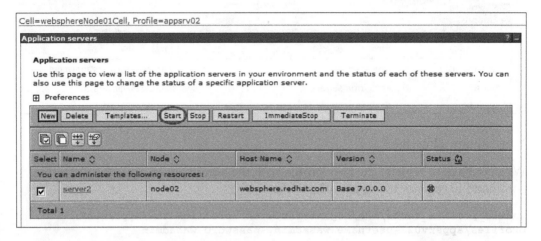

Now that we have created and registered two application server profiles, we can now log in to the admin console of the admin agent and display the nodes that are managed by the admin agent.

Log out of any application server you are in and re-log in to the admin agent, as shown below.

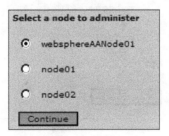

Once you have logged in, we can list the nodes administered by the administrative agent by navigating to the **System administration** section of the left-hand-side main navigation panel and clicking **Administrative agent link**. Then click the **Nodes** link located in the **Managed nodes** section of the **Admin Agents** page, as shown below.

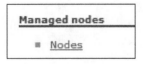

You will now be presented with a list of registered and managed application servers (nodes) as shown below.

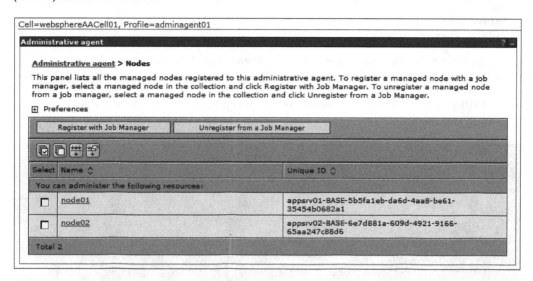

We have now demonstrated registering multiple nodes, which can be centrally managed.

Removing the administrative agent

To remove the administrative agent, we will need to unregister each application server from the administrative agent and then delete the unwanted profiles. Our goal is to be left with the single application server we started at the beginning of this chapter.

The command we are going to use is the `deregisterNode.sh` command.

```
Usage: deregisterNode -profilePath <path of profile to be deregistered>
[-host
          <adminagent host>] [-connType <SOAP | RMI | JSR160RMI | IPC>]
[-port
          <adminagent JMX port>] [-username <adminagent user name>]
[-password
          <adminagent password>] [-nodeusername <registered node user
name>]
          [-nodepassword <registered node password>] [-profileName
<adminagent
          profile name>] [-trace] [-help]
```

To de-register each server, navigate to the admin agents bin directory `<agent_profile_root>/bin` and type the following commands:

`./deregisterNode.sh -profilePath /apps/was7/profiles/appsrv01 –username wasadmin –password wasadmin`

`./deregisterNode.sh -profilePath /apps/was7/profiles/appsrv02 –username wasadmin –password wasadmin`

Once an application server profile has been de-registered, you will see the following report:

```
[root@localhost bin]# ./deregisterNode.sh -profilePath /apps/was7/profiles/appsrv02 -username wasadmin -pas
sword wasadmin
ADMU0116I: Tool information is being logged in file
           /apps/was7/profiles/adminagent01/logs/deregisterNode.log
ADMU0128I: Starting tool with the adminagent01 profile
ADMU8053I: Successfully connected to AdminAgent Server: localhost:8877
ADMU0505I: Servers found in configuration:
ADMU0506I: Server name: server2
ADMU2010I: Stopping all server processes for node localhostNode01
ADMU0512I: Server server2 cannot be reached. It appears to be stopped.
ADMU8052I: Removing signers exchanged during node registration.
ADMU8051I: Removed signers successfully.
ADMU8009I: Begin deregistration of Application Server with path
           /apps/was7/profiles/appsrv02.
ADMU0024I: Deleting the old backup directory.
ADMU8021I: Backing up the original config directory of the profile will be
           deregistered.
ADMU8038I: Deregistering the node with an adminagent.
ADMU8045I: Node has been successfully deregistered.
ADMU8043I: The administrative agent is stopping the administrative subsystem
           for the deregistered node.
ADMU8016I: The administrative subsystem for deregistered node has been
           successfully stopped.
ADMU8044I: The administrative agent is destroying the administrative subsystem
           for the deregistered node.
ADMU8017I: The administrative subsystem for deregistered node has been
           successfully destroyed.
ADMU8013I: Application Server with path /apps/was7/profiles/appsrv02 has been
           successfully deregistered.
```

Now that we have successfully removed both application server profiles away from the admin agent, we can stop the admin agent and remove its profile. To stop the admin agent, type the following command:

`<agent_profile_root>/bin/stopServer.sh adminagent`

Once the admin agent server has stopped, navigate to the `<was_install_root>/bin` folder and type the following command to list the current installed profiles:

`./manageprofiles.sh -listProfiles`

You will get the following list:

[appsrv01, adminagent01, appsrv02]

Type the following command to remove the **adminagent01** profile:

```
./manageprofiles.sh -delete -profileName adminagent01
```

Once the admin agent's profile has been removed, we can remove the **appsrv02** profile as well, using the same process. Once you have finished removing the **appsrv02** profile, we can re-run the listProfiles option of the manage profiles script and you should get the following list of profiles:

[appsrv01]

You should now have only one profile called **appsrv01** remaining, as shown above.

IBM HTTP Server

IBM HTTP Server is based on the Apache HTTP Server (httpd.apache.org), developed by the Apache Software Foundation. In this section, we are going to install IBM HTTP Server which will receive our web requests and allow a web application running on WebSphere to be served over port 80 as opposed to the web container port. The diagram below depicts the configuration we are trying to achieve.

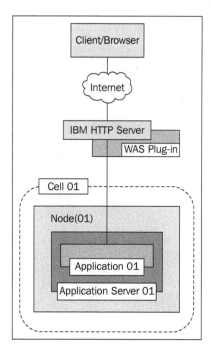

As shown in the diagram above, we will install IHS and the WebSphere plug-in to route HTTP requests to a single application server. In our example, we will be using IHS version 6.1, which can be downloaded from the IBM web site from the following URL.

`http://www-01.ibm.com/software/webservers/httpservers/.`

Download the install for Linux (`ihs.6100.linux.ia32.tar`). The download should not take too long as the size of the download is around 125 MB. Once you have downloaded the Linux tar file, upload it to your Linux machine to a folder called `/apps/ihs_install`.

 You will be able to use the same user id that you registered on IBM's web site when you downloaded the WebSphere 7 trial in Chapter 1.

Once you have uploaded the IHS install, un-tar the file using the commands learned in Chapter 1. Ensure that Xming is running and type the following command to install IHS:

`/apps/ihs_install/IHS_6.1.0.0/IHS/install`

You will then be presented with the graphical installer, as shown below.

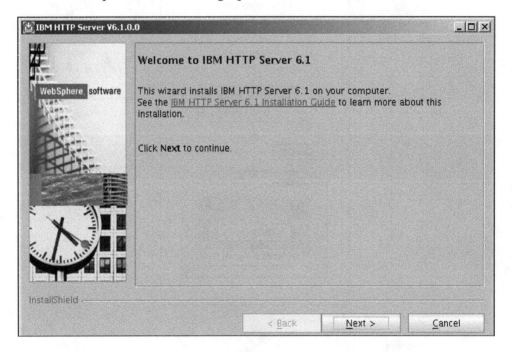

Click on **Next**, accept the license, and click **Next** again to move on to the **System Prerequisites check** page. Then click **Next** again after the prerequisites have passed and enter /apps/ihs in the **Product install location** field, as shown below.

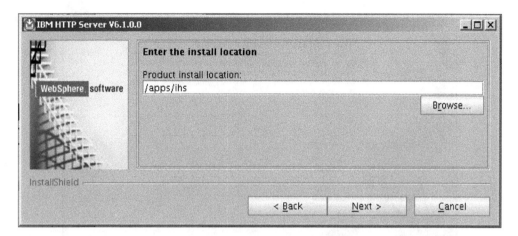

Click on **Next** to move on to the **Port Values Assignment** page, where you will leave the defaults.

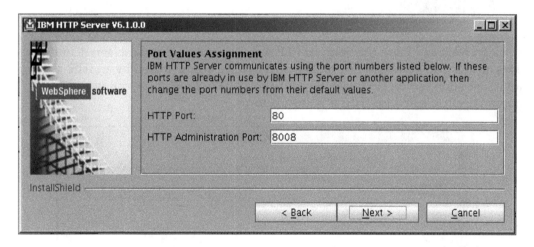

Click on **Next**. Then, you will be asked to type in a username and password for IHS administration from WebSphere. Type **wasadmin** for both the username and password, as shown below.

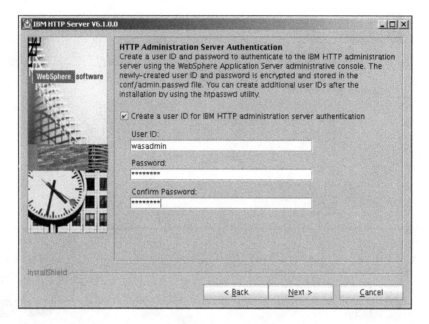

Click on **Next** and leave the **Setup HTTP Administration Server** screen defaulted. This means that we will not be setting up IHS to be administered by an IHS administration server. However, we will allow a new Linux user and group to be automatically created for IHS, as shown below.

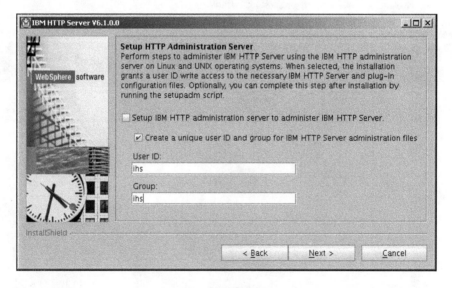

Enter **ihs** in both the **User ID** and **Group** fields and then click on **Next**. Review the summary and click on **Next** to begin the IHS installation. When the installation has finished, click on **Finish** to close the wizard.

> If you have any trouble with the wizard configuring IHS, then you can use the following commands from the `<ihs_install_root>/bin` directory.
>
> The first command creates a clear text password that is used by a file called `admin.conf` which WebSphere uses to connect to remote web servers.
>
> `./htpasswd -cpb <ihs_install_root>/conf/admin.passwd wasadmin wasadmin`
>
> The second command creates the `admin.conf` file used for remote administration of IHS.
>
> `./setupadm -create -usr ihs -grp ihs -cfg /apps/ihs/conf/httpd.conf -adm <ihs_install_root>/conf/admin.conf`
>
> By definition, IHS is local to your example, but it is good to know how the wizard would configure IHS for remote administration, for situations when IHS is not installed on the same machine as WebSphere Application Server.

Starting IBM HTTP Server

To start IHS, navigate to the `<ihs_home>/bin` folder and type the following command:

`./apachectl start`

If you have any issues with starting IHS, you can check the logs located in the `<ihs_install_root>/logs` folder.

To test if IHS is running, open the following URL:

`http://<host_name>:80`

If you see the page below, you know that you have successfully installed and started IHS.

Now that we have installed IHS, we need to download and configure the WebSphere plug-in.

The WebSphere plugin

The WebSphere plugin provides the mechanism for IHS to route requests to WebSphere Application Server and holds configuration information which directs HTTP traffic to applications running in WAS.

The WebSphere plugin can be downloaded from the same IBM site we downloaded the WebSphere 7 Trial from. To download the plug-in use the following URL:

`http://www.ibm.com/developerworks/downloads/ws/was/`

On the home page, at the time of the writing of this book, there is a link on the WAS home page which takes you to the plugin download.

Look for a download called **WebServer Plugin for WebSphere Application Server for Linux**. Once again, you will need to use the IBM user id you registered when you first downloaded the WebSphere 7 trial in Chapter 7. The name of the plugin installer tar file will be called `trial_plugins_linux.ia32.tar.gz`. Download the TAR file and copy it to your Linux server into a folder called `/apps/plugin_install`. The download will be very quick as the file is around 80 MB in size.

Installing the WebSphere plugin

Once you have uploaded the tar file to your Linux server, un-tar the file as you did for the IHS installation previously in the chapter. Once you have expanded the installation files, navigate to `<plugin_install_root>/plugin`. Then ensure that Xming is running and type the following command:

`./install`

You will then be presented with the WebSphere plug-in install wizard, as shown below.

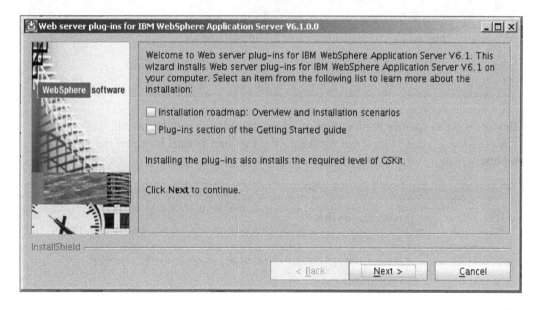

De-select all the checkboxes and click on **Next** and accept the license. Click on **Next** until you reach the following screen and select **None** from the available server types, as shown below. This will stop the wizard from trying to automatically configure WebSphere. We will do the plugin configuration manually after the binaries have been installed. The reason we are doing this manually is to show you some of the inner working of how the plugin is configured. You can choose to use the wizard, however, you should read through the next steps to gain an understanding of what the wizard is trying to do for you.

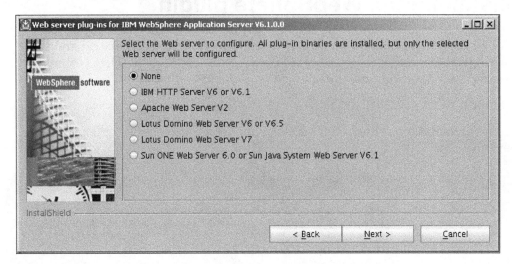

Click on **Next** to specify the location of where the plugin will be installed. Type the `<ihs_install_root/Plugins>` path into the **Product install location** field and click on **Next**.

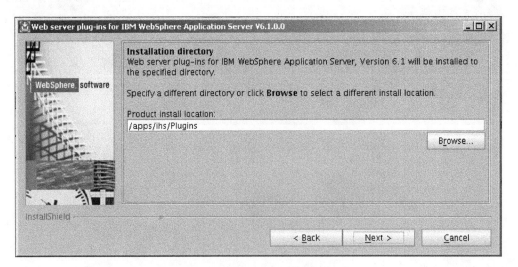

Click on **Next** to confirm the settings and then **Next** again to begin the installation and then click on **Finish** when it is complete.

We now have to manually complete the plugin configuration

Manual configuration of the plugin

Now that we have installed the plugin binaries, we can log in to the admin console and prepare the web server definition, which will allow us to administer the propagation of the `plugin-cfg.xml` file to IHS. The `plugin-cfg.xml` is used to tell IHS what URI paths are available to applications running in the application server. To create a web server definition, we must start server1 so that we can once again use the admin console of the application server, defined by the appsrv01 profile. To start server1, navigate to the `<was_profile_root>/appsrv01/bin` directory and type the following command:

`./startServer.sh server1`

Once the application has started, we can log in to the admin console using the following URL: `https://<host_name>:9043/ibm/console/`.

Once you have logged in to the console, navigate to the **Server | Server types** category in the lefthand side navigation panel and click on **Web servers**. You will then be presented with the option to define a new web server definition. Click the **New** button to enter the **Create new Web server definition** screen. Type **webserver1** into the **Server name** field, ensure that the **Type** field has **IBM HTTP Server** selected, type the **Host name** or IP address of your server, and select **Linux** as the **Platform**, as shown below.

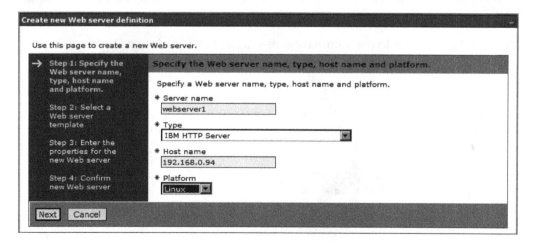

Click **Next** and skip the next screen to move on to the **Enter the properties for the new Web server** screen. Type **/apps/ihs** in the **Web server installation location** field and type **/apps/ihs/Plugins** in the **Plug-in installation location** field. Use **wasadmin** as the value for both the username and password fields, as shown below.

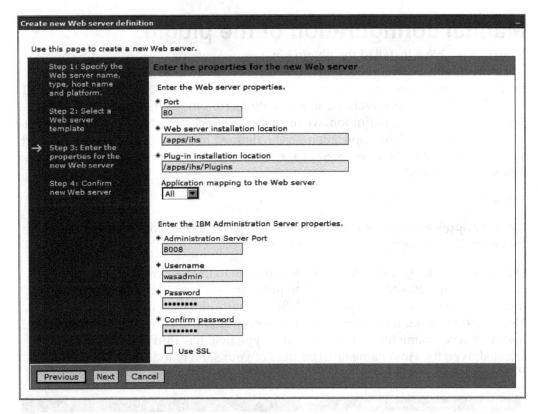

Click **Next** to proceed to the summary screen and click **Finish** to complete the wizard. Once the configuration has been made, click **Save** in order to retain the web server definition. We now need to install the default application to test our configuration. As instructed in Chapter 2, install the default application EAR file and when you get to the **Map modules to servers** screen, ensure that the application is mapped to the web server, as shown in the following screenshot:

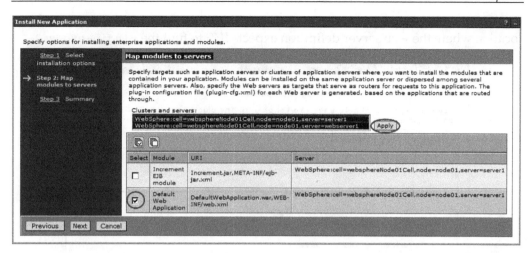

Once the default application EAR has been installed, start the application.

Now, we can go back to the web server definition list screen, for example, **Server | Server Types | Web servers.** Update the configuration of the web server definition we created earlier to ensure that the `plugin-cfg.xml` file can be propagated correctly to IHS. As shown below, click on the **webserver1** link to enter the web server definition configuration page.

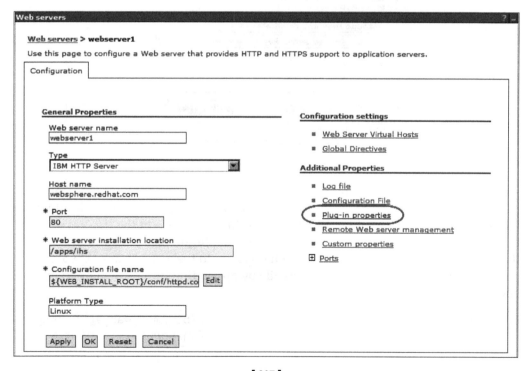

Click on the **Plug-in properties** link, as shown above, and you will be able to see the location where the web server definition expects IHS to find the plugin-cfg.xml.

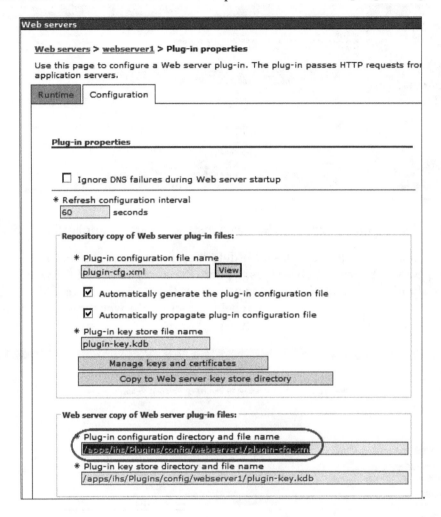

As shown above, we can see that the plugin-cfg.xml file is configured to be propagated to the <ihs_install_root>/Plugins/config/webserver1 location within the ihs/Plugins folder. What we need to do now is edit the IHS httpd.conf file which tells IHS where the plug-in binaries and plug-in files are located. To edit the httpd.conf file, navigate to the IHS file system to the <ihs_install_root>/conf/ location and edit the httpd.conf file by appending the following two lines and saving the file.

```
LoadModule was_ap20_module /apps/ihs/Plugins/bin/mod_was_ap20_http.so
WebSpherePluginConfig /apps/ihs/Plugins/config/webserver1/plugin-cfg.
xml
```

Save the `httpd.conf` file and restart IBM HTTP Server using the following commands:

```
<ihs_install_root>/bin/apachectl stop
<ihs_install_root>/bin/apachectl start
```

Once IHS has restarted, you will be able to open the snoop servlet in the browser using the following URL: `http://<host_name>/snoop`.

Notice how we no longer need to specify port 9080 as we did in Chapter 2. We can now use the default HTTP port 80, which means that the request is being routed through IHS. Because we mapped the default application EAR to both the application server and the web server, we can also use the application server web container port using the following URL: `http://<host_name>:9080/snoop`.

If we don't want this to happen, we can go into the application settings and remap the application web module to webserver1 and restart the application server. Regenerate the `plugin-cfg.xml` file and propagate it to IBM IHS.

Generate plugin

Remember that to make any changes to the applications web module mappings or context root changes (new application), you will need go to the web server definition and click the **Generate Plugin** button, and then the **Propagate Plugin** button, as shown below

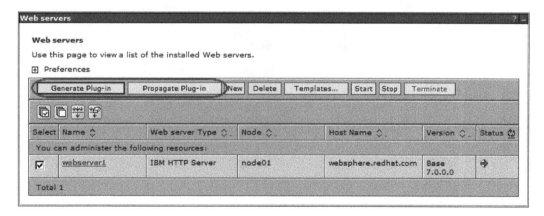

Once the `plugin-cfg.xml` has been updated, you can restart IBM HTTP Server and re-test the URLs.

Summary

In this chapter, we covered the administrative agent, which allows the use of a single administrative console to be used to administer multiple application servers. When a server is registered (federated) to the admin agent, we can start and stop servers without losing access to the admin console. The admin agent allows us to also configure other aspects of WebSphere Application Server in a centralized fashion. We also covered a simple example of how to use IHS as a web server in front of the Application Server, thus allowing HTTP requests to applications mapped to the web server on port 80 as opposed to going to the web container. We learned that IBM HTTP Server can use the WebSphere plug-in which is the mechanism by which IHS can route requests to the application server. By creating a web server definition, we were able to propagate (copy) a file called `plugin-cfg.xml` which contains the URIs (context root and URLs) of all the applications which have web modules mapped to a given web server.

9
Administration Tools

In the preceding chapters, we have covered the core concepts of administering WebSphere Application Server. However, there are a number of other tools available which we have not yet covered. In this chapter, we will be covering a few of the command line tools shipped with WebSphere which provide useful utilities to help you in problem diagnosis when WebSphere or applications are not running as they should.

In this chapter, we will cover the following topics:

- Dumping namespaces
- EAR expander
- Application Server Toolkit
- Log analysis
- Symptom databases
- Inspecting J2EE (Enterprise Edition) applications

Dumping namespaces

To diagnose a problem, you might need to collect WebSphere JNDI information. WebSphere Application Server provides a utility that dumps the JNDI namespace. The dumpNamespace.sh script dumps information about the WebSphere namespace and is very useful when debugging applications when JNDI errors are seen in the WebSphere logs. You can use the utility to dump the namespace so you can see the JNDI tree that the name server (JNDI lookup service provider) is providing to the application. This tool is very useful in JNDI problem determination; for example, debugging incorrect JNDI resource mappings in the case where an application resource is not mapped correctly to a WebSphere configured JNDI resource or the application is using direct JNDI lookups when really it should be using indirect JNDI lookups. For this tool to work, the naming service for the WebSphere server host must be up when this utility is run. In the case of the WebSphere Application Server base, the naming server is the server itself and so it must be running. To run the utility, use the following syntax:

```
./dumpNameSpace.sh -<command_option>
```

There are many options for this tool and the table below lists the command line options available by typing the command <was_root>/dumpsnameSpace.sh -help.

Command option	Description
-host <host>	Bootstrap host, that is, the WebSphere host whose namespace you want to dump. Defaults to localhost.
-port <port>	Bootstrap port. Defaults to 2809.
-user <name>	Username for authentication if security is enabled in the server. Acts the same way as the -username keyword.
-username <name>	Username for authentication if security is enabled in the server. Acts the same way as the -user keyword.
-password <password>	Password for authentication if security is enabled in the server.
-factory <factory>	The initial context factory to be used to get the JNDI initial context. Defaults to com.ibm.websphere.naming.WsnInitialContextFactory and normally does not need to be changed.
-root [cell | server | node | host | legacy | tree | default]	Scope of the namespace to dump.

Command option	Description
For WS 5.0 or later:	
`cell:`	DumpNameSpace default. Dump the tree starting at the `cell` root context.
`server:`	Dump the tree starting at the `server` root context.
`node:`	Dump the tree starting at the `node` root context. (Synonymous with **host**)
For WS 4.0 or later:	
`legacy:`	DumpNameSpace default. Dump the tree starting at the `legacy` root context.
`host:`	Dump the tree starting at the bootstrap `host` root context. (Synonymous with **node**)
`tree:`	Dump the tree starting at the `tree` root context.
For all WebSphere and other name servers:	
`default:`	Dump the tree starting at the initial context which JNDI returns by default for that server type. This is the only -root choice that is compatible with WebSphere servers prior to 4.0 and with non-WebSphere name servers. The WebSphere initial JNDI context factory (default) obtains the desired root by specifying a key specific to the server type when requesting an initial CosNaming NamingContext reference. The default roots and the corresponding keys used for the various server types are listed below: • WebSphere 5.0: Server root context. This is the initial reference registered under the key of `NameServiceServerRoot` on the server. • WebSphere 4.0: Legacy root context. This context is bound under the name `domain/legacyRoot` in the initial context registered on the server under the key `NameService`. • WebSphere 3.5: Initial reference registered under the key of `NameService` on the server. • Non-WebSphere: Initial reference registered under the key of `NameService` on the server.

Command option	Description
-url <url>	The value for the java.naming.provider. url property used to get the initial JNDI context. This option can be used in place of the -host, -port, and -root options. If the -url option is specified, the -host, -port, and -root options are ignored.
-startAt <some/subcontext/ in/the/tree>	The path from the requested root context to the top- level context where the dump should begin. Recursively dumps (displays a tree-like structure) the sub-contexts of each namespace context. Defaults to empty string, i.e., root context requested with the -root option.
-format [jndi | ins]	jndi: Display name components as atomic strings.
	ins: Display name components parsed per INS rules (id.kind)
	The default format is jndi.
-report [short | long]	short: Dumps the binding name and bound object type, which is essentially what JNDI Context.list() provides.
	long: Dumps the binding name, bound object type, local object type, and string representation of the local object that is, Interoperable Object References (IORs) string values, etc., are printed).
	The default report option is short.
-traceString <some. package.to.trace.*=all>	Trace string of the same format used with servers, with output going to the DumpNameSpaceTrace.out file.

Example name space dump

To see the result of using the namespace tool, navigate to the <was_root>/bin directory on your Linux server and type the following command:

```
./dumpNameSpace.sh -root cell -report short -username wasadmin -password
wasadmin >> jnditree.txt
```

The following report, as shown in the screenshot below, is a segment of the contents of the jnditree.txt file which contains the output of the above command. In your example, you should be able to see the JNDI names for the JDBC data sources we created for the application in Chapter 2 and the JNDI names for the JMS and MQ connection factories and destination we created in Chapter 6.

```
=======================================================================
Beginning of Name Space Dump
=======================================================================

1  (top)
2  (top)/legacyRoot.naming.Context
2  Linked to context: websphereNode01Cell/persisten
3  (top)/cells  x javax.naming.Context
4  (top)/cell javax.naming.Context
4  Linked to context: websphereNode01Cell
5  (top)/cellname java.lang.String
6  (top)/persistentjavax.naming.Context
7  (top)/persistent/cell  javax.naming.Context
7  Linked to context: websphereNode01Cell
8  (top)/nodesjavax.naming.Context
9  (top)/nodes/node01 javax.naming.Context
10 (top)/nodes/node01/celljavax.naming.Context
10 Linked to context: websphereNode01Cell
11 (top)/nodes/node01/nodejavax.naming.Context
11 Linked to context: websphereNode01Cell/nodes/node01
12 (top)/nodes/node01/nodenamejava.lang.String
13 (top)/nodes/node01/servers javax.naming.Context
14 (top)/nodes/node01/servers/server1 javax.naming.Context
15 (top)/nodes/node01/servers/server1/jms javax.naming.Context
16 (top)/nodes/node01/servers/server1/jms/QCF.Testjavax.jms.QueueConnectionFactory
17 (top)/nodes/node01/servers/server1/jms/QCF.LQTest  javax.jms.QueueConnectionFactory
18 (top)/nodes/node01/servers/server1/jms/Q.Test  com.ibm.ws.sib.api.jms.impl.JmsQueueImpl
19 (top)/nodes/node01/servers/server1/jms/LQ.Test com.ibm.mq.jms.MQQueue
20 (top)/nodes/node01/servers/server1/iscportletservice
20 javax.naming.Context
21 (top)/nodes/node01/servers/server1/iscportletservice/com.ibm.portal.propertybroker.service.PropertyBrokerService
21 com.ibm.iscportal.portlet.service.PortletServiceHomeImpl
22 (top)/nodes/node01/servers/server1/iscportletservice/com.ibm.portal.portlet.service.DynamicUIManagerFactoryService
22com.ibm.iscportal.portlet.service.PortletServiceHomeImpl
23 (top)/nodes/node01/servers/server1/iscportletservice/com.ibm.portal.portlet.service.URLGeneratorFactoryService
23com.ibm.iscportal.portlet.service.PortletServiceHomeImpl
24 (top)/nodes/node01/servers/server1/thisNodejavax.naming.Context
24Linked to context: websphereNode01Cell/nodes/node01
25 (top)/nodes/node01/servers/server1/SecurityServer  com.ibm.ws.security.server._SecurityServer_Stub
26 (top)/nodes/node01/servers/server1/DefaultDatasource
26 javax.resource.cci.ConnectionFactory
27 (top)/nodes/node01/servers/server1/UserRegistrycom.ibm.websphere.security._UserRegistry_Stub
28 (top)/nodes/node01/servers/server1/servername  java.lang.String
29 (top)/nodes/node01/servers/server1/Incrementcom.ibm.defaultapplication.IncrementHome
```

EAR expander

Sometimes during application debugging or automated application deployment, you may need to enquire about the contents of an Enterprise Archive (EAR) file. An EAR file is made up of one or more WAR files (web applications), one or more EJBS, and there can be shared JAR files as well. Also, within each WAR file, there may be JAR files as well. The EARExpander.sh utility allows all artifacts to be fully decompressed much like expanding a TAR file.

```
Usage syntax:

  EARExpander -ear (name of the input EAR file for the expand
  operation or name of the output EAR file for the collapse operation)
  -operationDir (directory to which the EAR file is expanded or
  directory from which the EAR file is collapsed) -operation (expand |
  collapse) [-expansionFlags (all | war)] [-verbose]
```

To demonstrate the utility, we will expand the `HRListerEAR.ear` file we installed in Chapter 2. Ensure that you have uploaded the `HRListerEAR.ear` file to a new folder called `/tmp/EARExpander` folder on your Linux sever or appropriate alternative location and run the following command.

```
<was_root>/bin/EARExpander.sh -ear /tmp/HRListerEAR.ear -operationDir /
tmp/expanded -operation expand -expansionFlags all -verbose
```

The result will be an expanded on-disc structure of the contents of the entire EAR file as shown below:

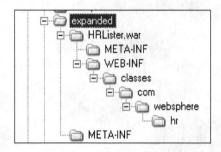

An example of everyday use could be that `EARExpander.sh` is used as part of a deployment script where an EAR file is expanded and hard-coded properties files are searched and replaced, then the EAR is re-packaged up using the EARExpander `-operation collapse` option to recreate the EAR file once the find-and-replace routine has completed. An example of how to collapse an expanded EAR is as follows:

```
<was_root>/bin/EARExpander.sh -ear /tmp/collapsed/HRListerEAR.ear
-operationDir /tmp/expanded -operation collapse -expansionFlags all -
verbose
```

In the example above, the folder called `EARExpander` contains an expanded `HRListerEAR.ear` file which was created when we used the `-expand` option. To collapse the files back into an EAR file, we have used the `-collapse` option as shown above; however, we have expanded the file into the `tmp` folder. The result is a file called `HRListerEAR.ear` in the `/tmp` folder which is created from collapsing the folder contents back into an EAR file.

Oveview of the WebSphere Application Server toolkit

The WebSphere Application Server toolkit is a tool that can be used to help with basic packaging of the J2EE application and provides tooling for publishing to your application server. You can also use the tool to perform basic unit testing, debugging, and profiling functions. With WebSphere 7, there has been a new product release called the Rational Application Developer Assembly and Deploy (RADAD) tool, which ships with WebSphere Application Server V7.0 and is fully licensed with WebSphere Application Server 7. It can be used to build, test, and deploy Java Platform Enterprise Edition (Java EE) applications on a WebSphere Application Server V7.0 environment. RADAD provides support for all Java EE artifacts supported by WebSphere Application Server V7.0, such as servlets, Java Server Pages (JSPs), Enterprise JavaBeans (EJBs), XML, and web services. It also supports developing Java EE 5 applications. However, the tool cannot be used for previous versions of WebSphere. Since this product is only available with purchased WebSphere 7 media and is not yet available for trial, we will demonstrate the previous version, the Application Server Toolkit (ASTK), which can be used for WebSphere 7 as well and at the time of writing is still available for download. We are going to use the ASTK tool for Windows to evaluate some WAS logs, and demonstrate how to inspect an EAR file. The reason we are using the Windows version is because x-windows does not perform very well for complex GUI applications and often most development of scripts, debugging of scripts and application packaging, and so on, is often done on your workstation, using a Windows version of ASTK and a windows version of WebSphere, and when you are satisfied you have your scripts or application packaging working as intended, you can implement the script or deploy a newly packaged application in your Linux server environments.

You can download the ASTK 6.1.1.0 for Windows from the following URL: `http://www-01.ibm.com/support/docview.wss?uid=swg24014241`

You will have to use your IBM id created when you download the WebSphere 7 trial for Linux and the download for the ASTK is about 800MB, so it will take time. Once you have downloaded the `esd.image.ast.win32.zip` file, you can expand it using your favorite windows ZIP tool, like WinRAR or WinZip for instance. To begin the installation, look for the install icon as shown below, and click to begin the installation wizard. The `install.exe` file should be located in the `disk1` folder.

Installing the WebSphere Application Server toolkit

Once the installation wizard has loaded, click **Next**, accept the license agreement, and then click **Next** again to set to the upgrade options page as shown below.

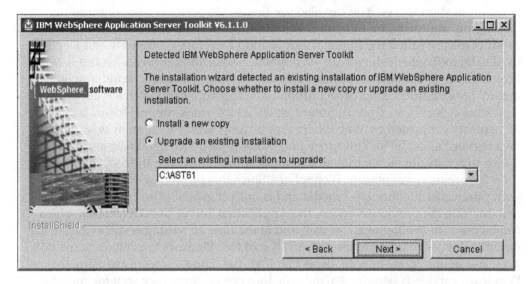

In this example, the wizard detects a previous version of the Application Server toolkit installed. You can choose to upgrade an existing version or you can choose to install a new copy. Select **Install a new copy** and then click **Next** to go to the installation location page. Type **C:\AST6110** as the path for your install in the installation destination field and click **Next** to view the summary page. Then, click **Next** again if you are happy with the summary. The installation will then begin. Once the installation has finished, you can then click **Finish** to exit the install wizard.

Running the Application Server toolkit

The ASTK can be located in the **Start | Programs | IBM Websphere | Application Server Toolkit version 6.1.1** program group. Click the **Application Server Toolkit** icon to start the ASTK. When the ASTL starts for the first time, you will be prompted for the location of your workspace. ASTK is based on Eclipse and so a workspace is used to store all the projects that you create with the ASTK. It is recommended that you select or name a new folder that will contain all your project files. The folder should not be present in the same directory as the ASTK, so that when you uninstall it, you can keep all our project files, without them being removed as part of the uninstall process. In our example, we are using the path **C:\workspace\ASTK6110** as shown below.

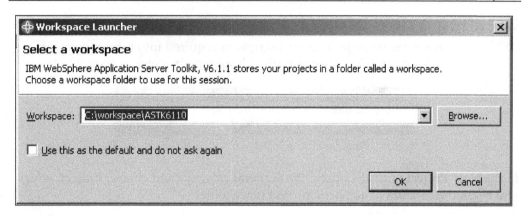

Once you have decided on your workspace path, click on **OK** and the workspace folder will be created if it does not exist. When the ASTK has loaded, close the welcome screen and you will see the main Eclipse-based workbench.

Log analysis using the ASTK

The ASTK can be used to analyze WebSphere JVM logs. The types of logs the ASTK can analyze are:

- **First Failure Data Capture (FFDC)** logs
- Diagnostic trace
- Java TM Virtual Machine (JVM) logs (for example, SystemOut.log)
- Process logs
- IBM Service logs (for example, Activity.log)

For your first project, we are going to create a project called Logs which we will use to import an example SystemOut.log from our Application Server. Before we begin, download a sample SystemOut.log from your Linux server using winscp or other secure copy program into your C:\temp folder in preparation for importing into the Logs project.

Creating a new project

ASTK uses projects to organize files and scripts as required into local groupings. To create a new project, select **New | Project** from the file menu as shown below.

In the **New Project** wizard, expand the **General** category and choose **Project**, which will begin the creation of a generic project placeholder.

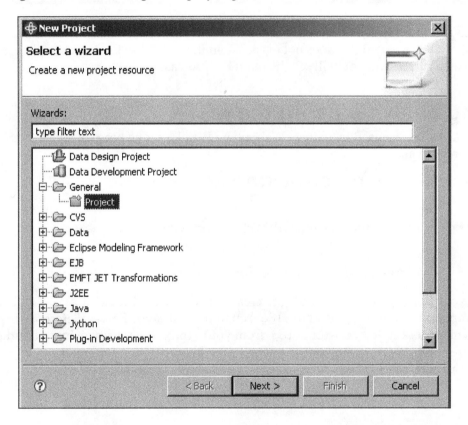

Click on **Next** to move on to the **New Project** screen. As shown in the following screenshot, type **Logs** for the **Project name field** and click on **Finish** to create the empty project.

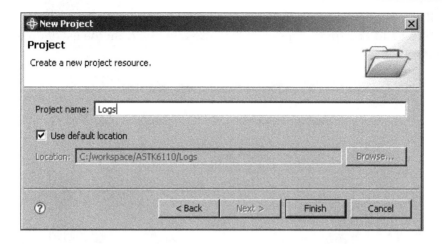

Importing log files

Once the **Logs** project has been created, it will appear in the lefthand side **Project Navigation** panel. Right-click the **Logs** project and select **Import** as shown below.

You will be presented with the type of source files you want to import. Expand the **Profiling and Logging** category and choose **Log File** from the list of options as shown below.

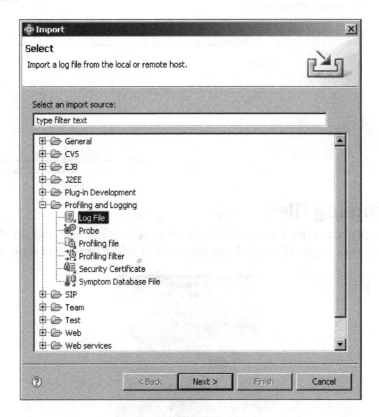

You will then be prompted to add a new log set. A log set defines the type of logs you are importing for analysis. As shown below, click the **Add** button in the **Import Log File** screen, select **IBM WebSphere Application Server systemout.log** option from the **Log types** pick-list, and then browse for the SystemOut.log file you downloaded from your Linux server, as shown in the following screenshot:

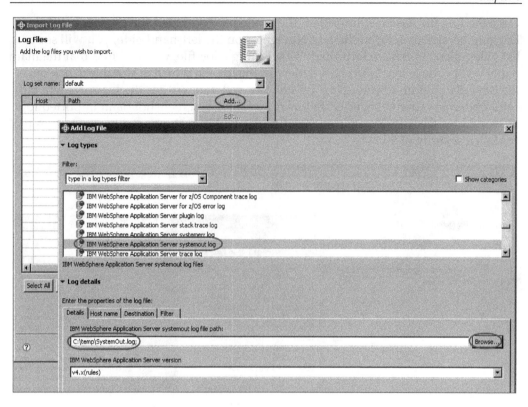

Click **OK** to return from the **Log types** and **Log details** settings screen and then click **Finish** to complete the **Log import** screen and return back to the project to see your imported log file. You will then be prompted with the option to switch to the **Profiling and Logging Perspective**, which will display specific context menus and options to log analysis. Click **Yes** as shown below.

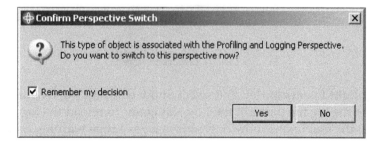

Once the Log file has been imported, the workspace will load the Profiling and Logging perspective. From the Log Navigator on the left-hand-side, you will see a list of log file(s) you have imported. By selecting a log file, you will find that the main panel will produce a column-based view of the log file which is storable. Click on the **Severity** column to sort errors by severity and you will see the log rows will be color-coded in order of severity. Below is an example screenshot of an imported log file sorted by severity. You can see the **Severity** column shows red for log entries that contain a severity of **50**.

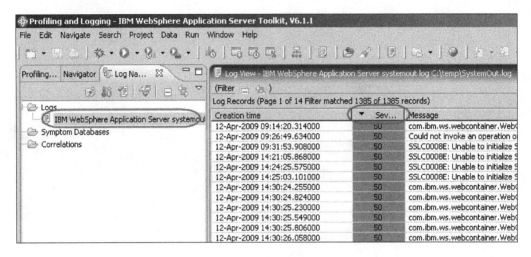

Applying filters

You can use the toolbar to change the log display attributes. By clicking on the **Highlight Events** toolbar button as seen below, you can select to filter certain types of log entries.

Click the **Highlight Events** button and select **Show warning log records only.** Then double-click on the log file name in the Log Navigator to reload the log file and you will notice that the main panel now only shows logs of type warning (severity 10).

Selecting columns

By clicking on the **Choose Columns** button as seen below, you can select columns
you wish to display.

Click the **Choose Columns** button and select the **Creation time** and **Message**
columns as shown below.

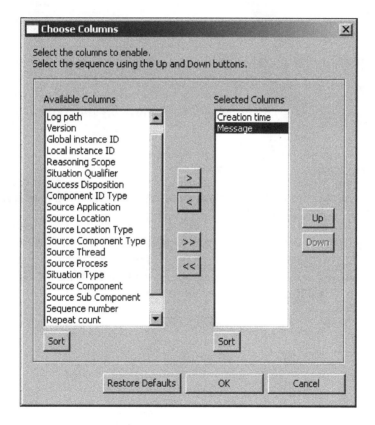

When you have finished selecting which columns you want, click **OK** and the main
log panel will refresh to display the new columns.

Loading symptom databases

Just viewing logs using the ASTK is not a useful problem analysis activity until the log is correlated against a database. IBM WebSphere Service and Support maintains the symptom database. You can import symptom databases into the ASTK. The symptom database is in XML format and you can download the most recent version from the IBM web site.

The symptom database contains three key types of information:

- Symptoms
    - Common problem or error messages
- Solutions
    - Reasons why the error may have occurred
- Directives or resolutions
    - Possible resolutions for the error

You can download the latest symptom database XML file for WebSphere 7 at the following URL:

```
ftp://ftp.software.ibm.com/software/autonomic/symptomcatalog/v2/
websphere_application_server/v7/en/
```

It is best to download the ZIP file (for example, `websphere_application_ server_7_0_en.zip`) and expand it into `c:\temp`.

To import a symptom database for log analysis and correlation, you can right-mouse-click on the **Symptom Databases** folder in the left-hand-side log navigation panel and select import. Select the **Symptom Database File** option from the **Profiling and logging** category as shown below.

In the **Import Symptom Database file** wizard, select **IBM WebSphere Application Server 61** (WebSphere 7 format is not yet available) and select IBM WebSphere propriety format import from the import form pick-list, as shown below, and then click on **Finish**.

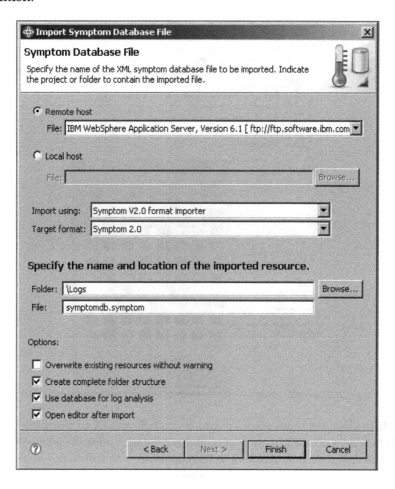

Once you have imported the symptom database, you can change the log filter by once again clicking on the **Highlight Events** toolbar button and selecting the **Show correlated log records only** option and choose an appropriate color for identification as shown below.

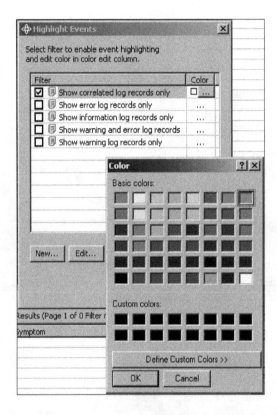

Click on **OK** to close the color selector and then click on **OK** to complete and start the analysis. When the correlation analysis has completed, you will see all the log entries (rows) records that match symptoms in the database. The following screenshot shows that as you click on each log entry you can now see recommended solutions.

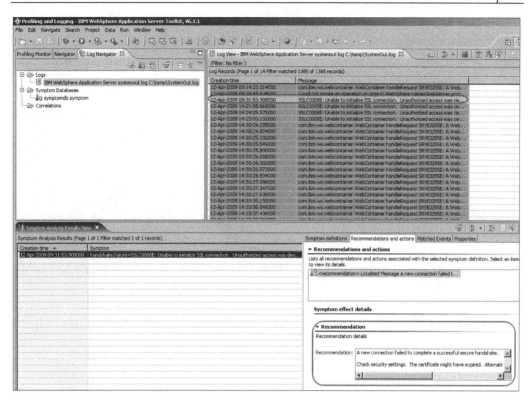

Inspecting J2EE applications

The ASTK can also be used to create J2EE artefacts like JARs, EJBs, WAR files, and can package them into an EAR file. Essentially, it is a cut-down version of the Rational Application Development tool suite and thus provides some useful development-related features. For our demonstration, we are going to import the JSM Test Tool EAR file which we used in Chapter 6 and will examine the EAR file's contents.

To import the `JMSTesterEAR.ear` file from Chapter 6, select **Import** from the **File** menu and then select the **EAR file** from the **J2EE** category as the import source, as shown below.

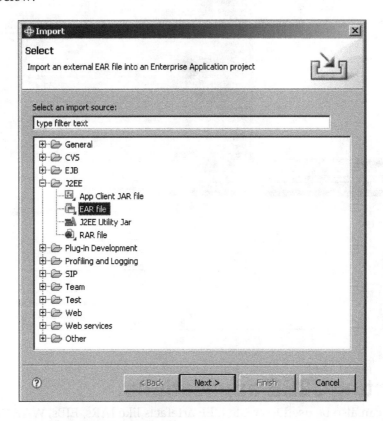

Click **Next** to go to the **Enterprise Application Import** screen as shown below and browse for the `JMSTesterEAR.ear` file. The wizard will automatically assign a project name as **JMSTesterEAR**. Click **Next** to move on to the next screen.

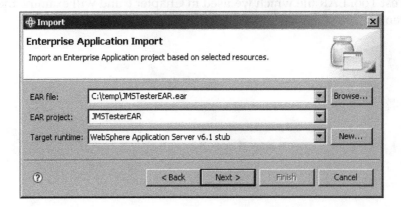

Since the `JMSTesterEAR.ear` file has utility JAR files, the **Utility JARs and web libraries** screen will be presented. Click on the **Select All** button to ensure that the appropriate `lib` folder is created, as shown below.

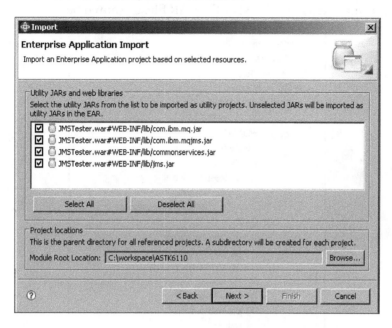

Click on **Next** to move on to the **EAR Module and Utility JAR Projects** window shown below and click on **Finish** to complete the import.

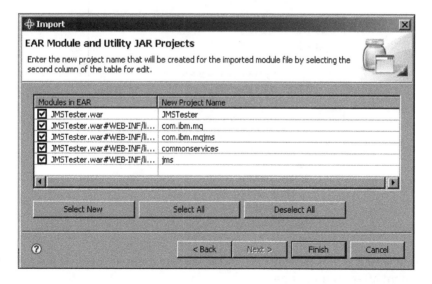

Because we have now had a J2EE project created as a result of the import, you will be prompted to use the J2EE perspective, which provides context menus and tool bars suited for a J2EE project. Click **Yes**. The result will be a collection of projects which make up the components (artefacts) of the EAR file, as shown below.

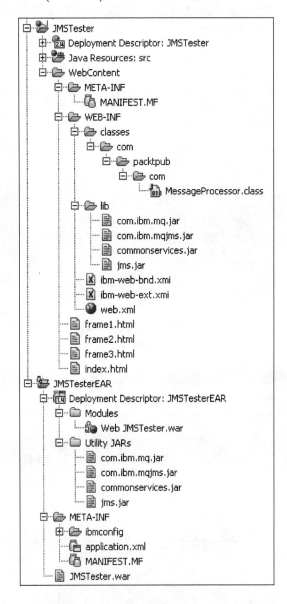

You can now edit the files as required and re-export them as an EAR file for re-deployment after your changes.

Summary

In this chapter, we saw that WebSphere Application Server comes with some useful command-line tools. The dumpNameSpace.sh utility can be used to view the JNDI tree of a running application server, which is very useful to help with debugging the root cause of application failures that involve JNDI resource lookups. Another tool we looked at was the EARExpander.sh utility which can be used to unpack an EAR file during automated deployments to manipulate the EAR file and repackage it up on the fly. It can also be used during problem diagnosis if the supplied EAR file has problems during deployment. We also learned that IBM provides a graphical tool called the Application Server Toolkit, which is a very powerful instrument that can be used to create J2EE applications and inspect the contents or make changes to an existing EAR file and re-package it for deployment. Another not so well-known fact is that the ASTK can also be used to analyze key log file types produced by WebSphere Application Server, and when correlated with a symptoms database, suggestions from IBM Support can be made available to help correct problems with both application and server configurations.

10
Product Maintenance

An important role of a WebSphere administrator is to ensure that the product is up-to-date and patched accordingly. IBM frequently makes product updates available as they release improvements as part of their product lifecycles. The goal of this chapter is to instruct you on the options available to you to locate and download product updates, then apply them in the correct manner to your WebSphere Application Server installation.

In this chapter, we will cover the following topics:

- Locating and downloading updates
- Update installers
- Applying updates
- Verification of updates
- Silent updates
- Feature packs
- Interim features and fixes
- Backing up your system
- Installer logs
- Troubleshooting tips

Understanding updates

All software products can have defects often termed as bugs. Product updates are often released to address known defects. IBM WebSphere has an aggressive product update strategy to keep your product up-to-date, stable, and secure, which will ensure that applications run without issues introduced by defects in the underlying application server. Security is also paramount in WebSphere. Since WebSphere is often part of the public-facing web portal solution for many companies, it is important to ensure that the product has no security holes that can be used by hackers to circumvent security. By understanding how to locate, download, and apply product updates to your WebSphere Application Server, you will need to ensure that, as a product, it is running as error-free as possible. It is also important to understand that application design and configuration can also cause problems. However, by applying updates you will find that the errors are less likely to be caused by a defect in WAS itself and more to do with the actual code of deployed applications or improper configuration of WebSphere, and so having a good update strategy is paramount.

Update process overview

The update process can basically be broken down into the following list of steps:

1. Locate, download, and install (if required) the latest Update Installer.
2. Read relevant supporting documentation.
3. Locate and download product updates.
4. Verify the current version of WAS using the `versionInfo.sh` command script.
5. Ensure you have stopped all WebSphere (JAVA) processes.
6. Create a backup.
7. Apply updates.
8. Verify the new version of WAS using the `versionInfo.sh` command script.
9. Optionally, check WebSphere logs to ensure that there are no installation errors.

We will now step through the list above in detail to explain, with a demonstration, the process of upgrading install of the WAS1 trial from 7.0.0.0 to version 7.0.0.1.

Product update types

Before we continue, it is important to note that there are several types of product updates. You need to be familiar with the terms used in the maintenance of these packages , such as fix packs, features packs, interim fixes, and interim features. The table below explains the different types of product updates in case you come across these terms on web sites, installers, and/or documentation.

Type of Update	Description
Release	Essentially, a new product version. • A new WebSphere Application Server that includes major new functions, such as V7.0. • This is a separate installation that can coexist with other Application Server releases. • Full testing of all applications with a new release is recommended.
Fix pack	A product update that fixes defects. • This is the standard delivery for updates—it has been regression tested. • A fix pack is a cumulative package of fixes, such as Fix Pack 2 (7.0.0.2). • Fix packs also install on top of a previous fix pack, such as applying V7.0.0.2 to V7.0.0.1. • Fix packs are cumulative, so V7.0.0.2 includes all fixes in V7.0.0.1. • Fix packs uninstall all Interim Fixes applied to the release since the last fix pack was installed. Therefore, it is necessary to check the list of delivered fixes to determine if an interim fix needs to be reinstalled. Note: Brief testing of critical functions with the new fix pack is recommended.
Feature pack	A new set of features added to your WAS. • WebSphere Application Server V7.0 releases feature packs, which are free, downloadable product extensions (on top of V7.0) that provide incremental new features. • Note: Regression testing of critical functions with new feature packs is strongly recommended before you release environments for production use.

Type of Update	Description
Fix	Emergency fixes to names and recorded defects.
	• A single published emergency fix, such as PK41267 (sample number).
	• A fix is an interim fix or test fix that resolves one or more product defects.
	• A fix can be applied to a release or fix pack where applicable.
	• Interim fix = IFnnnn (for example: 7.0 IF0001.)
	• Test fix = TFnnnn (for example: 7.0 TF0002).
	• Interim fixes are created when a standalone fix is required between fix packs. They are validated by at least one customer prior to being published by IBM.
	• It is recommended that you test functions affected by the WebSphere Application Server component which is fixed by an interim fix. You do not need to apply interim fixes, unless you have a requirement.
	• It is recommended that you frequently visit the WebSphere recommended fixes page (Fix Central) for currently available fixes. When urgent, the fix will also be flashed on IBM Support pages.

If you wish to learn more about the product update strategy, it is recommended you consult the IBM support web site located at the following URL:

`http://www.ibm.com/support/us/en/`

Preparing for updates

Before you apply any updates, you should query your WebSphere product to see what the current version is. This will help you decide which product updates you may wish to apply. You can use the WebSphere command script `<was_root>/bin/versionInfo.sh` to evaluate what has been installed and which updates have already been applied.

The result of running `versionInfo.sh` will be a report similar to the example report, as shown in the screenshot below.

```
[root@websphere bin]# ./versionInfo.sh
WVER0010I: Copyright (c) IBM Corporation 2002, 2005, 2008; All rights reserved.
WVER0012I: VersionInfo reporter version 1.15.1.26, dated 8/9/08


--------------------------------------------------------------------------------
IBM WebSphere Application Server Product Installation Status Report
--------------------------------------------------------------------------------


Report at date and time July 8, 2009 5:18:19 PM BST

Installation
--------------------------------------------------------------------------------
Product Directory            /apps/was7
Version Directory            /apps/was7/properties/version
DTD Directory                /apps/was7/properties/version/dtd
Log Directory                /apps/was7/logs
Backup Directory             /apps/was7/properties/version/nif/backup
TMP Directory                /tmp

Product List
--------------------------------------------------------------------------------
BASETRIAL                    installed

Installed Product
--------------------------------------------------------------------------------
Name                         IBM WebSphere Application Server
Version                      7.0.0.0
ID                           BASETRIAL
Build Level                  r0835.03
Build Date                   8/31/08
Architecture                 Intel (32 bit)


--------------------------------------------------------------------------------
End Installation Status Report
--------------------------------------------------------------------------------
```

The section of the report that we are most interested in is the **Installed Product** section, which details the current base version and any applied fix packs or feature packs. By using this section, we can see what updates have already been applied. It is also useful for audit purposes to confirm the status of recently applied updates and to confirm that the updates have successfully been registered.

Locating updates

IBM has provided a detailed section on their **Fix Central** web portal. Fix Central features an interface that is designed to help you locate your product updates. The WebSphere product suite is huge and there are many hundreds of product updates available for many releases at any given time. Fix Central's goal is to help you find your product updates relevant to your particular WebSphere product as easily as possible. In our case, we are only interested in updates for WAS 7.0 and it must be noted that IBM's web site is in a constant state of flux and thus may not look exactly the same when you go to find your updates. The screenshots in this chapter are used to help you see the typical style that IBM uses in its support pages and hopefully serve as a guide going forward; as it is likely the IBM web site pages and processes will change over time.

Helpful hint: At the time of writing this book, there is an article on IBM's web site that covers how to use Fix Central located at the following URL: `http://www.ibm.com/developerworks/websphere/techjournal/0711_supauth/0711_supauth.html#seca`

Fix Central

Fix Central is found at `http://www-933.ibm.com/support/fixcentral/`.

To find the latest fix packs available for Websphere 7, navigate to the Fix Central URL mentioned above. When you open the **Fix Central** landing page, you will need to select the product group, product, and version using the pick-lists provided. When you click **Continue**, you will be taken to a filter page where you can decide what kind of updates you are looking for. In our example, we are looking to see if there are any updates to WAS 7.0.0.0, as shown in the following screenshot:

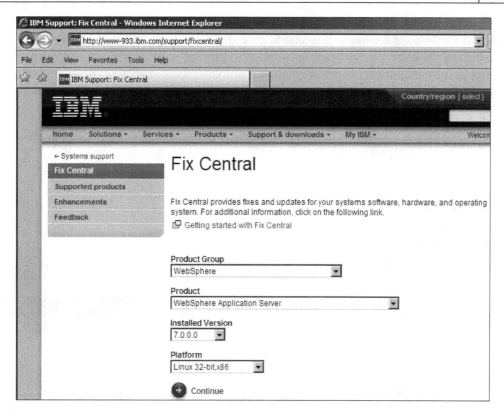

Eventually, you will get to a screen as shown below which will list available updates. In our example, there were updates available for WAS7 when we went to Fix Central.

We are interested in downloading **7.0.0-WS-WAS-LinuxX32-FP0000001**, which will update our WAS 7.0.0.0 to 7.0.0.1.

Click **Continue** to move on to the fixes download page.

Once you have located the download page, you can choose to use direct HTTP or the IBM **Download Director**, a reusable downloader supplied by IBM. Using the **Download Director** is highly recommended to ensure your download continues if there is a loss of connection during your download. Using direct HTTP means that your download can be interrupted if network connectivity is lost and you will have to restart the download all over again.

In the screenshot below, you can see an example of the IBM **Download Director** in action as we downloaded our fix pack.

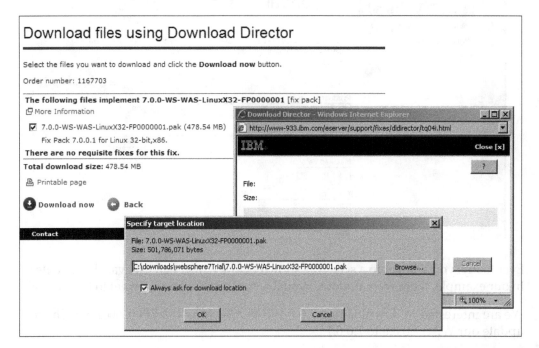

Update installers

Product updates are installed using the **IBM Update Installer for WebSphere Software** tool. Since new updates are made to the update installer tool over time, it may be required to download the latest version of the update installer.

The V7.0 Update Installer is a JAVA application and will run on multiple platforms. The latest version of the Update Installer available at the time of writing this book is backward compatible with V6.0.2.21 and newer maintenance and any maintenance for V6.1.0.x and V7.0 releases.

Just like the WAS installer covered in Chapter 1, the Update Installer wizard runs with either as a graphical user interface or in silent mode with a response file.

Creating a backup

Before making any changes to an existing WebSphere installation, it is wise to make a backup. You can back up WAS using the `backupConfig.sh` shell command. This will create a ZIP file of your full WAS configuration in case there are problems and you need to resort back to a previously known copy. If you run `backupConfig.sh` without any parameters, it will automatically create a date and time stamped `.zip` file.

You can get the help for the command by typing `./backupConfig.sh -help`.

```
Usage: backupConfig [backup_file] [-nostop] [-quiet] [-logfile
<filename>]
          [-replacelog] [-trace] [-username <username>] [-password
<password>]
          [-profileName <profile>] [-help]
```

An example of running the `backupConfig.sh` utility is shown below:

```
[root@websphere bin]# ./backupConfig.sh
ADMU0116I: Tool information is being logged in file
           /apps/was7/profiles/appsrv01/logs/backupConfig.log
ADMU0128I: Starting tool with the appsrv01 profile
ADMU5001I: Backing up config directory /apps/was7/profiles/appsrv01/config to
           file /apps/was7/bin/WebSphereConfig_2009-07-08.zip
ADMU0505I: Servers found in configuration:
ADMU0506I: Server name: server1
ADMU2010I: Stopping all server processes for node websphereNode01
ADMU0512I: Server server1 cannot be reached. It appears to be stopped.
.............................................................................
.............................................................................
.............................................................................
.................................
ADMU5002I: 499 files successfully backed up
```

Even though Websphere provides a profile backup facility, it is recommended that you have a backup of the actual file system from a Linux point of view. Often it is easier to not use the Websphere profile backup facility and just TAR the Websphere installation folders, so you have a rollback scenario. We all know that things can go wrong and so having multiple ways to roll back to a known point in time is a good thing.

 If you are using a Linux VM on VMWare or similar virtual server technology, you can action a snapshot which saves the entire state of the virtual machine. If an error occurs at any time during upgrades, you can roll back to a known point of time for the entire virtual machine.

Installing a new Update Installer

Before installing any updates installers, you may have to stop all WebSphere processes related to the WAS environment that you are going to update as the installer will not work if you have WAS processes running while you are trying to apply the updates.

> Before applying updates, please consider that if you have not already chosen to install the sample applications, they might not work if installed at later stage after a fix pack has been applied. The best approach is to ensure that all samples and features are installed before fix packs are applied.

Downloading the Update Installer

It is good practice to use the latest update installer. However, saying that, it all depends on the cycle of IBM's update release schedules and versions. During a product's lifecycle, IBM often changes track with their install technology and so it is recommended that you read all supporting documentation made available on the page where the download is located to understand whether you need to use the update installer that comes with WebSphere or download the latest from IBM. At the time of writing, the latest WebSphere 7 Update Installer was available at the following IBM web site URL:

```
http://www-01.ibm.com/support/docview.wss?rs=180&uid=swg24020446.
```

As mentioned in the *Fix Central* section above, you can do a quick search on IBM's Fix Central site to search for the latest update installer. Often the actual fix pack download page has a link to the latest update installer as well.

> For further information on how to use the Update Installer, you can also follow the instructions that are included in the **readme** file, which is available in the install directory:
>
> `<installer_home>/docs/readme_updateinstaller.pdf.`

Installing the graphical Update Installer

To apply a product update, you must first download, unpack, and install the latest version of the update installer. For our demonstration, we have downloaded and unpacked the latest version of the update installer. At the time of writing, the latest version was 7.0.0.1 and the following download was available:

```
7.0.0.1-WS-UPDI-LinuxIA32.tar.gz
```

It is often common practice to untar the update installer into the root folder of the WebSphere binaries path you used in Chapter 1, so that the update installer's install process can use the WebSphere installer's JVM. An example path could be as follows:

```
/<was_root>/UpdateInstaller
```

To begin the installation of the Update Installer, run the `./install` command to start the installation wizard for the Update Installer.

> Since we are using a manual graphical install, you will need to ensure that you have Xming running as the graphical installation wizard uses XWindows, just like the WebSphere installation wizard covered in Chapter 1.

When the Update Installer's installation wizard has loaded, you will be presented with a license screen. Accept the license and click on **Next** to continue to the **Installation Directory** screen as shown below.

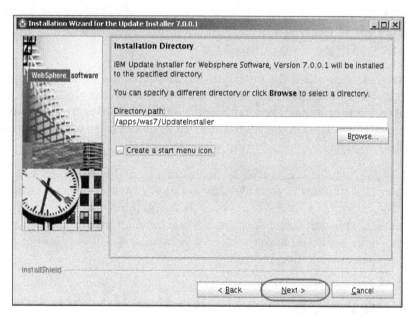

To proceed, click **Next** to move on to the installation and follow through the screens until completion of the wizard steps, where you will be presented with a summary screen as shown below.

Note: If you have already downloaded a fix pack, you can save time by checking the **Launch IBM Update Installer for WebSphere Software on exit** option and this will automatically launch the Update Installer.

The next step is to download the most current version of the update that you wish to apply from the appropriate support site and copy it into the Update Installer's maintenance directory. In fact, you can unpack the update files anywhere as the newer versions of the Update Installer allow for fix packs to be located via a browse button in the Graphical Installer during a fix pack installation.

Once the Update Installer has been installed as mentioned in the steps above, it is recommended practice to copy the downloaded *.pak files (for example, 7.0.0-WS-WAS-LinuxX32-FP0000001.pak) to the maintenance folder within the Update Installer. This will then allow the Update Installer to automatically detect available fix packs, without having to expressly browse the file system for them during the fix pack installation process.

Applying an update using the Update Installer

Before the installation of a fix pack, it is required that you stop all running WebSphere processes. Use the following Linux command to check if there are any WAS processes running:

```
ps -ef | grep -i java | grep -i websphere
```

Once you have ensured that there are no running WebSphere processes, launch the Update Installer if it is not already running. Once the Update Installer has loaded, you will be presented with the following screen as shown below. Click on **Next** to move on to the **Product Selection** screen.

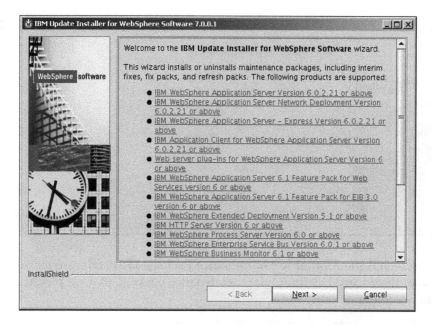

Once you are in the **Product Selection** screen, select the appropriate path where WebSphere is installed as shown in the screenshot below. This is the folder that the fix pack will be applied to. In Chapter 1, we used `/apps/was7` as our `<was_root>` path. If you have changed this path, please use the path you used in Chapter 1.

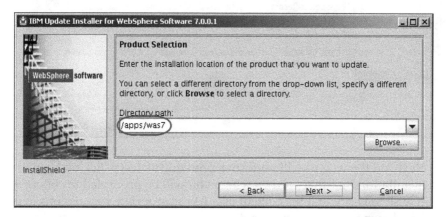

Click on **Next** to move on to the **Maintenance Operation Selection** screen. Here, you need to select whether you are applying a fix pack or removing it. Since we are applying a fix pack, we accept the default setting of **Install maintenance package**, and then click on **Next** to view the available fix packs.

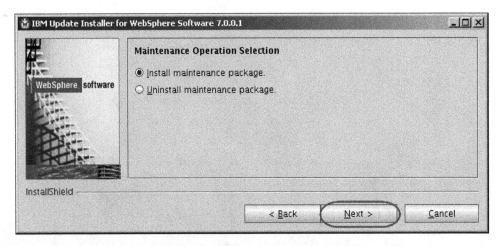

The next screen is the **Available Maintenance Package to Install** screen. Here, you can see that the wizard has found the maintenance package that we placed in the maintenance folder earlier.

Click on **Next** and the wizard will perform a prerequisite test. Click on **Next** to go to the final **Installation Summary** screen where you will be prompted to choose whether or not you wish to verify that the current user has appropriate permissions to perform the install as shown in the screenshot below. We are using root access so there is no issue with permissions. Click **Next** and the installation of the fix pack will occur.

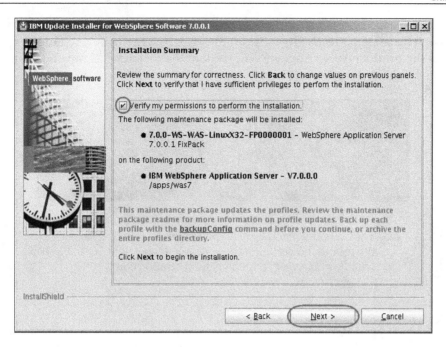

At the end, the Update Installer will report **Success** or **Failure**. Click on **Finish** to complete the fix pack installation as shown in the screenshot below.

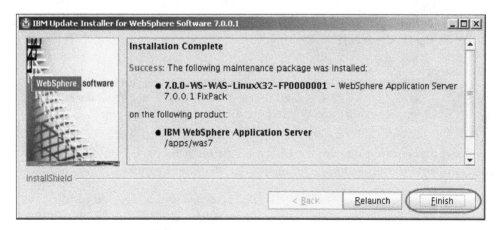

 Useful hint: It is important to know that the Update Installer creates a backup file in the `<was_root>/properties/version/nif/backup` directory. This backup file is used by the uninstall process.

Now that we have completed applying the fix pack, it is good practice to verify that it has been installed correctly. If we rerun the `versionInfo.sh` command script and evaluate the product list section, we will see that the fix pack has now been applied, as shown by the screenshot below:

```
Installed Product
---------------------------------------------------------------------
Name                    IBM WebSphere Application Server
Version                 7.0.0.1
ID                      BASETRIAL
Build Level             cf010845.08
Build Date              11/12/08
Architecture            Intel (32 bit)
```

 The current version of WebSphere will be reported in the right-hand corner of the welcome screen, which can be seen when you next log in to the Administration console.

Silent updates

Instead of using the graphical installer, you can use the **Update Installer for WebSphere Software** in silent mode to install fixes and features. Below is an overview of the tasks required to implement updates via the silent install process.

Remember, before applying fix packs, install the most recent version of the Update Installer on the WAS server.

 When you run the Update Installer, make sure you run it using the same user which was used to install WAS. Otherwise, file ownership issues can arise and will require correction by the root user.

Download the required interim fix, interim feature, or fix pack from the IBM Fix Central site into the `<installer_root>/maintenance` directory.

A sample response file exists called `install.txt` and will be located in the `<was_root>/UpdateInstaller/responsefiles` directory if you have installed the update installer in the `<was_root>` directory. Edit the response file, changing any of the fields as required. The following table explains the two key options which can be changed as required for the silent install to work correctly.

Property	Description
`-W maintenance.package=`	Specify a single maintenance package full filename, or a semi-colon delimited list, or a folder containing the updates, for example `<installer_root>\maintenance\<file_name>.pak`.
`-W product.location=`	Identify the WAS install location that will be updated.

The options above are the two main options that you will need to change. There are other options you can adjust as required. The provided sample response file (`install.txt`) is very descriptive and is self-explanatory.

Remember to stop all WebSphere processes. It is required that all WebSphere processes must be stopped so that there are no conflicts with file system updates.

Run the Update Installer silently using the following command:

```
<installer_root>/update -options <installer_root>//responsefiles/install.
txt -silent
```

Logs

As a general rule, it is wise to check the installer logs after an installation of an update to verify that the install is successful. The log can be found in the following folder: `<installer_root>/logs/update/install`.

For reference, below are some key error words you may find in the log, along with their explanations.

Status	Description
`INSTCONFSUCCESS`	The complete installation is a success.
`INSTCONFPARTIALSUCCESS`	The installation is partially successful; refer to the installer log for more details.
`INSTCONFFAILED`	The installation has failed; refer to the installer log for more details. Some of the most common reasons for errors are running out of disk space, folder permissions and environment paths, script syntax and mismatched versions of update installers.
	The best thing to do before any installation is to check you have enough disk space on the file system and ensure you have read any notes about the update, often listed on the update's download page. Sometimes it is useful to read the `readme.txt` in the Update Installer, as IBM can often change the update process between versions.

If the maintenance package is not applied to the WebSphere installation, a log file found in `<installer_root>logs/tempX` will contain the reason(s) for the failure. A log file of the naming sequence `tmpX` will exist to reflect the status of installs. `x` refers to the first available empty directory.

Here is an example of the logs directory after the 7.0.0.1 fix pack was applied.

```
/apps/was7/UpdateInstaller/logs
[root@websphere logs]# ls -ltr
total 32
drwxr-xr-x  2 root root 4096 Jan  1 10:35 install
drwxr-xr-x  2 root root 4096 Jan  1 10:57 tmp
-rwxrwxrwx  1 root root   89 Jan  2 03:19 lastMaintenanceDir.properties
drwxr-xr-x  2 root root 4096 Jan  2 03:29 tmp1
```

Troubleshooting tips

Update installers can sometimes be problematic and often it is hard to deduce the root cause of a fix pack installation failing. The obvious reason for failure are often the amount of disk space left on the file system, folder permissions and environment variables, namely system paths. However, there are a few other kinds of errors that are less intuitive. Below is a list of common problems and their solutions, to help you with problem-solving upgrade failures. Following are some common problems:

- Problem: Silent Install
  - When using the silent option of installing a fix pack, the installer may not report accurately in the logs the root cause of a failed installation.
- Resolution: Silent Install
  - You can opt to try a graphical installation using X Windows. Using the manual install approach can often shed light on errors that are reported in the GUI, but not in the silent installer.
- Problem: GUI Install
  - Launchpad installation wizard will not start or fail when using GUI.
- Resolution: GUI Install
  - Problems starting the launchpad or installation wizard can usually be traced back to missing prerequisite system or application levels, and permissions.

- Problem: Installation wizard fails

  ○ The installation fails with INSTCONFPARTIALSUCCESS or INSTCONFFAILED.

- Resolution: Installation wizard fails

  ○ JVM errors can cause the installation to stop and can be due to system paths or permissions. To solve JVM issues related to the installer, you can ensure that you have the correct permissions and your Linux profile has not been altered and is not causing an environmental variable conflict.

  ○ File system errors can mean the installer has not completed. Check disk space, mounting of file systems and permissions.

- Problem: Installation wizard hangs

  ○ During installation, a progress indicator shows you how far the install has progressed. If there is no change in the progress indicator for a very long time, the installation process could have hung.

- Resolution: Installation wizard hangs

  ○ The most common reason is that system resources are low. Check memory, swap space and file system disk space.

  ○ Another reason can be that X Windows is running slow, due to network traffic. This can be your workstation being affected by your local desktops' local network and also your desktop's resources. Ensure that your machine has a good network connection and plenty of memory.

For further reading on detailed problems and resolutions, you can consult the IBM Redbooks site using the following URL:

```
http://www.redbooks.ibm.com/redbooks.nsf/portals/.
```

If you search the Redbooks site using the **Advanced search** option and use the search words **WebSphere Application Server Installation Problem Determination**, you will find that many Redbooks and Redpapers are listed which contain problems and resolutions of typical WebSphere installer issues. At the time of writing this book, there were no WebSphere 7 problem determination guides. However, if you check this site every quarter, you will find that there are always new Redbooks and Redpapers available. It is important to know that often referring to Redbooks covering the previous version of WebSphere will frequently provide valuable information which is still relevant to the next version of Websphere.

Helpful hint: To keep up-to-date with product updates as they become available, you can subscribe to an email support account on IBM's web site. The URL below covers how you can set up notifications:

http://www-01.ibm.com/support/docview.
wss?rs=180&uid=swg21159292

Summary

In this chapter, we introduced the need for fix packs and how to locate, download, and apply them using the IBM Update Installer for WebSphere software. We have demonstrated an easy approach to maintenance, and by using these steps you should be confident to prepare for maintenance in your environments. We did not cover all variation of applying updates; however, using these steps we are confident you would be able to apply any other updates not demonstrated if required.

It is recommended that you plan your update strategy for when you move into production as it can be a complex task organizing production updates, often due to the fact that change requests are required and change windows may be infrequent for many live environments.

Since there are many releases, updates, and fixes throughout a given product's lifecycle, it is a good idea to officially assign the task to administrative personnel to ensure that your WAS product is up-to-date and to schedule time to continually assess and improve your WebSphere estate. It may mean that you need to provide **proof of concept** and/or **test environments** (sand boxes) to ensure that your applications will still work with new binaries and fix packs. Any updates you make should go through the complete lifecycle of testing, just like with other application deployment.

Index

Symbols

./chmod 755 ./listapps.sh command 127
/home/wasscripts/linux/listapps.sh command 127
./wsadmin.sh -lang jython -c 'AdminApp.list() command 126
./wsadmin.sh -lang jython command 124

A

AdminApp object 123
AdminConfig object 123
admin console 40, 41
AdminControl object 123
administration profile
  about 241
  administrative agent console 246, 247
  administrative agent, starting 245
  application server node, registering 247-250
  creating 241
  creating, PMT used 241-244
  PMT 241
administrative agent
  about 240
  administration profile, creating 241
  removing 255, 256
  second application server node, creating 250-255
administrative agent console 246, 247
administrative roles
  about 108
  administrator 109
  Admin Security Manager 109
  auditor 109
  configurator 109
  deployer 109
  Iscadmins 109
  managing 110
  monitor 109
  operator 109
  users, mapping 110
administrator role, administrative roles 109
Admin Security Manager role, administrative roles 109
AdminTask object 123
analysis tool, by IBM
  about 234
  Database Connection Pool Analyzer for IBM WebSphere Application Server 235
  HeapAnalyzer 235
  IBM Pattern Modelling and Analysis Tool for Java Garbage Collector 235
  IBM Trace and Request Analyzer for WebSphere Application Server 235
  IBM Web Server Plug-in Analyzer for WebSphere Application Server 235
  Performance Analysis Tool for Java 235
  Processor Time Analysis Tool for Linux 235
Ant targets
  installEAR 122
  listApplications 122
  uninstallEAR 122
application
  asset 52
  business application 52
  deploying 52
  deployment options 55
  detailed, installing options 54
  EAR file, deploying 52, 53
  EAR file, installing 54

EAR file, installing options 54
fast path, installing options 54
fast path, selecting 54
installing, Jython used 129-131
mapping, to application server 57
starting 58, 59
types 52
application class loader
about 163
class loading mode field 164
configuring 163
WAR class loader policy 164
application file types
EAR file 51
JAR file 51
WAR file 51
application, options
export 59
export DDL 59
export file 59
install 58
remove file 58
rollout update 58
start 58
stop 58
uninstall 58
update 58
application server class loader
about 161
class loading mode field 162
configuring 162
application server node
registering 247-250
Application Server Toolkit. *See* **ASTK**
ASTK
about 277
downloading 277
installing 278
J2EE applications, inspecting 289
log analysis 279
running 278
auditor role, administrative roles 109
authentication, J2EE security model 83
authorisation, J2EE security model 83
automation
about 116
wsadmin tool 116, 123

ws_ant tool 116

B

backup, WebSphere
creating 303

C

cell level XML files
about 145
admin-authz.xml 145
cesprofileRegistry.xml 145
resources.xml 145
security.xml 145
variables.xml 145
virtualhosts.xml 145
wimconfig.xml 145
class loader order field, web module class loader
about 165
classes loaded with local class loader first (parent last) 165
classes loaded with parent class loader first 165
classloader policy field, application server class loader
about 162
multiple 162
single 162
class loaders, WebSphere configuration
about 159
loading basics 160
class loading isolation
about 165
types 165
class loading isolation, types
full 165
minimal 165
partial 165
class loading mode field, application class loader
about 164
classes loaded with local class loader first (parent last) 164
classes loaded with parent class loader first 164

class loading mode field, application server class loader
about 162
classes loaded with local class loader first (parent last) 162
classes loaded with parent class loader first 162
command line options, dumpNamespace. sh script
cell root context 273
default 273
-factory <factory> 272
-format [jndi | ins] 274
-host <host> 272
host root context 273
legacy root context 273
node root context 273
-password <password> 272
-port <port> 272
-report [short | long] 274
-root [cell | server | node | host | legacy | tree | default] 272
server root context 273
-startAt <some/subcontext/in/the/tree> 274
tree root context 273
-url <url> 274
-user <name> 272
-username <name> 272
command script files, wsadmin tool
application, installing Jython used 129
application status, querying 132-139
installed applications, listing 129
components, WebSphere Application Server
environment settings 49
JNDI 50
JVM 49
resources 50
virtual host 49
web container 49
configurator role, administrative roles 109
connection factory interface 172
connection interface 172
custom JVM properties
about 224
adding 226, 228
IBM_HEAP_DUMP 225

IBM_HEAPDUMPDIR 225
IBM_HEAPDUMP_OUTOFMEMORY 225
IBM_JAVADUMP_OUTOFMEMORY 225

D

data access application
about 61
data source, creating 72
data sources 61
deploying 75
diagrammatic representation 61
employing 80
J2C alias, creating 70
JDBC providers 66
sample database, preparing 62-65
data access application, deploying
context roots, mapping for web modules 79
deployment steps, reviewing 79, 80
installation options, selecting 76
JSP reloading options, providing for web modules 77
modules, mapping to servers 77
resource references, mapping to resources 78
shared libraries, mapping 77
virtual hosts, mapping for web modules 78
Database Connection Pool Analyzer for IBM WebSphere Application Server 235
data source
component-managed alias, selecting 74
creating 72-75
J2C alias, applying 74
J2C alias, applying options 74
testing 75
default JMS provider 173
deployer role, administrative roles 109
deployment options
allow dispatching includes to remote resources 56
allow EJB reference targets to resolve automatically 56
allow servicing includes from remote resources 56
application build ID 56
application name 55

asynchronous request dispatch type 56
business level application name 56
create MBeans for resources 55
deploy enterprise beans 55
directory to install application 55
distribute application 55
file permission 56
override class reloading settings for Web
    and EJB modules 55
precompile JavaServer Pages files 55
process embedded configuration 56
reload interval in seconds 56
use binary configuration 55
destination interface 172
dumpNamespace.sh script
about 272
command line options 272
features 272
dynamic caching
about 221
enabling 221

E

EAR expander 275
EAR file 51
environment settings 49
export DDL option 59
export file option 59
export option 59

F

FFDC logs 153
file structure, WebSphere
about 141
product binaries file structure 142
profile file structure 143
WebSphere file system 142
First Failure Data Capture. *See* **FFDC logs**
Fix Central 300

G

global security
about 84
enabling 89
registry types 84

requisites 84
standalone custom registry, selecting 87
standalone LDAP 94
starting issue 89
stoping issue 89
troubleshooting 89
turning on 85, 86
turning on, with local operating system
    option 92
X connection error 89
Graphical Update Installer
about 304
installing 304-306
graphic installation, WebSphere
    Application Server
about 10
base binaries, installing 11
installation directory, changing 21
installation logs 39
installation registry files 38
installation wizard welcome screen 18
installing, as root 16
launchpad, running 17
optional features 20
PMT files 40
PMT logs 40
profile, creating 25,-36
profile creation, verifying 36, 37
software license agreemen, accepting 18
system prerequisites, checking 19
trial install, uploading to Linux server 13,
    14
WAS, downloading for Linux trial 11, 12
WAS environments 21

H

HeapAnalyzer 235
Help object 123

I

IBM HTTP Server
about 257, 258
configuration 257, 258
installing 258-261
starting 261

IBM Pattern Modelling and Analysis Tool
    for Java Garbage Collector 235
IBM Thread and Monitor Dump Analyzer
    for Java 229
IBM Trace and Request Analyzer for Web-
    Sphere Application Server 235
IBM Update Installer for WebSphere Soft-
    ware tool 302
IBM Web Server Plug-in Analyzer for Web-
    Sphere Application Server 235
individual commands, wsadmin tool
    about 126
    ./chmod 755 ./listapps.sh 127
    /home/wasscripts/linux/listapps.sh 127
    ./wsadmin.sh -lang jython -c 'AdminApp.
        list()' 126
installation directory
    changing 21
installation logs, graphic installation 39
installation registry files, graphic
    installation 38
installation types, WAS
    base binaries 21
    management profile 21
    standalone application server 21
installation wizard welcome screen 18
installed application
    listing, Jython used 129
install option 58
interactive commands, wsadmin tool
    print 125
    print Help.AdminApp() 126
    print Help.AdminConfig() 126
    print Help.AdminControl() 126
    print Help.AdminTask() 126
    print Help.help() 125
    ./wsadmin.sh -lang jython 124
interfaces, javax.jms package
    connection factory interface 172
    connection interface 172
    destination interface 172
    message consumer interface 172
    message producer interface 172
Iscadmins role, administrative roles 109

J

J2C alias
    creating 70-72
J2EE applications
    inspecting, ASTK used 289-292
    JSM Test Tool EAR file, importing 289-291
J2EE security model
    about 83
    authentication 83
    authorisation 83
JAR file 51
Java application
    file types 50
Java core dump
    about 222
    generating, for viewing thread lock 229-234
    generating, Jython used 222, 223
    requesting, kill command used 224
Java core (thread) dump
    analysing 228
Java heap dump
    generating, Jython used 223
Java Message Service. *See* JMS
Java messaging
    about 168
    JMS 168
Java Naming and Directory Interface. *See*
    JNDI
Java Virtual Machines. *See* JVM
javax.jms package
    about 172
    interfaces 172
JCA tool
    installing 229
JDBC providers
    about 66
    Connection pool data source, implementa-
        tion types 68
    creating 66-69
    implementation types 68
    XA Datasource, implementation types 68
Jexplorer 99
JMS
    about 168
    concepts 170
    configuring 177

features 168-170
JMS activation specification 174
JMS application
   components 169
   JMS clients 169
   JMS provider 169
JMS concepts
   point-to-point or queuing model 170
   publish/subscribe model 171
JMS, configuring
   about 177
   queue connection factories, creating
      177-179
   queue destinations, creating 179
   queue destinations, viewing 179
JMS connection factory 174
JMS demo application
   about 180
   installing 180-183
   reconfiguring 196-198
JMS features 170
JMS messaging
   features 168
JMS objects
   about 169
   connection factories 169
   destinations 169
JMS queue 174
JMS queue connection factory 174
JMS resources
   about 174
   types 174
JMS resource types
   JMS activation specification 174
   JMS connection factory 174
   JMS provider 174
   JMS queue 174
   JMS queue connection factory 174
   JMS topic 174
   JMS topic connection factory 174
JMS Test Tool application
   about 180-184
   configuring 184
   left-hand-side frame 184
   right-hand-side frame 184
   top-most frame 184

JMS topic 174
JMS topic connection factory 174
JNDI 50
JVM
   about 49
   core dumps 222
   heap dumps 222
JVM logs
   about 148
   configuring 150
   Linux grep command 156
   Linux tail command, used for viewing
      154-156
   viewing, in admin console 154
   viewing, on file system 154
JVM parameters
   initial.heap.size 158
   maximum.heap.size 158
   verbose class loading 158
   verbose garbage collection 158
   verbose.JNI 158
JVM-triggered heap dump 224
JVM tuning
   about 222
   heap size, tuning 236
   IBM Thread and Monitor Dump Analyzer
      for Java 229
   initial heap size, setting 236
   Java core dump, analysing 228, 229
   Java core dump, generating for viewing
      thread lock 229
   Java core dump, requesting Jython used
      222, 223
   Java core dump, requesting kill command
      used 224
   Java heap dump, requesting Jython used
      223
   JCA tool, installing 229
   JVM-triggered heap dump 224
   maximum heap size, setting 236
JVP settings, WebSphere
   about 157
   JVM parameters 158
Jython code
   code line 136
   key lines 132, 133
Jython commands 128

Jython script
  key concepts 136

K

key directories, WebSphere root path
  bin 142
  logs 142
  profileTemplates 143
  properties 143
  samples 142
  scriptLibaries 143
  uninstall 143
key folders, profile file structure
  bin 143
  config 143
  firststeps 143
  installableApps 143
  installedApps 144
  logs 144
  properties 144
  samples 144
  temp 144
  tranlog 144
  wstemp 144

L

launchpad installation 17
LDAP registry
  configuring, in WebSphere 104-108
LDIF files
  about 97
  attributes 98
LDIF files, attributes
  CN 98
  DN 98
  O 98
  objectclass 98
  SN 98
Linux grep command 156
Linux port
  opening 101
Linux tail command
  about 154
  employing 154
Linux user
  creating 92-94

local operating system option, global security
  about 92
  Linux user, creating 92
log analysis, ASTK used
  about 279
  columns, selecting 285
  filters, applying 284
  log files, importing 281-284
  new project, creating 280
  symptom databases, loading 286, 288
logs, product updates 311, 312
logs, WebSphere configuration
  about 148
  configuring 150
  FFDC logs 153
  JVM logs 148
  JVM logs, viewing 154
  log file location, changing 151
  log styles, changing 153
  native_stderr.log 149
  native _stdout.log 149
  <server_name>.pid 150
  startServer.log 149
  stopServer.log 149
  SystemErr.log 149
  SystemOut_<date_time_stamp>.log 150
  SystemOut.log 150

M

manual configuration, WebSphere plugin
  about 265-269
  generate plug-in button 269
message consumer interface 172
message producer interface 172
messaging 168
messaging system 168
monitor role, administrative roles 109
MQ Series 185

N

name space dump example 274
node level XML files
  about 146
  namestore.xml 146
  resources.xml 146

serverindex.xml 146
variables.xml 146

O

Open LDAP
  about 94
  configuring 95, 96
  downloading 94
  installing 95
operator role, administrative roles 109
optional features installation 20
OracleXE
  about 62
  downloading 62
  installing 62

P

Performance Analysis Tool for Java 235
performance counters, TPV
  JVM runtime 205
  Servlet Session Manager 206
  system data 206
  thread pools 206
  transaction manager 206
  web applications 206
performance modules, TPV
  about 205
  counters, adding 205
  counters, removing 205
Performance Monitoring Infrastructure. *See*
    PMI
PerfServlet
  installing 219
PMI
  configuration page 202
  enabling 202
PMT
  about 25
  profile, creating 27
  profile, creating options 27
  running 25
  starting 241
point-to-point or queuing model
  about 170
  diagrammatic representation 170
print 125

print Help.AdminApp() command 126
print Help.AdminConfig() command 126
print Help.AdminControl() command 126
print Help.AdminTask() command 126
print Help.help() command 125
Processor Time Analysis Tool for Linux 235
product binaries file structure, WebSphere
  about 142
  key directories 142
product updates, WebSphere
  about 296
  installer used 306-310
  locating 300
  locating, Fix Central used 300
  logs 311
  preparing for 298
  silent updates 310
  types 297
  update installers 302
  update process overview 296
product update types, WebSphere
  feature pack 297
  fix 298
  fix pack 297
  release 297
profile file structure, WebSphere 143
profile manager files, graphic installation 40
profile manager logs, graphic installation 40
profile scripts, wsadmin tool 128
properties files, WebSphere configuration
    147
  sas.client.props file 147
  soap.client.props file 147
publish/subscribe messaging model
  about 171
  diagrammatic representation 171
  javax.jms package 172
PuTTY
  downloading 12
  installing 12

Q

queue connection factories
  creating 177-179
queue destinations
  creating 179

presenting, in SIB 180
TCF, creating 180
TD, creating 180
viewing 179

R

registry types, global security
about 84
federated repositories 85
local operating system 85
standalone custom registry 85
standalone LDAP registry 85
remove file option 58
request metrics
about 215
components, measuring 216
destinations 217
enabling 216
features 215
in SystemOut.log 217, 218
performance data, retrieving with PerfServlet 219, 220
trace level field 217
request metrics, components
EJB 216
JDBC 217
JMS 217
JNDI 217
portlet 217
servlet 217
servlet filter 217
SIB 217
web services 217
resources
about 50
JDBC 50
JMS providers 50
mail providers 50
types 50
URL providers 50
rollout update option 58

S

sas.client.props file 147
scripting objects, wsadmin tool
AdminApp 123

AdminConfig 123
AdminControl 123
AdminTask 123
Help 123
second application server node
creating 250-255
security, WebSphere Application Server
about 83
global security 84
J2EE security model 83
server level XML files
sabout 146
resources.xml 146
server.xml 146
variables.xml 146
service integration bus. *See* **SIB**
SIB
about 174
creating 175, 177
**silent installation, WebSphere Application
  Server**
about 43
installation logs, examining 45
installer, running in silent mode 45
response file, creating 44
response file, editing 45
sections, customizing 44
silent updates 310
slapd
about 96
starting 96
stopping 96
snoop servlet
about 60
attributes 60
soap.client.props file
about 89
editing 89
soap.client.props fileabout 147
software lincense agreement 18
standalone custom registry
about 87
configuring 88
groups.props file, creating 88
user.props file, creating 87
standalone LDAP
about 94

connection, configuring 100
jexplorer, launching 99
LDAP registry, configuring in WebSphere 104
testing 99
user, adding 99-103
webpshere.ldif file, creating 98
windows installer, running 99
start option 58
stop option 58
summary reports section, TPV
about 205
connection pool 205
EJB methods 205
thread pool 205
symptom database
about 286
importing 286
key types information 286
SystemOut.log file 218
system prerequisites
checking 19

T

TCF 180
TD 180
Tivoli Performance Viewer
about 200
categories 200
collection status column 207
enabling 201-203
features 200
guide to the PMI, for monitoring 214
PMI, enabling 202
starting 207-214
start monitoring 207
Topic Destinations. *See* **TD**
Topics Connection Factories. *See* **TCF**
TPV categories
application data 201
log settings 204
performance modules 204, 205
settings 204
summary reports 204, 205
system resources 200
WebSphere pools and queues 200

trial install, WAS
uploading to Linux server 13-16
troubleshooting, update installer
about 312, 313

U

uninstall option 58
update installer, WebSphere
downloading 304
Graphical Update Installer, installing 304-306
installing 304
troubleshooting tips 312, 313
update, applying 306
update option 58
users
mapping, to administrative roles 110-113

V

virtual host 49

W

WAR class loader policy, application class loader
about 164
class loader for each WAR file in application 164
single class loader for application 164
WAR file 51
WAS environments
about 21-23
installation types 21
WAS web container 49
web module class loader
about 164
class loader order field 165
configuring 165
Web Services Validation Tool for WSDL and SOAP 235
WebSphere
administrative agent 240
backup, creating 303
dynamic caching 221
file structure 141
JVM tuning 222

namespaces, dumping 272
new update installer, installing 304
product updates 296
profile backup facility 303
request metrics 215
Tivoli Performance Viewer 200
update, applying 306
WebSphere Application Server
  security 83
  anatomy 48
  architecture 48
  components 48
  downloading, for Linux trial 11, 12
**WebSphere Application Server, download-
    ing for Linux trial**
  about 11
  PuTTY, installing 12
  WinSCP, installing 12
WebSphere Application Server installation
  about 7
  graphic installation 10
  planning 8
  prerequisites 10
  profile types 10
  scenarios 9
  silent installation 43
**WebSphere Application Server Installation
    Problem Determination 313**
WebSphere Application Server toolkit
  about 277
  overview 277
WebSphere class loaders
  about 161
  application server class loader 161
  class loading isolation 165
  enterprise application class loader 161
  web module class loader 161
WebSphere configuration
  class loaders 159
  file structure 141
  JVM settings 157
  logs 148
  properties files 147
  XML configuration files 144
WebSphere file system 142
WebSphere messaging
  about 173

default JMS provider 173
JMS, configuring 177
JMS demo application, installing 180
JMS Test Tool application 183
WebSphere SIB 174
WebSphere MQ. *See* **WMQ**
WebSphere plugin
  about 262
  features 262
  installing 263, 264
  manual configuration 265-269
WebSphere SIB
  about 174
  SIB, creating 175-177
WinSCP
  downloading 12
  installing 12
WMQ
  about 167, 185
  demonstrating 185
  example overview 185
  installing 185, 186, 187
  JMS demo application, reconfiguring 196-
    198
  overview 185
  WMQ connection factory, creating 192
  WMQ queue destination, creating 195, 196
WMQ connection factory
  creating 192-194
WMQ installation
  about 185, 186
  queue manager, creating 188-191
  WMQ installer, running 187
WMQ queue destination
  creating 195, 196
WMQ Queue Manager
  about 188
  creating 188-191
  starting 189
wsadmin tool
  about 123
  advantages 123
  command script files 128
  individual commands 126, 127
  individual scripting commands, running
    124
  interactive commands 124-126

modes, of running 124
profile scripts 128
running, in different modes 124
scripting commands, running in profile
    script 124
scripting commands, running in script file
    124
scripting commands, running interactively
    124
scripting objects 123
ws_ant tasks
about 117
wsInstallApp 117
wsListApps 117
wsStartServer 117
wsStopServer 117
wsUninstallApp 117
ws_ant tool
about 116
advantages 116
application, deploying wsInstallApp used
    118-122
application, deploying wsInstallApp used
    119
demonstrating 117
HR application, deploying 117, 118
wsInstallApps, ws_ant tasks
employing 118-122

X

Xming
about 14
download link 14
Xming-fonts 15
**XML configuration files, WebSphere
    configuration**
about 144
cell level XML files 145
node level XML files 146
server level XML files 146
X Windows system 13

Thank you for buying

WebSphere Application Server
7.0 Administration Guide

About Packt Publishing

Packt, pronounced 'packed', published its first book "*Mastering phpMyAdmin for Effective MySQL Management*" in April 2004 and subsequently continued to specialize in publishing highly focused books on specific technologies and solutions.

Our books and publications share the experiences of your fellow IT professionals in adapting and customizing today's systems, applications, and frameworks. Our solution based books give you the knowledge and power to customize the software and technologies you're using to get the job done. Packt books are more specific and less general than the IT books you have seen in the past. Our unique business model allows us to bring you more focused information, giving you more of what you need to know, and less of what you don't.

Packt is a modern, yet unique publishing company, which focuses on producing quality, cutting-edge books for communities of developers, administrators, and newbies alike. For more information, please visit our website: www.packtpub.com.

Writing for Packt

We welcome all inquiries from people who are interested in authoring. Book proposals should be sent to author@packtpub.com. If your book idea is still at an early stage and you would like to discuss it first before writing a formal book proposal, contact us; one of our commissioning editors will get in touch with you.

We're not just looking for published authors; if you have strong technical skills but no writing experience, our experienced editors can help you develop a writing career, or simply get some additional reward for your expertise.

JasperReports for Java Developers

ISBN: 978-1-904811-90-9   Paperback: 344 pages

Create, Design, Format and Export Reports with the world's most popular Java reporting library

1.   Get started with JasperReports, and develop the skills to get the most from it

2.   Create, design, format, and export reports

3.   Generate report data from a wide range of datasources

4.   Integrate Jasper Reports with Spring, Hibernate, Java Server Faces, or Struts

Apache JMeter

ISBN: 978-1-847192-95-0   Paperback: 140 pages

A practical beginner's guide to automated testing and performance measurement for your websites

1.   Test your website and measure its performance

2.   Master the JMeter environment and learn all its features

3.   Build test plan for measuring the performance

4.   Step-by-step instructions and careful explanations

Please check **www.PacktPub.com** for information on our titles

Java EE 5 Development using GlassFish Application Server

ISBN: 978-1-847192-60-8   Paperback: 424 pages

The complete guide to installing and configuring the GlassFish Application Server and developing Java EE 5 applications to be deployed to this server

1. Concise guide covering all major aspects of Java EE 5 development

2. Uses the enterprise open-source GlassFish application server

3. Explains GlassFish installation and configuration

4. Covers all major Java EE 5 APIs

Java EE 5 Development with NetBeans 6

ISBN: 978-1-847195-46-3   Paperback: 400 pages

Develop professional enterprise Java EE applications quickly and easily with this popular IDE

1. Use features of the popular NetBeans IDE to improve Java EE development

2. Careful instructions and screenshots lead you through the options available

3. Covers the major Java EE APIs such as JSF, EJB 3 and JPA, and how to work with them in NetBeans

4. Covers the NetBeans Visual Web designer in detail

Please check **www.PacktPub.com** for information on our titles